8.50
01

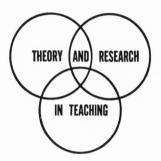

THEORY AND RESEARCH IN TEACHING

Teachers College, Columbia University
Arno A. Bellack, editor

Recent years have witnessed a resurgence of
interest on the part of educational researchers
in the teaching process. Volumes in the *Theory
and Research in Teaching* series report significant studies of instructional procedures in a
variety of educational settings, at various organizational levels in the schools, and in many
of the subjects included in the curriculum.
These studies present fresh perspectives on
teaching both to educational researchers and
to practitioners in the schools.

VERBAL COMMUNICATION IN INSTRUCTIONAL SUPERVISION

**An Observational System for
and Research Study of
Clinical Supervision in Groups**

RICHARD H. WELLER

TEACHERS COLLEGE PRESS
Teachers College, Columbia University
New York, New York

Contents

List of Illustrations

List of Tables

Preface

Most educators would agree that supervised student teaching is an important—perhaps the most important—component in programs for the preparation of teachers. Teachers in training consistently express the opinion that supervised student teaching is the most significant and helpful aspect of their training program. In spite of the importance attached to the supervision of student teachers, however, very little research has focused directly on the supervisory process. A major gap in supervisory research to date has been the absence of valid, reliable data on the process itself; and this gap is due in large measure to the lack of effective data-gathering instruments. The study reported by Dr. Weller in this volume is designed to meet this need for a reliable and valid instrument to guide the observation and analysis of supervisory conferences. Although intended primarily for the study of group supervision of student teachers, the framework for analysis developed in this research is applicable to both individual and group supervision of experienced teachers as well as teachers in training.

Dr. Weller's research is significant because it provides a potentially fruitful method for studying the complexities of instructional supervision—a process that has been too long neglected by educational researchers.

Arno A. Bellack

August 1971

**VERBAL
COMMUNICATION
IN INSTRUCTIONAL
SUPERVISION**

•1•

Introduction

Few aspects of school operation have been simultaneously so condemned and so extolled as instructional supervision. While some consider supervision to be a potential panacea of improvement and enlightenment for teachers, others, usually the teachers themselves, view the process with hostility and often outright contempt. Volumes have been written on the subject, but research on the effects and on the processes of supervision is virtually nonexistent. Supervision is rarely observed except by those who are actually involved in the process. One might even infer that with the possible exception of novice teacher training programs where "supervised student teaching" is a universal prerequisite for certification, instructional supervision barely even exists in American schools.

The reasons for this nebulous state of affairs are deep and pervasive. Decades of philosophizing and research on the objectives and effectiveness of instruction have produced little consensus and remarkably few generalizable research results on which effective supervision might be based. Lacking a specifically identifiable "product" in an area where changes are difficult to justify, produce, or even measure, and where prompt feedback is practically nonexistent, both supervisor and supervisee face formidable obstacles.

In reality, very little is known about what actually happens in instructional supervision:

The work of supervisors is characterized by very diverse human relationships, a multiplicity of kinds of tasks, and no fixed locus of operation. The supervisor works in many organizational climates, deals extensively with subordinates, peers, and superordinates, ranges over a wide variety of substantive and procedural problems, produces no readily visible product, is held only vaguely accountable for certain on-going events in the school, and is almost immune to systematic evaluation. [Harris, 1965, p. 87]

1

It might be added that the supervisor performs his diverse functions by poorly conceptualized or inadequately validated processes, mostly idiosyncratically and with unknown effects.

The need for research on supervision is obvious. Harris (1963, p. 129) noted that between 1953 and 1963 there was an average of only thirty-six articles a year listed under the heading of "Supervision and Supervisors" in the *Education Index*. An average of only one article per year was considered "supervision research," and of these, almost none deals directly with the actual process of supervision. In reaction to the absence of systematic research, Harris emphasized:

The problem calls for elaborate descriptive studies which have not yet been attempted. . . . Most studies of supervisory behavior look at the supervisor as an isolated person or the supervisor as a homogeneous class of professionals, and both views are terribly unrealistic. [Ibid., pp. 87–88]

This book develops and tests a research methodology designed to examine this problem. It focuses on a particular type of instructional supervision, called "clinical supervision," which is operationally defined, well-exemplified in practice, and considered by many educators to meet the criterion of "best existing practice." According to Cogan, clinical supervision, developed and practiced at the Harvard-Newton Summer School, "is probably the most sophisticated and concentrated program of supervision in the country" (1966, p. 10).

The succeeding chapters will examine the definition and practices of clinical supervision as well as the available research relating to it. A major gap in the existing supervisory research is the absence of valid, reliable data on the process itself: what actually happens when supervisor and supervisee engage in the activity called clinical supervision. This research gap is caused to a large extent by the almost total lack of any effective data-gathering instruments.

The present study develops such an instrument: an observational category system based on the characteristics and purposes of clinical supervision. This system, called M.O.S.A.I.C.S. (*M*ultidimensional *O*bservational *S*ystem for the *A*nalysis of *I*nteractions in *C*linical *S*upervision), produces several basic matrices or mosaics of interaction data as well as fundamental ratios that may be used as indices of supervisory behavior.

The resultant data analysis may be used as an adjunct to research on teaching or as a clinical examination of the processes of supervision. It is so designed that the output may be directly compared with similar data produced in research on teaching.

The potentialities and use of this instrument are demonstrated in a longitudinal study of five supervisory groups at the Harvard-Newton Summer School. The similarities and differences among these groups are examined through the M.O.S.A.I.C.S. output. These data are then compared with similar data taken from teaching groups in a study by Arno Bellack (1966), whose observational instrument for the analysis of instructional interactions was used as a framework for the M.O.S.A.I.C.S. instrument.

•2•

An Observational Approach to Research on Supervision

INSTRUCTIONAL SUPERVISION

The literature on instructional supervision is as diverse as it is voluminous. There is little consensus among the major writers either about what the supervisor is supposed to do or how he should proceed. Ayer's attempt to summarize the nature of instructional supervision and its historical development reflects this nebulous situation:

The improvement of instruction lies at the focus of leading definitions and concepts of prefessional supervision. Supervision in this sense is taken to include all aspects of instruction . . . all persons concerned in the instructional program, and all efforts to help people to gain and exercise creative ingenuity. Early treatments of instructional supervision centered largely upon the expert inspection and improvement of classroom teaching. This was followed by a period in which the chief emphasis was placed upon creativity. In recent years the literature on supervision has centered upon democratic leadership, purposeful supervision, and better human relations. [1954, p. 5]

This statement sheds little light on the process of supervision, but it effectively reflects many of its basic problems. It might well be rewritten as follows: Instructional supervision is a poorly defined and inadequately conceptualized process. It has grown and fragmented under pragmatic pressures and diverse theoretical orientations. Supervision now encompasses numerous functions, vaguely related to an objective that is only superficially understood.

4

It is instructive to look at some of these problems in more detail. Lucio and McNeil (1959, chap. 1) carefully document the historical pressures that have changed supervisory practice. Supervision appears to have changed more by reaction to outside forces than by a natural evolutionary process. Often supervision is equated with coercion and inspection:

Psychologically [instructional supervision] is almost inevitably viewed as an active threat to the teacher, possibly endangering his professional standing and undermining his confidence in himself. Other factors [include] uncertainty about whether one-to-one supervision really does any good, the apparent conflict between the competence of the teacher and the need for supervision, and abuses by poorly trained supervisors. [Cogan, 1961, p. 2]

These uncertainties and conflicts are actually well-founded. Cogan has argued that "the processes through which a supervisor makes a series of observations of a teacher's performance and then sets about directly and straightforwardly to devise a program of planned efforts to improve that performance have almost atrophied" (ibid.). In so arguing he appears to assume that effective processes of supervision and valid criteria of teaching effectiveness already exist but have simply fallen into disuse. The major problem may actually lie in our ignorance of these factors rather than in apathy or compliance to adverse pressures.

There is ample evidence of this ignorance in the vagueness and diversity of the stated objectives for supervision found in the literature. There appears to be no generally accepted statement of objectives in anything resembling operational terms. The closest approach to such a fundamental statement that might be accepted by most writers is one proposed by Lucio and McNeil: "Through conferences and consultations, [the supervisor] seeks to improve the quality of instruction" (1959, p. 26).

Statements such as this raise immediate problems by implying the existence of criteria of effectiveness by which teaching behavior may be evaluated. These criteria may be thought of as being arrayed along a continuum of importance, from ultimate to proximate (Gage, 1963, pp. 116–118). The ultimate or fundamental criteria of teaching effectiveness are generally taken to be the teacher's effect on pupil achievement or the realization of some basic educational value. Proximate or less fundamental criteria may range from the teacher's effect on pupil attitudes toward school to the pupils' liking the teacher.

The supervisor actually works with such correlates of these criteria as the teacher's classroom behavior or interpersonal relations with pupils. These correlates might be called the "content" of supervision, the observable actions or interactions that are amenable to change and that provide a focus for supervisory action.

A fundamental difficulty for supervisory practice is that these correlates of effectiveness are virtually unknown. Decades of intensive educational research in this area have produced very few significant results (ibid., chaps. 6, 7, 9, 10, 11, 13). Lacking basic research evidence for these correlates, or a fundamental theory of effectiveness from which they might be derived, the supervisor's "content focus" has become an eclectic jumble of factors representing his synthesis of personal experience or his own theory of effectiveness. In practice the correlates that are focused upon rarely have more than a dubious connection with ultimate criteria.

The determination of supervisory "method" encounters similar problems. Methods depend upon the specific objectives that are considered important. When objectives can be operationally specified, procedures may be hypothesized, tested, and refined with some measure of precision. The more precise objectives, however, are often those which have a tenuous relationship to ultimate criteria. High reliability may thus be achieved at the expense of objective validity. The supervisor may, on the other hand, base his methods on more subjective goals that appear to him to have a certain measure of face validity. These methods rarely offer any means for evaluation other than the subjective judgments of participants.

Many writers on supervision appear to have reacted to these problems by turning from questions of teaching effectiveness to questions of teacher adjustment. This portion of the supervisory literature focuses on such global teacher objectives as mental health, personal development, and cooperative action toward group goals. Generalized supervisory methods have been proposed for these objectives from the fields of group process, leadership, and human relations.

These omnibus approaches place more emphasis on the method than on the problem itself. Supervision is commonly abhorred if authoritarian, praised if democratic, and viewed with suspicion if "scientific." It is a consoling but rather naïve hope that all cognitive, behavioral, and social-emotional problems teachers have may be subsumed under a single methodological blanket. A more promising approach appears to lie in the identification of different supervisory functions related to problems of teaching and the proposal of methodologies appropriate to each.

It might be argued that considerable differentiation of functions already exists. Instructional supervision is often defined by reference to particular supervisory roles found in the schools. Gwynn summarized the diversity of these roles as follows:

Some authorities would make the supervisor a strictly professional official, highly trained to do a major administrative job. Another group would go far in the opposite direction, divorcing the supervisor from administrative duties and responsibilities; this action would result in a supervisor whose main responsibility is to help teachers meet their problems. A third group of educators would make the supervisor's position mainly that of a teacher of teachers, improving instruction through programs of in-service education. A fourth group, active and vocal, would center the emphasis around human relations; they would interpret the supervisor's responsibility as the effective use of group processes with teachers, pupils, and other school personnel. A fifth group regards supervision as a task including supervision and curriculum revision or curriculum rebuilding; in this dual role the supervisor has to add to the responsibility of helping teachers the allied responsibility of stimulating curriculum development. [1961, pp. 27–28]

This type of role differentiation does little more than add to the confusion surrounding instructional supervision. It is actually a role diffusion, adding auxiliary duties but not clarifying the nature of the supervisory process.

Educators are reacting to the primitive state of instructional supervision in several ways. New approaches to teacher education have been proposed that emphasize concentrated training before practice and limit supervision to the testing of specific behavioral competencies (for example, LaGrone, 1965, pp. 219–229). Other educators have recognized the contention of Lucio and McNeil that "supervision has no independent thought of its own" (1959, p. 11), and have emphasized research on the supervision of teachers.

This research is receiving considerable impetus from recent studies in the analysis of teaching and from technological developments. Before examining current research approaches to instructional supervision, however, it is appropriate to differentiate certain problems experienced by teachers in their initial years. These problems will indicate that the responsibilities or functions of the supervisor lie in different areas, which require different supervisory approaches and different research methodologies.

The functions of the supervisor appear to be separable into three areas, which may be called counseling, teaching, and training. Although there is some overlap, operational distinctions are evident. These functions represent a multidimensional continuum: from emphasis on personal adjustment, to emphasis on understanding instructional phenomena, to emphasis on specific teaching behaviors; and from concepts derived from social and counseling psychology, to those derived from educational and cognitive psychology, to those derived from training and behavioral psychology. Supervisors can rarely expect to be equally competent in all three functions, yet neither can they afford to be ignorant of any one.

1. The Counseling Function

The initial years of teaching frequently produce great personal stress. The individual who has set high standards for himself finds that his work is never done to his satisfaction. Feedback concerning his failures is often much more obvious and persistent than that concerning his successes. This may be the first instance of failure for the novice who has had an academic history of success, and such perceptions of failure are frequently taken in an intensely personal way.

It is a potential area of strong value conflicts: a commitment to the individual is frustrated by interaction with large numbers of students for short periods of time; values of personal autonomy and freedom conflict with the requirements for maintaining discipline and order; the value of being liked and respected by one's pupils comes into conflict with the control, teaching, and grading functions of the job; and a commitment to the teacher's academic discipline confronts pupil disinterest and even distaste.

The novice teacher may experience problems in role adjustment. He is essentially passing through a role reversal from student to teacher of students. He may assume that his pupils have the same orientation that he has had, and experience difficulty both in differentiating their roles from his collegiate role and in understanding their different orientations toward school.

Another area of conflict lies in the different role expectations of the novice teacher, the college, and the school. It is not uncommon to find various authorities expecting radically different behaviors from him, while his own preference may lie in still another direction. His objectives may conflict with the realities of his job, and he may find himself unable to accomplish even those objectives which he has personally reconciled from the conflicting pressures acting upon him.

The initial years of teaching force the individual to confront his personal objectives: his reasons for entering teaching, his expectations of satisfaction from his job, and his basic commitment to this career. This is an intensely personal adjustment, a period during which the novice learns whether he can adapt his own needs to his career or his career to his needs while still remaining an autonomous individual.

A basic premise of the counseling function of supervision is that the individual must solve these conflicts satisfactorily before he can become an effective teacher. This assumption states that what the individual is affects what he does, that psychological changes are as important as cognitive or behavioral changes, and that a supervisory focus on these psychological changes is, in some cases, the only effective means of achieving changes in teaching behavior.

Supervisory methods may be adapted from the methodologies of counseling and psychotherapy. Judson Shaplin proposed the relevancy of a psychotherapy approach as follows:

> Practice provides an opportunity to analyse the characteristic defenses which a teacher employs in the face of stress, to test the appropriateness of these defenses, and to develop a rational, controlled behavior to handle the stress conditions. In many ways the situation is similar to the process of psychotherapy, though with less intent to change the basic personality: the examination of the appropriateness of reactions and defenses, the inquiry into why things are this way, the achievement of emotional insight, and the search for new adaptive behavior congenial to the emotional growth that takes place. [1961, p. 35]

Mosher's application of ego counseling (1964) and Binnington's use of client-centered counseling (1965) are examples of counseling approaches in instructional supervision that appear to have merit. These studies will be discussed in a later section on research. An essential point to be made here is that the importance of the counseling function is often overlooked by supervisors, who generally consider it to be outside their range of competencies.

An encouraging possibility is the use of teams of supervisors with different capabilities and interests. Grey and Greenblatt (1963, pp. 154–162), for example, used a team composed of a psychologist and a curriculum specialist in joint meetings with student teachers. Their differing diagnoses appeared to be helpful both to the student teachers and their cooperating teachers. One of the encouraging aspects of this work is the possibility that interaction with others on the team might provide training for the instructional supervisors themselves.

In general, however, most supervisors will probably avoid becoming too involved with the counseling function. There is a strong and well-founded reluctance to meddle around with "amateur psychologizing" without proper training, and a possible trend away from general supervision toward supervision by subject specialists will probably increase this reluctance. Although the counseling function of supervision is often crucial, there seems little promise that it will assume a major portion of the supervisory repertoire in the near future.

2. The Teaching Function

Teaching is a complex interaction of many poorly specified and little understood variables. The novice begins teaching with some theoretical preparation but faces the difficult task of translating theory into practice in a real situation.

The teacher must interact with pupils of different backgrounds, characteristics, and personal problems. He is faced with the difficult task of understanding their interests and capabilities and diagnosing learning and behavior problems. In essence he must learn not only a great deal about the characteristics and problems of children but also how to recognize their behavioral manifestations, relate these to possible causes, and propose and test alternate courses of action.

Teaching content is a frequent area of difficulty. The novice must view his subject through a new set of eyes: those of a learner, much younger than himself, who may not see the relationships, the relevance, or the motivational factors that seem obvious to the teacher. He may be required for the first time to justify the teaching of a subject he had always assumed to be important in its own right. He will be confronted by deficiencies in his own understanding of the subject as well as in his ability to organize it in ways that are meaningful to his pupils.

The teacher must learn to recognize and relate variables of classroom interaction. This involves the observation and analysis of classroom phenomena, patterns of teaching and learning, and the conditions of learning. It further requires the application of concepts from other behavioral sciences in an attempt to conceptualize the relationships among these interacting variables.

A basic assumption of the teaching function of supervision is that instruction, a complex interaction of teacher behaviors, learner behaviors, and content and environmental variables, is patterned. As such it is capable of being analyzed and subjected to a tentative explanatory scheme. The teaching function is therefore concerned with cognition: the understanding of the instructional process. In the words of Judson Shaplin, one of the foremost proponents of this teaching function:

Teaching requires highly specialized knowledge as well as specialized methods of presentation dictated by the nature of the knowledge selected, the essentials of learning, and the capacities of the students. The planning, the process, and the analysis of teaching depend upon findings, concepts, and generalizations from many disciplines, including the academic subject fields, the behavioral sciences, and the corresponding subdisciplines within professional education. One of our major difficulties is that the relevant concepts and generalizations have usually been developed in contexts other than teaching. . . . The teaching act requires a practical synthesis by the teacher of this material from many fields. [1961, p. 36]

A further assumption is that an individual cannot be a fully effective, autonomous teacher until he recognizes and attempts to understand these variables in the teaching act. One function of the supervisor, therefore, is to teach these skills of behavioral analysis to the practice teacher:

It is inefficient and unrealistic to expect the novice teacher to achieve his own synthesis of the many disciplines contributing to teaching, and to analyze and improve his own teaching behavior, without systematic help from more experienced and expert professors and teachers who have specialized in both the content and process of teaching, and who have attempted to make the kind of synthesis which is required of the novice . . . [it is essential to recognize] that the analysis of teaching requires highly specialized knowledge, skill, and training. [Ibid.]

The absence of a general theory or methodology for teaching is a crucial problem for the teaching function of supervision. The techniques of clinical supervision appear to be the most directly pertinent to it. Clinical supervision has been defined by Morris Cogan as "supervision focused upon the improvement of the classroom performance of the teacher by way of observation, analysis, and treatment of that performance (1964, p. 118). This is a generic term only recently come into general use in programs that have long used procedures that could be called "clinical," or based on actual observations of behavior. In effect, clinical supervision has been defined by example; the term applies to supervision as developed and practiced in specific programs, such as the Harvard-Newton Summer School (Cogan, 1961).

Few detailed descriptions or analyses of clinical supervision are to be found in the literature, although there are indications that many student teaching programs are based on clinical techniques (for example, *Evaluating Student Teaching*, 1960). It would appear that clinical supervision has become an important factor in teacher training without having been carefully specified or adequately researched.

The major distinguishing factors of clinical supervision are the emphasis on the analysis of instructional interactions and the rational modification of procedures based on this analysis. Supervision is conducted through a systematic sequence of observation, objective feedback, analysis, and planning for modification. It has been carried out in various arrangements of individual and group interaction, frequently using a staff of supervisors trained in different supervisory specialties (Cogan, 1964, pp. 3–9).

The lack of knowledge about this type of supervision was outlined by Cogan and reported by Oliver and Shaver in 1961:

Both the problems and the importance . . . [of studying the processes of supervision in a more systematic way] derive from the fact that there is neither a developed body of theory and research nor a systematic body of clinical practice that will help supervisors to improve the performance of the teacher in the classroom. . . . One of the reasons for such meagre accomplishment is simply that the practices of clinical supervision have been only poorly developed. For example, supervisors have not been able to set up any widely accepted and continuously refined strategies and techniques for observing the teacher, making a convincing analysis of his performance, and using this analysis as a basis for the improvement of the teacher's classroom performance. [1961, p. 440]

An approach to research relating to these problems is a major focus of this book.

3. The Training Function

The novice teacher needs a command of many behavioral skills, both simple and complex. Unconscious gestures, movements, and speech patterns may be partial determinants of teaching difficulties. An experienced supervisor is usually able to identify many of these very quickly and the novice teacher himself can often make the necessary changes without help.

More complex skills include the novice's ability to question, to illustrate points he is making, and to express himself logically and clearly. He must learn to vary the pattern and frequency of his interaction with pupils, to utilize different techniques of reward and punishment, to elicit and make use of pupils' contributions, and to find ways of maintaining pupil attention and motivation.

Included in this area is a wide range of behaviors that are usually called "teaching methods." This term encompasses such large-scale patterns of behavior as leading discussions, lecturing, and conducting laboratory exercises, as well as the specific competencies involved in the use of audiovisual materials, test construction, and laboratory setups. In essence the training function attempts to develop in the novice teacher a version of Goodlad's "well-stocked pharmacy of successful diagnostic and prescriptive techniques" (1966, p. 21).

A basic assumption of the training function is that teaching is complex behavior and as such can be broken down into elemental behaviors that can be systematically developed in the teacher by training techniques. These elements may then be used to develop sequences or subroutines, patterns of interactions that will ultimately be used by the teacher in achieving his objectives with pupils.

It is at the latter point that the training function begins to overlap with the teaching function. The training and teaching functions of supervision may be differentiated on the one hand by the specificity of the desired behaviors:

When the end-products of learning can be specified in terms of particular instances of . . . performance, then instructional procedures can be designed to directly train or build in these behaviors. [Training] When the end-product behaviors cannot be specified precisely because they are too complex or because the behaviors that result in successful accomplishment in many instances are not known, then the individual is expected to transfer his learning to the performance of the behavior which was found difficult to analyze. [Teaching] [Glaser, 1964, p. 5]

The teaching function focuses on the analysis and interpretation of instructional interactions as they occur with respect to objectives, whereas the training function focuses on these specific objectives themselves and the means for attaining them.

On the other hand, the two functions may be distinguished by differing emphases on cognition or behavior. The training function places greater emphasis on a repertoire of behavioral capabilities in the novice, while the teaching function stresses the groundwork of understanding within which the individual may operate in the application of these capabilities.

One of the major problems of the training function is the identification and specification of relevant behaviors and capabilities. Supervisors have long been involved with such "how to do it" problems as how to discipline the troublemaker, how to conduct a panel discussion, how to run a filmstrip projector, and how to pith a frog. This has been called the "nutsy-boltsy" school of supervision.

Attempts are now being made to identify and specify more basic instructional capabilities. Recent work at Stanford illustrates this growing trend. The Stanford Microteaching Clinic attempts to train novices in such skills as establishing set, establishing frames of reference, achieving closure, using questions effectively, recognizing and obtaining attending behavior, controlling participation, providing feedback, employing rewards and punishments, and setting a model (Bush and Allen, 1964). This sample of behaviors indicates the particular emphases of those educators. Numerous other behaviors are also possible training foci.

One of the chief strengths of the training function is that procedures have been fairly well established for the training process once the skills themselves have been identified. Procedures have been developed in the field of behavioral psychology that are as potentially useful in teaching as they are in technical and military training. The following procedures might be a guide for a supervisor-trainer:

1. A task analysis of the proposed teaching performance in terms of terminal behaviors for the purpose of identifying classes of response options in behavioral terms.

2. The assessment of the novice's entering behavior as a guide to determining the steps to be taken in building up the response repertoire.

3. The training of the novice through specific activities designed to help him attain the response repertoire. Training procedures might include cue discrimination, reinforcement, response guidance and shaping, practice, and feedback as knowledge of correct results. The viewing of models performing the desired behaviors has also been found to be effective.

4. The assessment of the novice's proficiency in performing these behaviors in a controlled situation. [Glaser, 1965, chaps. 1, 2, 6]

As the novice begins to use his repertoire of skills in a real teaching situation, the function of the supervisor begins to shift from training to teaching. The novice must then use perception and judgment in selecting proper responses, making strategic and tactical decisions, and evaluating the process of instruction (Fitts, 1961, p. 185). The supervisor acts as a source of information feedback, an examiner of instructional interactions, and an evaluator of particular behaviors in the given teaching context.

Supervisors, while often concentrating on the training function, rarely proceed in as systematic a manner as outlined above. Many educators now feel that such training should be a primary responsibility of schools of education and should precede actual practice teaching. For example, the Teacher Education and Media Project of the American Association of Colleges for Teacher Education recommended that practice teaching involve:

A tempering experience that introduces all the complexities of several rather than one teaching situation after certain basic competencies have been developed and refined in the preceding courses. The prospective teacher approaches this experience with confidence in his knowledge and abilities rather than the anxiety we now observe. [LaGrone, 1965, p. 228]

As technology and procedures for training become further improved, this function will probably become increasingly the responsibility of the training colleges themselves, where time, controlled conditions, and adequate facilities are available.

With this discussion as a frame of reference, the next section focuses specifically on the teaching function of supervision by examining in detail the processes and assumptions of clinical supervision, defined and practiced in the intensive interaction of student-teacher training centers.

CLINICAL SUPERVISION

Clinical supervision may be defined as supervision focused upon the improvement of instruction by means of systematic cycles of planning, observation, and intensive intellectual analysis of actual teaching performances in the interest of rational modification. The distinctive nature of clinical supervision becomes more evident in the description of actual practice.

Clinical supervision is exemplified by practices at the Harvard-Newton Summer School, which was established in 1955 as a preliminary training experience for prospective teachers in Harvard's internship program. The practice of clinical supervision developed under the pressure of preparing some interns in a six-week summer period for immediate full-time teaching the following September. The actual processes of clinical supervision were developed and refined by the interaction between interns and supervisors with different backgrounds and styles in this unusually intense instructional environment.

Clinical supervision at the Harvard-Newton Summer School is based on the interaction between an instructional supervisor (called a "master teacher") and a small group of four to six interns. Supervision is essentially carried on *by* the group of interns, master teacher, and a cadre of specialized supervisory personnel including psychologists and subject specialists.

The program [is] one in which many carefully selected staff members possessing extensive resources of talent and experience are integrated into the total supervisory program set up for the interns. That is, the education of the interns is a direct responsibility of the total staff. [Cogan, 1961, p. 3]

The interns themselves are an essential part of the supervisory process:

Optimally, each intern enters deeply into all phases of the teaching cycle for every other intern in his group. This implies his critical and creative involvement in planning, to the extent that the success or failure of the lesson —no matter which intern does the actual teaching—is personally felt by all the interns. It means that the non-teaching interns are called upon to make most careful observations of the actual teaching performance of their co-interns, and to join actively in the evaluation sessions following the teaching. . . . It is of course clear that the intern who successfully enters into this role is profoundly and continuously involved in the improvement of instruction—that is, in supervision. [Ibid., p. 5]

Although all supervisors at Harvard-Newton do not behave in the same manner, some salient aspects have emerged that appear to be both generalizable and commonly exhibited in practice. Clinical supervision need not be carried out by groups. It can be and often is carried out on a one-to-one basis. Clinical supervision need not be restricted to pre-service teachers. It is theoretically adaptable to any teacher of any experience, and has, in fact, been used with teachers of a wide variety of experience. Clinical supervision is not necessarily remedial in nature. It can and probably should be a continual factor in every teacher's professional education.

There appear to be several assumptions about instruction upon which clinical supervision is based:

1. Instruction is an exceedingly complex interaction between teacher behavior, curriculum or content, and learner behavior, either singly or in groups.

2. Instruction is an intellectual, social, and psychological process that is amenable to rational analysis and some measure of comprehension.

3. Instruction is not a random process; it is patterned in terms of pedagogical, cognitive, affective, and social factors.

4. Instruction should be a rational, conscious, and planned process.

5. Through complex perception and rational analysis, an individual teacher may learn to understand, control, and ultimately improve his own teaching behavior.

Clinical supervisors characteristically view their role as that of a teacher of teachers. Although this is a common role perception of many instructional supervisors (for example, Lucio and McNeil, 1959, p. 3; Bartky, 1953, p. 26; Stratemeyer and Lindsey, 1958, p. 396), the emphasis in clinical supervision is more on the understanding of instructional phenomena than on changing observable teaching behaviors. Intern teachers are encouraged to develop their own teaching styles. What is taught is not necessarily teaching skills but rather the skills of behavioral analysis of instruction. Stress is placed on the making and testing of instructional hypotheses and tentative explanations for instructional interactions, based on observational evidence and findings from the behavioral sciences.

Clinical supervision ranges in practice over a broad continuum from nondirective to directive, supportive to high-pressured, and analytic to prescriptive. However, certain regularities are evident both in practice and in the meager literature available on the subject (for example, Berman and Usery, 1966, p. 25; Blaisdel, 1960; Cogan, 1964; Goldhammer, 1969). These regularities are partially the result of mutual supervision by the supervisors themselves. In intensive and continuing clinical supervision as practiced at the Harvard-Newton Summer School, supervisors have had the opportunity to observe, analyze, and actually supervise one another's practice. In effect, clinical supervisors learn to supervise and analyze supervision in the same way that the interns learn to teach and analyze instruction.

The basis of clinical supervision is the planning, observation, and analysis cycle. Each teaching session is preceded by a planning conference. The teaching is then observed by the conference participants and subsequently evaluated in an analysis conference following soon thereafter. The analysis conference leads naturally to planning for the next lesson. Each element of this cycle is crucial, and each builds upon those which precede it. Without planning, the observations are likely to be haphazard or meaningless, and the analysis session prone to problems of vagueness, misunderstandings of intent, and arbitrary evaluations; without observation there is no basis for analysis and little for planning; and without analysis there is little possibility of rational understanding and no basis for future planning that will build upon strengths and compensate for weakness.

The planning conference necessarily builds upon the past history of the particular group being taught. It ordinarily consists of two major foci: the proposed objectives and the methods of instruction. The subject matter of the lesson is analyzed and justified in terms of the aims of the school, the pupils' backgrounds, and the objectives and structure of the course or unit of which the lesson is a part. Objectives are frequently expressed as behavioral objectives, which identify specific pupil behaviors that might be expected during the lesson. Behavioral objectives provide a common framework both for observation and for the rational analysis and evaluation of the lesson. Their statement in a lesson plan is essentially a statement of hypotheses about how pupils will react to proposed content and methodology.

The planning conference also focuses on the methods and materials of instruction, including equipment, visual aids, teaching strategy, organization of content and method, motivational considerations, and planning for unforeseen contingencies. This involves what Shaplin has called the "psychologizing of curriculum": "the application of methods and techniques appropriate for the objectives and content of instruction and for the characteristics of the students specifically involved" (1961, p. 46).

The observation of the instructional process should produce highly relevant data for the analysis conference to follow. For this purpose supervisors often take verbatim notes, to provide evidence for significant patterns of interaction. Audio tapes, video tapes, and interaction analysis systems have also been employed for this purpose.

Extensive use is often made of focused observation, in which the supervisor and observing interns plan to observe specific parameters of the instructional process. It is a common practice for supervisors to use the pupils as the main focus of observation. At times the group will employ a division of labor, in which one observer might focus on the execution of specific objectives or evidence for specific hypotheses; another might take notes on such preselected factors as logical processes, content shifts, or particularly troublesome pupils; still another might focus on patterns of verbal interaction between teacher and pupils. The observational framework discussed by Cogan (1961) provides a useful guideline for this stage of clinical supervision, which is designed to provide comprehensive and valid data for the analysis of the lesson.

The analysis conference ordinarily follows very soon after the actual instructional period and focuses on the questions "What happened?" and "Why did it happen?" These questions might be asked with respect to the teacher's achievement of his objectives, the testing of previously formulated instructional hypotheses, or the analysis of persistent or unforeseen instructional problems.

The entire instructional process is subject to analysis in these conferences. The purpose of this analysis is mutual understanding of the complex cognitive, affective, and social interactions between teacher, pupils, and content or curriculum. The supervisors and interns are colleagues in this search for understanding, each offering his own perceptions, experience, and competencies to the analysis.

The supervisor's approach to these conferences may vary widely in terms of the parameters of instruction examined as well as the method of examination. Although clinical supervision is carried on by the group, the master teacher obviously sets the tone of supervisory strategy to a large extent, particularly in the early stages. Cogan (ibid., pp. 19–21) delineates a number of possible strategies he has observed. In order of his estimate of increasing potential effectiveness, these include the unconnected inventory of events (sometimes called "checking off the laundry list of faults"); the analysis of critical incidents, or "successive trauma technique"; the analysis of patterns of events with suggestions for improvement; and the selective pattern approach, in which focus is upon a small number of salient patterns both educationally important and realistically amenable to change.

The analysis conference may concentrate at times on training in specific behavioral skills of teaching. In general, however, its overriding function is to establish a basis of perception and understanding with which the participants will later analyze their own instruction and establish their own teaching styles. The movement is therefore from comprehension to creation, even as the supervisory cycle progresses from analysis to planning.

In general, although clinical supervision is as idiosyncratic and personalized as instruction itself, certain basic elements commonly appear. It is possible to abstract from the literature and from actual practice certain assumptions and working hypotheses that characterize the essential nature of this process:

1. The improvement of instruction requires that teachers learn specific intellectual and behavioral skills.

2. The primary function of the supervisor is to teach these skills to the teacher:

   a. Skills of complex analytic perception of the instructional process;

   b. Skills of rational analysis of the instructional process based on explicit observational evidence;

   c. Skills of curriculum innovation, implementation, and experimentation;

   d. Skills of teaching performance.

3. The supervisory focus is on what and how teachers teach; its main objective is to improve instruction, not change the teacher's personality.

4. The supervisory focus in planning and analysis is best anchored in the making and testing of instructional hypotheses based on observational evidence.

5. The supervisory focus is on instructional issues that are small in number, educationally vital, intellectually accessible to the teacher, and amenable to change.

6. The supervisory focus is on constructive analysis and the reinforcement of successful patterns rather than on the condemnation of unsuccessful patterns.

7. The supervisory focus is based on observational evidence, not on unsubstantiated value judgments.

8. The cycle of planning, teaching, and analysis is a continuing one that builds upon past experience.

9. Supervision is a dynamic process of give-and-take in which supervisors and interns are colleagues in search of mutual educational understanding.

10. The supervisory process is primarily one of verbal interaction centered on the analysis of instruction.

11. The individual teacher has both the freedom and the responsibility to initiate issues, analyze and improve his own teaching, and develop a personal teaching style.

12. The supervisor has the responsibility to determine which issues are best handled by the group, which are best handled individually, and which are best left entirely alone.

13. Group supervision is enhanced by individuals of diverse interests, experience, competencies, and viewpoints.

14. In group supervision, the cycle of planning, observation, and analysis is the responsibility of each member of the group.

15. Supervision is itself patterned and amenable to comparable processes of complex perception, rational analysis, and improvement.

16. The supervisor has both the freedom and the responsibility to analyze and evaluate his own supervision in a manner similar to a teacher's analysis and evaluation of his instruction.

Although clinical supervision may be rather explicitly characterized, it has never been adequately researched. Writers have reported their observations of the process and a few recordings and transcripts have been produced, but knowledge of the process rests mainly with those who have experienced it. The next section of this chapter will examine the limited body of research relevant to the processes of clinical supervision.

RESEARCH ON CLINICAL SUPERVISION

Very little research has been published on supervision, and most of that which is available does not focus on the actual process or activity of supervision. Harris has aptly summarized the state of the research:

Notable indeed is the lack of research on the supervisor and supervisory programs and practices in education. We continue to emphasize studies in this field which deal with teacher opinions of supervisors, principal's opinions, contrasting perception of roles, and role conflicts. . . . Neither the quality nor the significance of these studies warrants much more replication. [1963, p. 86]

The majority of this research has been unsystematic, unrelated to other research, globally evaluative, and of very limited scope. Extensive use has been made of questionnaires, subjective rating devices, checklists, and recall information. Significant research results are notably rare. The following broad classifications encompass most of the available supervisory research.

A. Correlational studies of supervisory ratings and student-teacher personality factors.

B. Correlation studies of supervisory ratings and supervisor personality or experience.

C. Comparisons of ratings by different types of supervisors.

D. Questionnaire studies of factors in the selection and training of supervisors.

E. Questionnaire studies of supervisors' role perceptions.

F. Correlational studies of student teacher attitudes and personalities with supervisor attitudes and personalities.

G. Evaluation studies of particular supervisory programs.

There is a significant lack of concern with the actual process of supervision in these research areas. They appear to epitomize the condition expressed in Gage's *Handbook of Research on Teaching* as "dust-bowl empiricism" in research on teaching:

. . . research too often proceeds without explicit theoretical framework, in intellectual disarray, to the testing of myriads of arbitrary, unrationalized hypotheses. The studies too often interact too little with each other, do not fall into place within any scheme, and hence add little to the understanding of the . . . process. [1963, p. 102]

Some research, however, does focus on the process of supervision itself. Other studies, chiefly in the fields of research on teaching and student teaching, deal with aspects of observation and analysis that may be considered germane to research on supervision. This section will briefly examine representative types of this research in order to provide a basis for the research focus of this book.

In general, research studies relating to the processes of clinical supervision fall into three categories: (1) status studies or evaluations of supervisory activities, (2) experimental studies of specific supervisory techniques, and (3) theoretically based studies of total supervisory methodology.

Status and evaluation studies have utilized both the reports of participants and direct observational techniques. For example, Swineford (1964, pp. 299–303) reported on supervisors' suggestions to student teachers for teaching improvement. These suggestions were recorded at a later date in essay form. They were then tabulated into the following categories in order of decreasing importance: teaching techniques and procedures, discipline and control, development of a classroom personality, planning, and development of a sound academic background. This study concluded with general implications for student teaching program development and supervision.

Hollister (1950, pp. 54–56) asked supervisors to report the topics discussed with student teachers. Thirty supervisors reported 510 topics that the author summarized into eighteen professional items, nine subject areas, and twenty-six teaching procedures. Frequencies are given for the number of times the topics were discussed, the number of different supervisors discussing them, and the weeks during which these discussions occurred. The analysis indicates extreme variability and a disconcerting lack of emphasis on topics directly related to the instructional process. Although the author stresses that the summary should only be suggestive of possible topic areas in the supervisory conference, this study reinforces the common notion that supervision is frequently a confused and irrelevant process.

Other studies have reported the reactions of student teachers to the process of supervision. McConnell (1960, pp. 84–86), Trimmer (1960, pp. 537–538; 1961, pp. 229–231), and Edmund and Hemink (1958, pp. 57–60) all found that student teachers want suggestions, constructive criticism, regular conferences, and freedom to show initiative while disliking rigidity, disorganization, and lack of candor. Little attempt was made to specify these categories more precisely, and the results appear to provide little substantial help to the supervisor.

Roth (1961, pp. 476–481) and Wright (1965) both studied student teachers' reports of supervisory activities they considered effective or ineffective, using the "critical incident technique." In both cases attempts were made to determine criteria of effectiveness for supervisors, a difficult objective for such a complex interaction. Wright limited herself to very general criteria (such as "reviewed lesson for evaluative purposes"), and Roth's more behaviorally defined criteria are based on only seventeen returns from student teachers. The critical incidents themselves provide revealing data on the problems and opinions of student teachers, but major implications for the process of supervision cannot be made from these studies.

Blumberg and Amidon took a different approach by focusing on perceptions of supervisory method. They assessed the research literature as follows:

In view of the obvious importance of the behavior of the supervisor in supervisor-teacher interaction, the paucity of research on the supervisory conference is surprising. . . . Nowhere does one find a clinical study of the supervisory confrontation. Neither are there systematic attempts to study the manner in which teachers perceive the conference itself, the supervisor's behavior, and the apparent consequences. [1965, pp. 1–8]

They chose the latter focus for their study. One hundred sixty-six in-service teachers reported their perceptions of actual and ideal supervisory conferences with their principals during the preceding year.

The questionnaire items were divided into two groups. The first set of items was adapted from Flanders' categories (1965). Included were items labeled "direct behavior," such as giving information or opinion, directions or commands, and criticism; and "indirect" behavior, such as accepting feelings and ideas, praising or encouraging, and asking questions. The second set of questions comprised "items relating to teacher evaluations of communicative freedom and supportiveness, learning outcome, amount of supervisory talk, and general productivity in the supervisory conference."

Blumberg and Amidon arrived at the following major conclusions:

1. High indirect supervisory behavior, whether combined with high direct behavior or not, is related to evaluations of greater conference productivity.
2. High indirect combined with high direct supervision behavior is related to learning about one's self both as a teacher and as a person.
3. Freedom of communication in the conference appeared to be curtailed only when the supervisor exhibited a combination of high direct and low indirect behavior.
4. The discrepancy between perceived and wished-for supervisory behavior was greatest for supervisors who de-emphasized indirect behavior. [1965, pp. 2, 3]

This study indicates that the interpersonal dynamics of supervisory conferences may have a substantial relationship to perceived productivity.

Studies directly analyzing supervisory conferences without resorting to report data are extremely rare. Kyte (1962, pp. 160–168) focused on the effects of conference "content." He collected thirty sets of tape recordings, each consisting of a lesson observed by a supervisor, a follow-up conference, and a second lesson taught shortly thereafter. All elementary grades, most subjects, and both city and rural schools were included in the sample. Typescripts were made of each recording and analyzed in the following ways:

A. Each lesson pair was randomly ordered and ten experienced supervisors rated the better lesson of the pair, giving reasons for their ratings.
B. A research analyst, a graduate student trained in elementary supervision, and the actual supervisor involved each listed conference "items"

according to order and frequency of occurrence, initiator, manner of introduction, the nature of the discussion, and the amount of stress (rated as
major stress, minor stress, and passing mention).

C. The research staff related conference "items" to changes in teaching
behavior.

Although this research approach appears to have great potential,
little use appears to have been made of the available data. Only the
number of "items" and amount of "stress" is actually reported. No
indication is given of the type of item or manner of presentation. The
"effectiveness" of supervisory "items" was determined in a very arbitrary way, and no information is given concerning the amount or type
of behavior change.

The results of this study all pertain to the optimal number of
"items" in a conference and the amount of stress that "should" be
given to each. Kyte's conclusions from this study are:

1. The conference should include not more than four or five items.

2. The first item in the conference should be planned to establish rap-
port and consequently should be given only minor stress or passing mention.

3. The second and third items in the conference should be given major
stress. If there is any difference in the amount of stress, the third item should
receive the greater stress.

4. The fourth item in the conference should be given either major stress
or minor stress, depending on the degree of influence desired on the subsequent teaching.

5. The fifth point in the conference should be given either minor stress
or passing mention and generally should be related to one of the preceding
items.

6. The last point introduced into the conference should be given either
minor stress or passing mention. It should have a pleasing effect on the
teacher irrespective of its influence on subsequent teaching.

7. When a number of items are included in a conference some of them
should be related to each other. The relatedness should be included especially when two or more major items are treated.

8. Repetition in the discussion of a major point should increase its
effectiveness on subsequent teaching. The repetition can occur in a brief
review of the item at or near the end of the conference. [Ibid, p. 168]

Kyte's conclusions appear to be unjustified. He assumes that all
instructional supervisors approach their task in the same manner and
that supervisory content and stress are the only important factors.
He also assumes that a definite format and ordering of topics can be
established that is effective for all supervisors and all supervisees.
These assumptions ignore the great complexity of instructional and

supervisory interactions. In short, this study is oversimplified and unjustifiably prescriptive.

Heidelbach (1967) and Brown and Hoffman (1966) both developed models for describing and analyzing the verbal behavior of supervisors in conferences with student teachers. These models were developed as part of a long-range team approach to research on supervision being carried out at Columbia University, and they will be examined later in this chapter. Neither model has yet been used in systematic research on actual supervisory conferences.

Experimental studies of specific supervisory technique are currently receiving much attention and appear to be having a definite impact on supervisory practice. Most of this research has focused on observational and analysis techniques. These studies are currently dominated by the concept of information feedback, derived mainly from engineering and the physical sciences. As used in these technical fields, feedback is usually defined as a sample of information from the output or results of a process that is compared with a specific plan or goal for the purpose of controlling the process itself. The sample is returned or "fed back" to the control mechanism, and the difference or error signal determines the kind and amount of change required.

The term has acquired a variety of different meanings in the educational literature, depending upon the purposes for which the feedback is used. Feedback has been applied to information used for confirmation or knowledge of correct results as well as for comparison with a goal or control of a process. It has also been applied to information presented to an individual about his actions for the purpose of refreshing his memory or challenging his own perceptions.

In research on supervision, feedback generally consists of information about a person's teaching that is presented to him after the fact. In some cases feedback is used to examine the way in which a particular planned course of action was executed. In other cases feedback is provided as a basis for the objective analysis and interpretation of instructional interactions.

The use of feedback in supervision has been accelerated by recent research in the descriptive analysis of teaching and by developments in instructional technology. Studies in teaching have provided both conceptional schemes for organizing information and category systems for the transmission of this information to teachers. Technological developments such as audio and video tape machines have provided objective channels for the transmission of feedback to teachers. These sources contain much more potential information than category systems, but the organization and interpretation of this information depends more on the individuals involved.

Research on supervision has employed feedback via time-lapse photography (MacGraw, 1965), kinescopes (Schueler and Gold, 1964, pp. 358–364), audio tapes (Moser, 1965), electrical signals indicating student understanding (Belanger, 1962), pupil opinionaires (Seager, 1965), and numerous category systems (see, for example, the following reports of research using the indicated category system: Withall's technique—Ishler, 1965; Flander's system—Yulo, 1967; Bellack's system—Brown, Cobban, and Waterman, 1966; OScAR—Morrison and Dixon, 1964, pp. 96–103). Because the volume of published or proposed studies in this area is becoming very large (for example, Simon and Boyer, 1967), only representative studies have been selected to illustrate different types of feedback information or different supervisory methodologies.

Seager and Belanger both used varieties of pupil feedback in supervision. Seager (1965) employed a short opinionaire of "improvement desirable" on various dimensions of student teacher behaviors. This was completed by the student teachers, their pupils, and their supervisors at the beginning and end of a six-week teaching period. The opinionaries were given to the student teachers as a form of feedback. Student teachers showed significant changes in certain teaching behaviors, as perceived by their pupils, in the direction of "needed improvement" indicated by these same pupils. In effect, Seager's study utilized both specific commitments for change by the student teachers (their own estimates of "needed improvements") and feedback. Pupil feedback was the most significant change variable.

In Belanger's study (1962) pupils used electrical switches to indicate when they did not understand the subject matter being presented by three intern teachers. A recorder registered the frequency of the "pupil switching response," which was later used both as feedback information and as a measure of teaching change. Although the signals could have been shown to the teacher as they occurred, they were recorded and shown after the class session. Each intern taught the same lesson twice, to different pupils, with a feedback conference preceding the second teaching episode. Feedback techniques consisted of combinations of pupil feedback and the supervisor's own record of the classroom proceedings. Switching responses were compared with written notes to provide a basis for the analysis of instruction.

The study revealed that over the experimental period each of the interns changed his teaching style from lecture to discussion. In the lectures there were significant decreases in pupils' switching responses after presentation of feedback in six out of nine cases, while in the discussions these differences were evident in only one out of nine cases. Switching responses were negatively related to the number of teacher questions.

This study indicated that the style of teaching may be an important variable in determining the effectiveness of feedback. The effectiveness of formal feedback also decreased as the interns became more perceptive of informal feedback from their pupils. Belanger's study appears to be unique in its use of pupil feedback with respect to specific objectives for understanding content.

Global audio or video feedback to teachers is becoming widely used as a supervisory technique, but much of the research to date has produced nonsignificant or ambivalent results. (For a summary of many of these studies see Schueler and Lesser, 1967, pp. 37–44.) These uncertain results may be caused by the lack of reliable dependent variables when the feedback is used as a basis for instructional analysis. Significant results have been achieved more often when feedback is used for a specific training purpose. This may be chiefly due to the specificity both of criterion and training variables. If one is willing to confine supervision to specific operational objectives, methodology may be tested with great precision.

The Hunter College study (Schueler and Gold, 1964) is often quoted as an instance in which a careful research design and analysis indicated no significant difference between the effects of different supervisors and different supervisory feedback techniques. Change in teaching behavior, measured by the Observation Schedule And Record (OScAR III), was used as a dependent variable. No difference was detected between supervisory methods using direct observation, kinescope recordings, or a combination of observations and kinescopes. Although significant teaching changes were noticed that were uniform for all teachers and that indicated "improvements" in teaching skill, no uniform effect was recorded of one supervisor over another. The one important factor seemed to be the individual class itself, the idiosyncratic combination of pupils and teacher producing what might be called a "classroom personality."

On the other hand, when specific training objectives are established in operational terms, significant results have been recorded with the use of feedback techniques. McDonald, Allen, and Orme (1965) studied the effects of different types of videotaped feedback on specific classroom teaching behaviors of practice teachers at Stanford University. The supervisory focus, also the dependent variable, was the teacher's positive reinforcement of pupil participatory responses. These were defined as "desirable" or "relevant" pupil responses. Of particular interest to this analysis are the types of feedback that were provided. The control group received general written instructions for viewing videotaped replays of their lessons and subsequently viewed the lessons alone. A self-feedback group received different instructions relating to pupil responses and rewarding these responses, and behavioral examples were provided. This group received a rating sheet for recording these behaviors and also viewed the playback alone. A reinforcement group received the same instructions as the preceding group but viewed the playbacks with a supervisor who positively reinforced each desired teacher response. A final group included a supervisor who not only provided differential reinforcement but also pointed out salient cues, made suggestions, and indicated effects on pupils.

This study showed that supervisory feedback which included both reinforcement and discrimination training was most effective in increasing student teachers' use of reinforcement techniques. The researchers hypothesized that the self-feedback condition was probably ineffective because of lack of cueing: the teachers may not have known when to produce the desired responses. Teachers also reacted differently to the different feedback techniques, a factor that may have influenced these results.

Second only in number of studies to videotaped feedback are those which have used various category systems as feedback instruments. The differences in significant results reported in these studies, like the studies using videotaped feedback, may be a function of the specificity of objectives and differences in the ways in which the feedback was actually used.

In Yulo's experiment (1967) Flander's Interaction Analysis instrument was used both as feedback and as a measure of teaching change. Yulo's interns were given minimal training in analyzing interaction matrices. The primary purpose of the feedback was to focus attention on classroom variables and to analyze classroom interaction without reference to specific training objectives. These objectives are implicit, however, both in the nature of the categories chosen and in the way in which they are scored and analyzed. A high indirect-to-direct teaching ratio, for example, is strongly valued in Flanders' work.

Yulo's experimental group of seven interns showed no significant differences from his control group, although he hypothesizes that the feedback may have helped minimize a "semester" effect found in other studies. Yulo's interns in the fall semester, for example, became less direct than a comparable group studied by Molchen (1967) a year later. Much of the importance of Yulo's study lies in his penetrating clinical analysis of the interns themselves and their reaction to feedback and to supervision.

Zahn (1965), at Temple University, also used the Flanders system for feedback with student teachers but provided his experimental group with over fifteen hours of intensive training in interaction analysis. This group did show significant changes in teaching behaviors in the direction considered positive by Flanders, such as a high ratio of indirect to direct teaching behavior and greater use of praise.

It may be hypothesized that the strong emphasis on the Flanders system at Temple University plus the training given to the experimental group combined to produce these effects. While Yulo consciously tried to avoid a strong bias in his supervision, there is no indication that Zahn did the same. This study may actually be measuring differential training effects rather than the effects of feedback alone.

The differences between these studies indicate that important elements are often missing in research of this type on specific supervisory techniques. Feedback is only a source of supervisory data. As such it provides a tool for supervision, but the effect of any tool depends on the ways in which it is used. The fundamental meaning of both significant and insignificant statistical results might often be enhanced by a more careful examination of other variables in the supervisory situation.

Studies of total supervisory methodologies germane to clinical supervision, which are carefully implemented and documented for the purpose of demonstrating the extent of actual implementation, are extremely rare.

Mosher (1964) used the methodology of ego counseling in the supervision of practice teachers. He hypothesized that success in practice teaching involves the individual's reasoning about and revising his own reality problems, plans, and actions. The supervisory foci are the practice teacher's self-perception in the teaching situation, the relationship of his actions to the attainment of his objectives, the examination of obstacles to these objectives, and the development of new ways of thinking about and acting in the role of a teacher. Mosher's method involved use of ego-counseling techniques of restatement of meaning, questioning, interpretation, and confrontation.

Mosher's experimental group of eleven practice teachers showed a grade point increase of 1.82 points, and a subgroup of seven atypically ineffectual teachers increased their practice teaching grade by 2.50 grade points. Both increases were significant beyond the .0005 level for the period of supervision. The increase for the atypical subgroup was significant at the .05 level when compared with a similar group in the previous year. The major evidence for the applicability of ego counseling in supervision was based on the analysis of conference transcripts, a rating scale, and a questionnaire. The transcripts gave evidence that the methodology was actually used in this experiment, evidence that is lacking in many studies of supervision. This is one of the few cases in which the actual interactions between supervisor and teacher are reasonably well documented.

Binnington (1965) reasoned that a positive self-concept is the most important variable in teaching success and that the supervisor's function is to maintain and enhance this self-concept. He therefore applied a model of client-centered counseling to a group of eleven teachers. Binnington used Gibb's counseling model, in which the social concerns of acceptance, data-processing, goal, and control are resolved in that specific order. The quality of the interpersonal relationship between the supervisor and the practice teachers was a major factor in this methodology. A comparison group attempted to resolve those same social concerns, but the temporal order was reversed. Binnington called his methodology with this group a "conventional" model of supervision, in which the concerns are resolved through the processes of observation, interpretation, and the making of suggestions.

Binnington used self-acceptance Q-sorts as a dependent variable. His experimental group showed a self-acceptance increase significant at the .025 level over the control group. Although written evaluations from both groups were positive, the experimental group desired more concrete suggestions, while the control group would have preferred more freedom. Binnington's assumption of positive self-concept as a critical variable in supervision must be considered experimentally unvalidated in this study, since he made no attempt to assess differences in success in student teaching.

With the exception of these two instances, the literature appears devoid of studies in which a carefully developed methodology, based on theory, was applied to broad aspects of teacher supervision. The general theoretical orientations found in much of the literature remain experimentally unvalidated and must be considered to be based mainly on intuition and hope.

In general, each of these three categories of research on supervision has its inherent advantages and disadvantages. Each would benefit from the incorporation of elements of the others. Unfortunately, much of the current research seems aimed at "proving a point" rather than at the understanding of very complex phenomena. As a result, research findings are often isolated, ungeneralizable, and unrelated to any developing conceptualization of the total process being studied. The next chapter proposes a research methodology that might help to pull these disparate elements together.

•3•

An Observational System for the Analysis of Clinical Supervision: Rationale and Choice of a System Framework

Clinical supervision, like teaching itself, is not founded on any one overriding theory translated into practice. It is rather a process that has evolved through experience, intuition, and trial and error. There is no one "style" of clinical supervision, but rather a variety of idiosyncratic styles that are individually developed much as individual teaching styles are developed.

Philip Jackson's distinction between "interactive" teaching and "preactive" teaching appears relevant to research on clinical supervision (1966, pp. 12–15). Jackson defines "preactive" teaching as the behavior of the teacher that is relevant to the task of teaching but carried on outside of the classroom. Examples of this category are such behaviors as making lesson plans, studying test reports, and analyzing aberrant behavior. Jackson regards this phase of teaching as analyzable in terms of models of the teacher as problem-solver or hypothesis-maker.

"Interactive" teaching, on the other hand, is behavior occurring vis-à-vis the students in classrooms. Jackson feels this behavior is more or less spontaneous, the teacher doing what he "feels" or "knows" is right rather than what he "thinks" is right. There are two major reasons for this. One is the fact that the students to some extent control what the teacher does. Much of the teacher's behavior is in response to pupils' requests and actions and could not have been planned ahead of time. Another reason is the evident rapidity of the events in the classroom. The teacher rarely has much time to think out all his actions and reactions in detail.

31

When this analysis is applied to supervision, clinical supervision may be considered an institutionalized form of "preactive" teaching.

During the preactive phase of teaching . . . models of rational inquiry do seem to have considerable descriptive power. As the teacher goes about deciding which textbook to use, how to group the children for reading, or whether to notify Billy's parents of his poor performance in arithmetic, his behavior is at least analyzable in terms that describe the rational problem solver. At such moments concepts such as evidence, evaluation, prediction, and feedback have real meaning for understanding what the teacher is doing. It is doubtful that they have similar meaning in the interactive setting. [Ibid., p. 15]

Clinical supervision is itself, however, similar to an interactive teaching situation. The interchange between participants is often quite rapid and spontaneous, and the process of the interaction is determined to a great extent by the actions of the supervisees. If clinical supervision is viewed as a relatively spontaneous interactive process, the potential deficiencies in theoretical and methodological research become more evident.

Methodological research based on models from such relevant disciplines as counseling psychology is prone to arguments such as those made by Travers with respect to curriculum research:

It is often difficult to determine just how curricula do differ. We must not be fooled by names and assume that, just because they differ in name (as do the so-called traditional and progressive curricula), they differ in significant stimulus characteristics as far as the pupil is concerned. The results of much research on curricula in the past have had little validity because the differences in curricula have been differences in name. [1958, p. 147]

The basic problem is one of execution. "Theory does not interpret or apply itself. Its meaning and utility reside in persons and depend on the ends they have in mind" (Thelen, 1963, p. 19). Both of the studies involving the application of counseling theory to supervision provided operational specification of supervisory actions and some evidence in the form of typescripts that these actions were indeed carried out. Further documentation of the nature and extent of the interaction between supervisor and supervisee would appear to be very valuable. This is particularly important if the effects of supervision on different individuals is to be examined.

Data of this sort are of crucial importance if more than one supervisor is included in future research. Different supervisors operating under the same theory might behave very differently in practice. Also, the behavior of any supervisor in an interactive situation will probably vary with both the situation and the individual being supervised. Studies of what actually happens during the interactive confrontation between supervisor and supervisee, especially over a length of time and under different conditions, appears to be a necessary factor in research of this type.

Supervisory research investigating a particular technique, such as the use of videotaped feedback, is hampered by similar uncertainties. Feedback devices and descriptive category schemes are being used as if they were effective in and of themselves. In reality, they are almost never used in isolation. Researchers have generally ignored the interaction between supervisor, supervisee, and feedback.

As an example, the Hunter College study (Schueler and Gold, 1964) showed no significant differences in the relative effect of one supervisor over another or of one supervisory treatment over another. This does not indicate that supervisors have no effect, for there is no specification of their individual objectives. Definite changes in teaching were found for all student teachers. Which of these changes, if any, were implemented by conscious supervision? Some changes appeared to be uniform. Were they the result of uniform supervisory actions or did different actions interact and modify one another? There was no relative effect of any one supervisory treatment. Did the interaction of supervisor, student teacher, and treatment alter the specific treatment effects? Are different treatments effective with individual student teachers at different stages of the supervisory process?

The evident differences between the studies of Schueler (ibid.) and McDonald, Allen, and Orme (1965) with video tapes and the studies by Yulo (1967) and Zahn (1965) with Flanders' Interaction Analysis appear to be based on questions of this type.

The status studies might provide a mechanism for answering some of the questions raised by theoretically based studies and research on supervisory techniques. The major difficulty lies in the fact that they too have tended to ignore the interactive and individualized nature of the supervisory process. Almost without exception these studies have viewed supervision as a stable referent and have attempted to develop guidelines or prescriptions for general practice. Critical incidents, reports of participants, and *post hoc* evaluations lose much of their meaning when divorced from the specifics of the situation itself.

One promising approach of this type has been almost totally neglected to date: research focusing on the direct observation and analysis of actual supervisory interactions. Research of this type might help to fill in present gaps in supervisory research. It would also open a new field of research that examines the competencies of experienced supervisors expressed in their interactive confrontations with supervisees.

Direct observation and analysis presents a number of distinct advantages. It yields data that is immediately pertinent to typical behavioral situations; it allows recording of data that is independent of the participants' willingness or ability to report; and it minimizes global evaluative judgments by relying on objective recordings of behaviors. Furthermore, it can be used both to test causal hypotheses and to make accurate descriptions of phenomena from which new hypotheses might be derived. The basic rationale for this research orientation is that precise data on actual supervisory interactions is a basis from which regularities may be determined, hypotheses proposed, and theories ultimately developed.

This latter point warrants further discussion. The major developing trend in research on supervision appears to be the study of a patchwork of isolated supervisory techniques. Studies too often attempt to "prove" that one technique or instrument is better than another, or that some resultant behaviors can be attributed to some given instrumental actions. A great deal of energy has been expended testing hypotheses having little relationship to any theoretical framework. There is no one overriding theory of supervision, and little basis from which one might presently be derived. The apparent educational value of supervision, however, indicates that the development of scientific theories is of crucial importance.

Maccia (1965, pp. 88–89) specified an adequate scientific theory as one exhibiting formal coherence, observational verification, and observational predictiveness. There are theories of supervision that exhibit formal coherence, but research has not progressed far enough to provide direct evidence either for verification or prediction. Clinical supervision exhibits both a measure of formal coherence and some evidence of systematic practice.

Northrop (1947, pp. 34–37) proposes that theory development proceeds in three phases which are roughly comparable to Maccia's specification: an analysis phase of a broad problem area that defines and organizes the basic theoretical root of a problem; a natural history phase employing observation, description, and classification that produces relevant data; and a stage of deductive theory from which inferences may be made, concepts deduced, and hypotheses tested.

Northrop notes that the majority of the social sciences are in the second stage of theory development. Major strides have been made in some fields through direct observation and analysis, particularly in such areas as social relations, child study, and group process (see, for example, such sources as Sellitz, Jahoda, Deutsch, and Cook, 1959, pp.

199–234; Wright, 1960, pp. 71–139). The long history of success in these fields contrasts sharply with the sporadic history of direct observation in the field of education.

Recently, however, direct observational research has begun to make impressive inroads on the teaching process. Studies by Flanders (1965), Smith and Meux (1959), Bellack (1966), and many others (for example, Medley and Mitzel, 1963, pp. 247–328) are opening up entirely new avenues of research on instruction. Data from these studies have not only been used to test existing hypotheses but have produced an information pool from which new hypotheses may be derived and theories of instruction ultimately developed.

One of the most productive aspects of these studies has been the development of complex observational systems as research tools. These systems, comprehensive and reliable, are based on an increasingly broad range of theoretical and observational variables. The diversity and sophistication of these systems indicates that educational researchers are finally making realistic attempts to examine the actual complexities of instructional interactions.

These observational category systems have several distinct advantages over less structured observational methods. There are obvious economies of data collection and abstraction in a structured system. These systems also allow researchers in widely varying situations to produce comparable data with a minimum of observer bias, less need for extensive observer training, and greater ease in maintaining observer reliability. Some systems are flexible enough to be modified for quite different purposes while retaining the essential nature of the data for purposes of comparison. Flanders' system, for example, has been modified by Amidon and Hunter (n.d.) and Hough (1965) for research on teaching, by Blumberg (1970) for research on supervision, and by Amidon (1965, pp. 50–55) for research on counseling.

Structured observational systems are entirely appropriate for the study of clinical supervision, which commonly occurs in rather structured conference settings. It reduces problems of equating the effects of a participant observer in group and individual conferences, both of which occur in supervision. The use of unmanned audio and video tape machines provides nonparticipant observers with the advantage of a permanent record that can be replayed for analysis by different theoretical frameworks and by systems too complex for a single live observer. Although structuring limits the range of available data sources, the greater amount of information available in the sources selected is a compensating advantage.

Observational systems expressly designed for research on clinical supervision do not currently exist. There are, however, three systems for the analysis of general supervision that would be applicable to clinical supervision. Arthur Blumberg (1970) has proposed a category system based on Flanders' instrument, and two "promissory models" have been developed as part of a research project at Columbia University.

Blumberg's system (see Appendix A) is an adaptation of Flanders' System of Interaction Analysis. It is a single-scoring, direct observational instrument in which a categorization is made every three seconds. The results are tabulated in a two-dimensional matrix of sequential categorizations.

Like Flanders, Blumberg seems to assume that the supervisee's learning is directly related to his level of independence in the conference. Flanders (1965) defines independence as a condition in which pupils see their activities as "self-directed," do not expect directions from the teacher, prefer to try their own solutions to problems before seeking help, and critically evaluate the teacher's help when it is given. He assumes that conditions of dependence or independence are created by the teacher's use of direct or indirect influence, operationally defined in terms of specific categories of the observational system. (See Appendix B.)

A comparison of the two systems shows that seven of the categories are essentially identical. Blumberg differentiates categories for questions and lectures into subgroups relating to the supervisor's focus on information, opinions, and suggestions. He also adds two categories for the supervisee's positive or negative social-emotional behavior.

A system of this type has several distinct advantages. Many supervisors consider supervision to be an instructional process, and the concept of direct-indirect influence is a useful way of examining this process. This system permits direct comparisons with the enormous amount of data currently being produced with the Flanders system. The Blumberg system can be readily learned and used with reliability and ease. The unique matrix analysis is both efficient and highly productive.

There are definite shortcomings, however, caused partially by the very simplicity of the system. Blumberg's system emphasizes the supervisor's verbal behavior, but it does not provide much detailed information on the supervisee. Clinical supervision places a high value on the initiative and active participation of all members of the conference. Blumberg's system does not permit the researcher to examine comparable parameters of each participant's verbal interaction, and thus it neglects crucial aspects of clinical supervision.

Blumberg's system also requires a forced choice between cognitive or task-oriented items (e.g., "asks for information") and social-emotional categories (e.g., "praise"). Although it is possible to score more than one item in each three-second interval, this forced choice is often difficult to make and possibly misleading.

While the categories themselves have proved useful for the analysis of generalized instructional interactions, they do not provide much research "leverage" on critical aspects of clinical supervision such as the rational analysis of specific instructional parameters. Although the system has certain advantages, particularly simplicity, direct coding, and ease of comparison with existing research, it is not ideally suitable to the analysis of the unique qualities of clinical supervision.

Brown and Hoffman (1966) developed a "promisory model" for analyzing and describing the verbal interaction between college supervisors and student teachers. The model was developed by abstracting generalized dimensions of performance for counselors and supervisors from the literature on counseling and general school supervision, and is designed to be used with typescripts of conferences. The authors propose two possible units for analysis: the "utterance," or uninterrupted verbal behavior of a participant, and the "thought unit," which expresses one complete idea.

The model consists of eleven "category procedures," which are subsumed under three "category domains": problem-solving, affective, and structuring. (See Appendix C.) This categorization has the advantage of separating the discourse into what are essentially cognitive, affective, and procedural dimensions. It is apparently possible to score a given utterance in more than one domain, but the authors do not indicate how this decision is made. Every cognitive procedure has at least some affective overtone, and optional scoring decisions present difficulties comparable to forced choices between categories.

The authors have not used their model in an actual research study, but a number of "utterances" were coded for reliability purposes and examples of verbal behavior are provided for each category. In general, the model is relatively simple and the breakdown into cognitive, affective, and procedural dimensions is a useful one. It is possible, however, that the "dimensions of counseling and supervisory performance" have been abstracted from the literature to the point that they have lost any unique pertinence to the process of supervision.

The Brown-Hoffman system is simple, but it must be used with typescripts of supervisory conferences, an expensive, frustrating, and time-consuming process. It is unfortunate that the system does not make more extensive use of this effort. Since the authors present no evidence of the utility of their model's output, it is doubtful that many researchers or supervisor-trainers will go to the trouble to use it with only eleven categories at their disposal. This would not necessarily be so if the system were directly related to a specific model of supervision or to theoretical formulations from the behavioral sciences. Although the system might be made more practical by adaptation to direct observation, its research utility must remain in doubt until demonstrated by future studies.

Heidelbach (1967) developed a "tentative model" for analyzing and describing the verbal behaviors of cooperating teachers engaged in individualized teaching with student teachers. The model contains two types of categories, operational categories and substantive areas. (See Appendix D.) Heidelbach arrived at her model by using procedures of content analysis and by "immersing herself" in a data pool of typescripts of supervisory conferences.

The model focuses only on the cooperating teacher's behavior— the student teacher is not considered at all. Analysis is made from typescripts in which the "larger unit of behavior" is the cooperating teacher's uninterrupted talk and the "smaller unit of behavior" consists of one operational category and one or more substantive areas.

Heidelbach's three operational categories (focusing, descriptive, and prescriptive operations) have potential utility, but they appear to have been somewhat inadequately conceptualized. She places most of her stress on the substantive areas, which contain categories ranging from "characteristics of children" to "school nurse" and "school monitor." Many seem germane only to the elementary school, and the choice of these particular categories seems to have depended primarily on their chance occurrence in the nine conferences she analyzed. A more general categorization, one that related items to some overall framework or established some hierarchy of importance having to do with the purposes of the conference, would appear to be much more useful to the researcher and the practitioner.

In an attempt to develop an instrument for research on the processes of clinical supervision that was meaningful, comprehensive, and reasonably easy to use, the author (1967) examined most of the available instruments for research on teaching and on group process. The observational system for research on teaching developed by Arno Bellack's research group (1966) was finally chosen as a basic framework. M.O.S.A.I.C.S. (Multidimensional Observational System for the Analysis of Interactions in Clinical Supervision) is an adaptation of the Bellack system designed for supervisory research.

There are many reasons for this choice. Bellack's system is designed for the analysis of teaching interactions. Although the clinical supervisor is at times a counselor, at times a trainer in behavioral skills, and at times an evaluator, the teaching role provides an initial research framework for what is generally considered the major function of clinical supervision and an important factor in most types of instructional supervision. Anderson presents a strong argument for the concept of supervision as the teaching of teachers about teaching:

(The) theoretical underpinnings are essentially the same constructs and ideas that undergird teaching itself. In other words, supervisory theory in this case derives from a concept of teaching, and its procedural elements are similar to those which guide teachers in their work with students. The supervisor is seen as a teacher, the dimensions of whose work are virtually the same as those one finds in the work of teachers. [1967, p. 33]

The use of an established framework for the analysis of instructional interactions also permits direct comparisons between research on teaching and research on supervision.

As Greenberg (1966, p. 100) points out, Bellack's is the only major system for research on teaching that does not make the assumption that each participant can and does control his verbal interaction in the classroom. It seems well suited to the analysis of the spontaneous, at times almost unconscious, nature of verbal discourse:

The use of the classroom game metaphor, coupled with [Bellack's definitions], indicates that the nature of the classroom enterprise, as seen in the Bellack study, has aspects which occur irrespective of the persons involved. It is the functioning of the enterprise itself which calls forth a certain kind of response rather than the persons involved. This aspect might be seen as being system oriented rather than person oriented. [Ibid., p. 101]

Most clinical supervision appears to be carried out through verbal interaction, and verbal behavior is thus an appropriate focus for at least the initial stages of observational research in this area. Other processes—such as modeling of teaching behavior, study of audio and video tapes, examining interaction analysis printout, and construction of teaching aids occur as well—and are not accounted for by this instrument. Neither are nonverbal cues, the often unconscious, unintended expressive acts that may be a crucial factor in social interaction. Their omission is basically a result of the limitations inherent in any one observational instrument.

Bellack's is one of the few major systems in which teacher-pupil behavior is not arbitrarily considered to begin with the teacher's behavior. Stress is on the different but complementary roles of participants in instructional interactions:

Clearly the verbal activities involved in teaching are reciprocal affairs involving both teachers and students. It follows, therefore, that the role played by the teacher can be adequately described only in relation to the role played by the students. Specifying the activities of teachers in the class-room without at the same time analyzing the actions of the students would give a distorted and incomplete view of the teaching process. [Bellack, 1966, p. 2]

This is a particularly important factor for the analysis of clinical super-vision because great stress is placed on the responsibility of all the participants for the entire process of planning and analysis.

One of the most important aspects of Bellack's system is his choice of "pedagogical moves" as a basic unit, and their analysis in cyclical patterns or combinations called "teaching cycles." Pedagogical moves are basic units of initiation and reaction, and their cycles occur with remarkable regularity in his research. Bellack's study indicated that teachers and students fill different but complementary roles, and that teaching appears to be governed by certain ground rules that guide the actions or moves made by the participants.

These regularities underscore the significance of Wittgenstein's metaphor of the "language game":

[The "language game" metaphor] points up the fact that linguistic activi-ties assume different forms and structures according to the functions they come to serve in different contexts. A game has a definite structure, and there are certain moves that a player is bound to make insofar as he is playing the game at all. . . . Learning to participate appropriately in various kinds of language activities is very much like learning to play a game. Players have to learn the rules, the purpose of the rules, and how the various parts of the game are related. Only by learning these rules can one play the game successfully. Similarly, successful communication in various types of linguistic activities depends on understanding the language rules that govern the use of words in these activities. [Ibid., p. 3]

The concept of the pedagogical move and the teaching cycle ap-pear as pertinent to the study of clinical supervision as they have proved to be in the study of teaching. If clinical supervision is indeed patterned, as many of its proponents assume, these patterns should be evident in a study using Bellack's instrument as a basic framework. One would expect that some "rules of the game" for supervision would be similar to those for teaching, while others would be very different. The examination of these similarities and differences might help to illuminate both fields.

Another reason for choosing the Bellack framework is the fact that it is both comprehensive and multidimensional. His system classifies each pedagogical move into separate categories according to the speaker, the pedagogical move, the content of the interaction, and the logical treatment of that content. It also permits the scoring of procedural categories concerned with instruction and classroom management, and their associated logical or extra-logical treatments.

This comprehensiveness allows the researcher to examine many different factors of any given interaction. It also permits him to add or substitute entire sections of the analysis system without changing its basic nature. For example, Bellack's original content categories were based on a specific unit on international trade. Categories in biology or French could easily be substituted without altering the basic framework of moves or teaching cycles. Similarly, one might add to or change the logical categories to suit a particular type of research. In this sense Bellack's instrument might be called a modular framework: one in which different modules, each pertaining to a different relevant dimension of meaning, could be substituted at will without altering the basic nature of the instrument itself.

Each of these individual modules can be relatively simple, with a reasonably small number of reliable categories that can be memorized and scored as a unit. The researcher is thus able to make repeated categorizations of the interaction, using different modules, without having to remember and differentiate all categories at the same time. Once scored in this simple and reliable way, the possible data combinations become enormous.

Modern computers perform this type of data manipulation with relative ease, and a huge data pool is produced for even short periods of interaction. These data are particularly useful for clinical research probing the interactions within a single group or a small number of groups in considerable depth. Data of this sort have not previously been available for any type of supervision.

Bellack's system provides a great deal of information on the pedagogical, content, and logical aspects of verbal interaction. This is entirely appropriate for the preactive nature of clinical supervision in which models of the teacher as a problem-solver or hypothesis-maker are germane. A major deficiency, however, is that categories for emotional meanings or feeling tone are not included. Although some provision is made for categorizing positive and negative reactions, the social-emotional factors of verbal interaction are essentially neglected.

Bellack had originally intended to include such social-emotional meanings in his system, but this did not prove feasible for a number of reasons. The major problem is that making inferences about social-emotional meanings from verbal discourse alone is extremely difficult. This is particularly true when such inferences are made from recordings or typescripts that are abstractions from reality, thus removing the researcher from the essential nature of the interaction itself. Although the use of video tapes might reduce this problem, the difficulties of inferring social-emotional meanings for different individuals remains. A positive reaction to one individual might be considered negative by another, and what appears positive to an outside observer might have an entirely different meaning when the past history of a particular group is considered.

There are also mechanical problems caused by the very nature of the scoring system. The pedagogical move is well adapted to the analysis of cognitive meanings expressed in verbal discourse. Social-emotional meanings, however, are often expressed much more subtly and fleetingly. They may change dramatically during a given pedagogical move, particularly when the move occupies a considerable period of time. It is difficult to give a single score in such a situation. While it is possible to determine fairly precisely when the content or logic changes in discourse, such determinations are much less certain in the social-emotional area.

Bellack finally used an entirely different instrument for this purpose: the Semantic Differential Technique (Osgood, Suci, and Tannenbaum, 1957) analyzed the *pupil's* impressions of the overall valence, potency, and activity of class sessions. This decision to use a separate instrument not only recognizes the limitations of any one instrument, but also underscores the need for a battery of different research tools, each performing a task for which it is particularly suited.

This basic framework for research on clinical supervision was chosen because it appears to be uniquely suited to the analysis of certain cognitive and pedagogical factors that are commonly assumed to be of critical importance. The neglect of social-emotional factors does not imply that they are unimportant. Indeed, they may actually be the most crucial factors in supervision. The instrument developed in this book should be considered only an initial step in the analysis of these complex interactions. The next section describes the changes that have been made in this framework and defines the basic categories of the M.O.S.A.I.C.S. instrument.

DESIGN OF THE SYSTEM CATEGORIES

The basic coding unit of the Bellack system is the pedagogical move, defined as an uninterrupted verbal utterance serving the function of structuring, soliciting, responding, or reacting to the verbal interaction between participants. An auxiliary coding unit is defined as the number of lines of 4½-inch segments of transcript in elite type that are contained in any pedagogical move. This unit gives an indication of the actual amount of time spent in each category, necessitated by the fact that pedagogical moves may range from a single word to several minutes in length.

A major procedural change in the M.O.S.A.I.C.S. instrument was the development of a method by which this system could be used directly with tape recordings or video recordings of supervisory conferences. The direct use of recordings avoids the exceedingly laborious, time-consuming, and expensive procedure of transcribing verbal discourse onto typescripts. A basic change necessary for this purpose was the substitution of a verbal unit for Bellack's "4½-inch line of elite typescript." This unit, derived from the "complete thought unit" defined by Bales, is not only relatively easy to use, but it is also a more fundamental unit in the process of communication. Bales defined the unit as follows:

> The unit to be scored is the smallest discriminable segment of verbal . . . behavior to which the observer, using the present set of categories after appropriate training, can assign a classification under conditions of continuous serial scoring. This unit may be called an act, or more properly, a single interaction, since all acts in the present scheme are regarded as interactions. The unit as defined here has also been called the single item of thought or the single item of behavior.
>
> Often the unit will be a single simple sentence expressing or conveying a complete simple thought. Usually there will be a subject and predicate, though sometimes one of these elements will only be implied. As an example, if the actor in a conversation says "What?", the observer translates "What was that?" or "I do not understand you" or "Would you repeat that?", thus filling out both subject and predicate. Complex sentences always involve more than one score. Dependent clauses are separately scored. If a series of predicates are asserted of a single subject, a separate score is given for each additional predicate on the reasoning that each one constitutes a new item of information or opinion. Compound sentences joined by "and," "but," etc., are broken down into their component simple parts, each of which is given a score. [1951, p. 37]

In the actual process of coding, however, grammatical form may give a clue but is not completely decisive. For example, unusual stress in a speaker's voice may indicate the presence of more than one thought unit, and adjective clauses that merely identify a participant are not separately scored. Complete coding instructions for the delineation of thought units are given in Appendix G.

The kinds of meanings scored in supervisory discourse are the same as those identified by Bellack in teaching discourse:

Four functionally different types of meaning are communicated by teachers in the classroom: (1) substantive with associated (2) substantive-logical meanings; and (3) instructional with associated (4) instructional-logical meanings. Within each pedagogical move these four types of meaning are identified when they appear in the discourse and coded according to the rules of analysis. . . . One or more pedagogical moves may occur within an utterance, which is defined as a complete statement by a [participant] at any one time in the discourse. Coding is done from the viewpoint of the observer, with pedagogical meaning inferred from the speaker's verbal behavior. [1966, pp. 15–16]

In the M.O.S.A.I.C.S. system, each speaker's pedagogical move is scored according to:

(1) Type of speaker
(2) Pedagogical move
(3) Substantive area (subject area being discussed)

If the speaker is actually discussing that substantive area, the following classifications are also made:

(4) Substantive-logical meaning (logical process involved in dealing with the substantive area)
(5) Number of thought units in (4)

If the speaker is talking about conference procedures or rating someone else's remarks, whether combined with discussion of the substantive area or not, the following classifications are included:

(6) Procedural area (items relating to conference management)
(7) Procedural-logical meaning (logical or rating process involved in dealing with procedural area)
(8) Number of thought units in (6) and (7)

Some examples of coded pedagogical moves are:

a. The supervisor (S) makes a structuring move (STR) giving facts (FAC) about the subject being taught (SBJ) for a total of three (3) thought units and also explains (XPL) conference procedures (PRC) for a total of two (2) thought units:
    (1) (2) (3) (4) (5) (6) (7) (8)
    S /STR/SBJ/FAC/ 3 /PRC/XPL/ 2
b. The teacher (T) reacts (REA) to this move about the subject (SBJ) by explaining (XPL) the facts in greater detail for six (6) units:
    (1) (2) (3) (4) (5) (6) (7) (8)
    T /REA/SBJ/XPL/ 6

c. An observer (O) who is participating in the conference reacts (REA) to the teacher's explanation of the subject (SBJ) by rating his statements (STA) very positively (POS) for one (1) thought unit:

(1) (2) (3) (4) (5) (6) (7) (8)

O /REA/SBJ/ – / – /STA/POS/ 1

The M.O.S.A.I.C.S. instrument retains Bellack's categories for pedagogical moves, and consequently retains his patterns of pedagogical moves or teaching cycles. Modifications have been made in each of the other category groups in an attempt to make the system more pertinent to clinical supervision and more practical to use. With the exception of the substantive meanings, which are not comparable to Bellack's system, these modifications have preserved as much of the original system as possible in order to permit direct comparisons.

The following sections define the actual categories of the M.O.S.A.I.C.S. system, which follows Bellack's basic analysis. Individual differences are explained within the context of each dimension of analysis. In general, definitions are taken directly from Bellack if the individual categories remain unchanged. Overall differences may be examined by comparing a summary of Bellack's system (Appendix E) with a summary of the M.O.S.A.I.C.S. system (Appendix F).

1. Speaker

M.O.S.A.I.C.S. contains three categories for identifying the participants in supervisory interactions:

S: Supervisor The supervisor or "master teacher" who has major responsibility for the planning or analysis conference.

T: Teacher The teacher (teachers if team teaching is being supervised) who is either planning or analyzing his instruction in the conference.

O: Observer In group supervision, observers are teachers and/or supervisors who have observed or plan to observe the instruction and who are an integral part of the supervisory interaction.

2. Pedagogical Moves

M.O.S.A.I.C.S. has retained Bellack's basic functional units and one of his auxiliary units. Bellack's "structuring-assigned," defined as structuring moves that are a result of an assignment such as student reports or debates, has been omitted.

STR: Structuring Structuring moves set the context for subsequent behavior by (1) launching or halting/excluding interacactions between participants, focusing attention on a problem; or (2) indicating the nature of the interaction in terms of time, agent, activity, topic and cognitive process, regulations, reasons, and instructional aids. Structuring moves form an implicit directive by launching discussion in specified directions and focusing on topics and procedures. Structuring may occur either by announcing or stating propositions for subsequent discussion. In general, structuring serves to move the discourse forward.

SOL: Soliciting   Soliciting moves are intended to elicit (1) an active verbal response on the part of persons addressed; (2) a cognitive response (e.g., encouraging persons to attend to something); (3) a physical response. Soliciting moves may be questions, commands, or requests. Rhetorical questions are not counted as solicitations.

RES: Responding   Responding moves bear a reciprocal relation to soliciting moves and occur only in relation to them. Their function is to fulfill the expectation of the solicitation. Responses may be in the form of anwers, statements of not knowing, etc. In general every solicitation must be intended to elicit a response, and every response must be directly elicited by a solicitation.

REA: Reacting   Reacting moves are *occasioned* by prior structuring, soliciting, responding, or reacting moves but are not directly elicited by them. Pedagogically, these moves serve to modify (by clarifying, synthesizing, or expanding) and/or to rate (positively or negatively) what has been said in the moves that occasioned them. Reacting moves may evaluate, discuss, rephrase, expand, state implications, interpret, or draw conclusions from a previous move.

RSM: Summary reaction   A summary reaction is occasioned by more than one previous move and serves the function of a genuine summary or review.

These pedagogical moves may also be classified in terms of their function of initiation or response. Structuring and soliciting are initiatory moves—they move the discourse forward and mark the beginnings of teaching cycles; responding and reacting are reflexive moves —they refer back to previous moves and comprise much of the substance of teaching cycles.

By dividing the number of initiatory moves by the number of reflexive moves, one arrives at a single index describing the extent of initiation for each participant. This ratio can be used to compare the pedagogical roles of the supervisor, teacher, and observer. It is formed in the following manner:

$$\text{I/R Ratio} = (\text{STR} + \text{SOL}) / (\text{RES} + \text{REA} + \text{RSM})$$

Comparison of roles in the supervisory conference is less straightforward than similar comparisons in teaching because of the size and nature of the supervisory group. Bellack studied groups composed of one teacher and a large number of pupils. Supervisory groups are composed of a supervisor and a variable number of both teachers and observers. The size of the group may range from two to more than ten. At times several teachers may be present, as is the case during supervision of team-teaching or multiple classrooms. The number of observers may vary widely, especially in such situations as the Harvard-Newton Summer School, where intervisitation and the participation of outside observers is common. Simple percentages are not adequate for the examination of roles in such conferences because these percentages say nothing about the number of participants of each type involved. For example, if teachers and observers make equal percentages of a given type of move, but the observers far outnumber the teachers, then that type of move may be considered to be more important for teachers than for observers.

A new ratio was therefore devised to examine the extent of interaction by each type of participant in clinical supervision. This ratio, called the participation index, is determined by dividing the percentage of moves in a given category made by each class of participants by the percent membership of the total group that class of participants comprises.

$$\text{Participation Index} = (\%\ \text{moves by S,T, or O}) / \%\ \text{membership of S,T, or O}.$$

For example, if the size of a supervisory group is five and there is one teacher in that group, the percent membership for teachers is 20 percent. If all types of participants had the same role for a given type of move, one would expect that the teacher would make 20 percent of those moves. In this case the participation index for that move for teachers would be 1. If the teacher actually made 40 percent of those moves, a participation index of 2 indicates that the move is an important part of the teacher's role in the supervisory conference. In effect, the teacher made twice as many moves of that type as would be expected on the basis of chance alone.

3. Teaching Cycles

Pedagogical moves occur in cyclical patterns and combinations in verbal discourse. Bellack has called these patterns "teaching cycles." Their utility lies in the way they describe the relationships between and among individual pedagogical moves. It is possible, for example, to determine the regularity with which solicitations elicit single or multiple responses, or the regularity with which single and multiple reactions follow other moves.

Teaching cycles are basic patterns of initiatory moves and the reflexive moves following them. They begin with either a structuring or a soliciting move, or both, and continue until the beginning of the next cycle. Twenty-one types of teaching cycles were defined by Bellack: three initiated by structuring moves alone, nine initiated by structuring followed by soliciting, and nine initiated by soliciting moves alone. Three periods following a given move indicate one or more additional moves of the kind designated. For example, RES . . . means one or more responses to the same solicitation.

The following teaching cycles were identified by Bellack:

1. STR
2. STR SOL
3. STR REA
4. STR REA REA . . .
5. STR SOL RES
6. STR SOL RES RES . . .
7. STR SOL REA
8. STR SOL REA REA . . .
9. STR SOL RES REA
10. STR SOL RES REA REA . . .
11. STR SOL RES REA RES . . .
12. STR SOL RES REA RES . . . REA . . .
13. SOL
14. SOL RES
15. SOL RES RES . . .
16. SOL REA
17. SOL REA REA . . .
18. SOL RES REA
19. SOL RES REA REA . . .
20. SOL RES REA RES . . .
21. SOL RES REA RES . . . REA . . .

Teaching cycles are coded by the initiator, the cycle number, and the number of thought units contained in the entire cycle. In the following examples the end of a thought unit is indicated by a single slash (/), and the end of a pedagogical move by a double slash (//).

Below is an example of a supervisor-initiated teaching cycle number 9 (STR–SOL–RES–REA) containing seven thought units: S/9/7

S/STR: One thing you could do . . . You might put a diagram of a microscope on the overhead projector/ and ask the kids to identify its parts.//
T/SOL: You mean . . . use this as a test?//
S/RES: Well, either as a test/ or as an individual assessment.//
T/REA: Yeah,/ at least it would probably wake them up!//

Below is an example of a supervisor-initiated teaching cycle number 19 (SOL–RES–REA–REA . . .) containing eleven thought units: S/19/11

S/SOL: Well, how do you think it went?//
T/RES: Oh, I guess it went okay./ I just wish they'd show a little more enthusiasm for this stuff!//
O/REA: Yeah!/ Were they dead today!//
O/REA: I don't know . . ./ they may not have been leaping out of their seats/ but they seemed pretty interested to me.//
T/REA: Well . . . I just didn't get the feeling they cared very much for it./ I guess I really don't blame them./ I was pretty bored with it myself.//

Below is an example of a teacher-initiated teaching cycle number 4 (STR–REA–REA . . .) containing fifteen thought units: T/4/15

T/STR: I just don't know what to do with that bunch of kids in the rear of the room./ They're never prepared,/ they're always talking . . ./I get more gas from them than from all the others combined.//
O/REA: Yeah./ They've been nothing but trouble all along.//
O/REA: Well, some of them are okay/ when you get them alone.//
O/REA: And they seem to work okay in small lab groups.//
T/REA: Yeah,/ but only when you can keep them so busy/ that they don't have time for anything else.//
S/RSM: You seem to be saying that they react differently in different situations:/ they make trouble in large groups/ but work all right in smaller groups.//

4. Substantive Areas (Content Analysis)

One of the most difficult problems in designing M.O.S.A.I.C.S. was the specification of meaningful and reliable categories for content analysis. Bellack's categories, dealing as they do with factors of international trade associated with a specially defined unit, are not applicable to the study of supervision.

Whereas the content of teaching varies extensively with the grade, subject, and situation, the content of clinical supervision is more readily specified. Clinical supervision focuses on the instructional process itself: the interaction of teacher, pupil(s), and curriculum. The content analysis section of M.O.S.A.I.C.S. was designed to be applicable to clinical supervision of any subject, grade, or instructional situation. With minor modifications it would be applicable to any type of instructional supervision.

Clinical supervision is essentially a formal process of "preactive teaching." The final content analysis system is a three-dimensional mosaic of categories that analyzes "preactive teaching" according to the dimensions of generality, focus, and domain. The dimension of generality relates to the analysis of instruction in a specific class (S) as opposed to the analysis of instruction in general (G). This might be considered "clinical analysis" vs. "curriculum and methods course." The dimension of instructional focus analyzes instruction according to content and objectives (O), methods and materials (M), and actual instructional interactions or execution (X). The dimension of instructional domain, adapted from Bloom (Bloom, et al., 1956; Krathwohl, et al., 1956), categorizes these instructional foci according to the cognitive (C), affective (A), or social and disciplinary domain (D) with which they are concerned.

The paradigm underlying this content analysis considers the teacher as a decision-maker (see figure 1). According to this paradigm the teacher possesses a body of information consisting of generalizations, past experience, and values concerning elements of instruction. This body of information may be broken down into subsets relating to content and objectives, methods and materials, and actual instructional interactions. This information pertains both to instruction in general and to the particular class being taught.

Planning for teaching involves the use of this body of information to make decisions on the objectives, content, methods, and materials for the particular class to be taught. It also involves the teacher's expectations of pupil reactions and interactions during instruction.

The teacher then implements his instructional decisions in a teaching session that is followed by analysis and evaluation. The results of this analysis are fed back into the teacher's storage of information on the particular class. This information may be either added to his general storage, or it may change some elements of that general understanding.

Based on this information, new decisions are made concerning the objectives, methods, and instructional expectations for the next class. This cycle presumably repeats itself throughout the teacher's professional life and is exemplified by the Planning–Observation–Analysis cycle in clinical supervision. In figure 1 this cycle is represented by a closed-loop feedback system.

The content-analysis system of M.O.S.A.I.C.S. consists of three separate classifications. Each pedagogical move that actually focuses on the analysis of instruction is categorized in the following three ways:

A. Instructional Areas
  1. Generality
    S (Specific): Pedagogical moves that focus on the objectives, methods, or instructional interactions for the particular class on which supervision is based. These may relate to the class either in the past or in the future.
    G (General): Pedagogical moves that focus on generalized objectives, methods, or instructional interactions. These may include generalizations, past experience, or applications of theory from educational thought and related behavioral sciences.
  2. Focus
    O (Objectives and Content): Expected educational outcomes and the content or subject matter related to these outcomes.
    M (Methods and Materials): Materials of instruction and strategic operations designed to achieve objectives.
    X (Execution and Instructional Interactions): Interactions between the teacher, pupil(s), and content or curriculum, either as the execution of a particular plan or as unexpected interactions and critical incidents.
  3. Domain
    C (Cognitive): Pertaining to cognition, knowledge, understanding, and learning. The cognitive domain is here restricted to cognitive interactions between pupil(s) and subject matter.
    A (Affective): Pertaining to interest, involvement, and motivation. Affective interaction between pupil(s) and subject matter.
    D (Social and Disciplinary): Pertaining to discipline, control, and social interactions. Interactions between teacher and pupil(s) or pupil(s) and pupil(s).

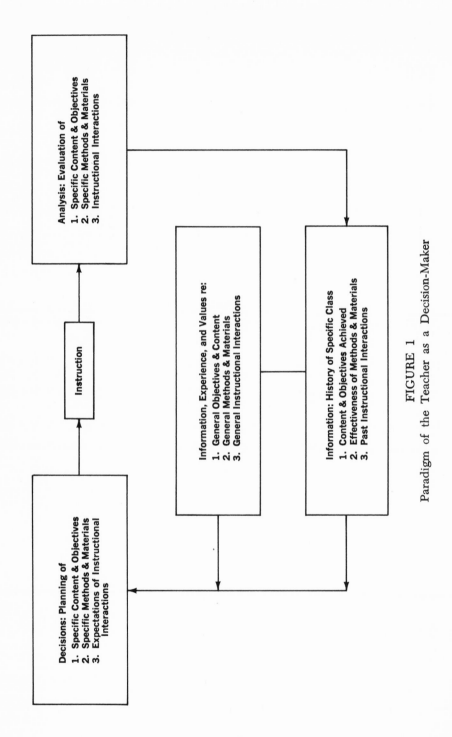

FIGURE 1

Paradigm of the Teacher as a Decision-Maker

52

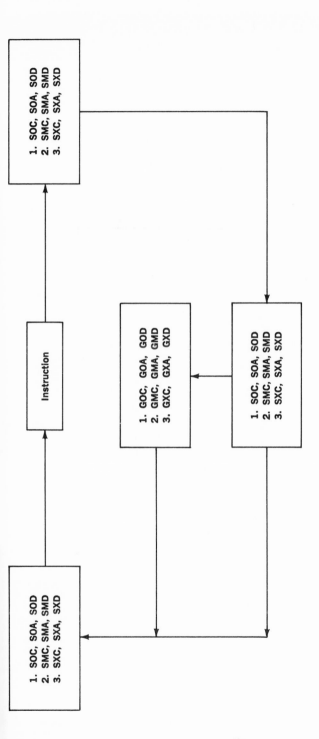

FIGURE 2

Paradigm of the Teacher as a Decision-Maker
in Terms of the Content Analysis System of M.O.S.A.I.C.S.

Instruction

1. SOC, SOA, SOD
2. SMC, SMA, SMD
3. SXC, SXA, SXD

1. GOC, GOA, GOD
2. GMC, GMA, GMD
3. GXC, GXA, GXD

1. SOC, SOA, SOD
2. SMC, SMA, SMD
3. SXC, SXA, SXD

1. SOC, SOA, SOD
2. SMC, SMA, SMD
3. SXC, SXA, SXD

S = Specific class
G = General

O = Objectives and content
M = Methods and materials
X = Execution (instr. interactions)

C = Cognitive
A = Affective
D = Social and disciplinary

53

Content focusing on the analysis of instruction is therefore classified into separate categories of specificity, focus, and domain. For example, pedagogical moves in a planning session might progress from specific cognitive interactions in the previous class (SXC: Specific–eXecution–Cognitive) to specific learning objectives (SOC: Specific–Objectives–Cognitive) to general methodologies for the implementation of these objectives (GMC: General–Methods–Cognitive) to decisions about specific materials to be used in the next class (SMC: Specific–Methods–Cognitive). In terms of this system, the paradigm of "preactive teaching" may be translated into specific categories of content-analysis (see figure 2).

This system allows the researcher to analyze the amount of stress in each category triplet (such as SOC) as well as the progression from one category to another (such as SXC–SOC–GMC–SMC). He is also able to sum across groups and determine the amount of stress given to each separate classification (such as Cognitive–Affective–Disciplinary, Objectives–Methods, eXecution, and Specific–General).

Additional categories, in some respects arbitrary, have been added to account for discussion that does not focus on the analysis of instruction. These added categories were established on the basis of observed emphasis in actual supervisory conferences:

B. Related Areas
    SBJ (*Subject*): Discussion of content and subject matter where the intent is to have the conference participants understand it.
    SPR (*Super*vision): Discussion of topics related to the Harvard-Newton Summer School, supervision, and teacher-training.
    GRL (General Topics *Rel*ated to Education): Discussion of topics such as school organization, faculty meetings, and custodial staff, which are only indirectly related to instruction.
    GNR (General Topics *N*ot *R*elated to Education): Discussion of topics unrelated to education or instruction.

A diagrammatic view of this content analysis system is presented in figure 3, and examples for each category triplet are given in Appendix G. Analysis by this system permits each triplet and subcategory to be related both to the preceding dimensions (the speaker and the pedagogical move) and to the following dimension—the logical treatment of that content area.

5. Substantive-Logical Meanings (Logical Analysis)

Bellack identified six basic logical treatments of content, which he grouped under three subheadings: analytic processes (definitions and intepretations), empirical processes (fact-stating and explaining),

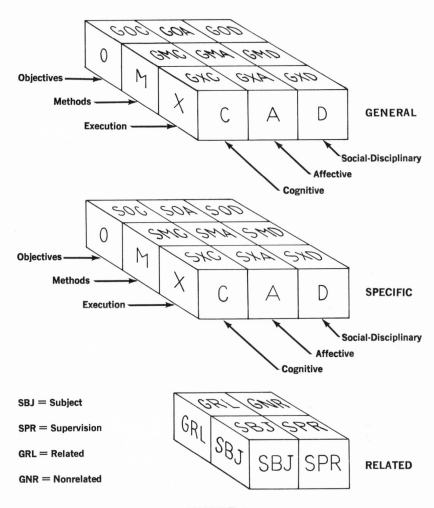

FIGURE 3
Diagram of the Substantive Categories (Content Analysis) of the
M.O.S.A.I.C.S. System

and evaluative processes (opining and justifying). These were adequate for use in the analysis of substantive interactions in teaching. Other teaching interactions, such as the giving of assignments, could be categorized as "instructional" or procedural in nature.

These categories, however, are not sufficient for the analysis of clinical supervision. The analysis of instruction involves definite commitments to action that are an integral part of the supervisory function. Much of the interaction in clinical supervision deals with suggestions and opinions of what could or should be *done,* as well as with explanations or evaluations of instructional interactions.

Bellack's substantive-logical categories were therefore both expanded and redefined in the M.O.S.A.I.C.S. instrument to include processes dealing with proposed actions. These new processes must be called quasi-logical, since they deal both with principles of reasoning and with directions for behavior.

The following substantive-logical categories are included in the M.O.S.A.I.C.S. instrument:

A. Processes relating to the proposed use of language. These statements are true or false by virtue of the words of which they are composed. They depend for their truth on an agreed-upon set of rules and follow logically from accepted definitions.

> DEF (Defining): A statement of what a word means, how it is used, or a verbal equivalent. Definitions may be in the form of the characteristics designated by a term or specific instances of the class designated by a term.
>
> INT (Interpreting): Rephrasing the meaning of a statement; a verbal equivalent which makes the meaning of a statement clear. Interpreting bears the same relationship to statements that defining does to terms.

B. Diagnostic processes focus on the analytical or evaluative examination of the instructional process itself. These processes are adapted from Bellack's substantive-logical processes and have no overtones of suggestions for individual action.

1. Analytical diagnostic processes give information about the world, based on one's actual experience. Analytical processes may be verified by tests conducted in terms of one's experience.

> FAC (Fact Stating): Giving an account, description, or report of an event or state of affairs which is verifiable in terms of experience or observational tests. Included are statements of what is, what was, or what will be, as well as generalizations and universal statements.
>
> XPL (Explaining): Explanations or reasons which relate one object, event, action, or state of affairs to another object, event, action, or state of affairs, or which show the relationship between an event or state of affairs and a principle or generalization. Included are conditional inferences, explicit instances of compare-and-contrast, and cause-and-effect relationships.

2. Evaluative diagnostic processes grade, praise, blame, commend, or criticize something. Evaluative statements are verified by reference to a set of criteria or principles of judgment.

> EVL (Evaluation): Statements about the fairness, worth, importance, value, or quality of something.
>
> JUS (Justification): Justification or vindication of an evaluation. Reasons for holding an evaluation; support or criticism for explicit or implicit opinions and evaluations.

C. Prescriptive processes focus on instructional actions that are proposed either for future classes or in retrospect for classes that are being critiqued. Prescriptive processes are quasi-logical and have either analytical or evaluative components.

   1. Analytical prescriptive processes relate to suggestions or tentative plans for action.

   > SUG (Suggestions): Suggestions, alternatives, and possible actions and goals which might be used or could have been used in the classroom.
   >
   > SGX (Explanations of Suggestions): Reasons for offering a suggestion; relationships between suggestion and other objects, events, actions, states of affairs, principles, or generalizations.

   2. Evaluative prescriptive processes relate to opinions of what should or ought to be done.

   > OPN (Opinions): Directives or opinions of what should be done or ought to have been done in a given situation. A definite evaluative overtone is presumed.
   >
   > OPJ (Justification for Opinions): Justification or vindication of an opinion; reasons for proposing opinion; support or criticism for opinions.

An overview of the substantive-logical meanings is given in diagrammatic form in figure 4. With the exception of DEF and INT, which pertain only to the use of language itself, these meanings may be visualized as a three-dimensional matrix along three separate dimensions of potential interest:

1. The analytical-evaluative dimension distinguishes between processes that are verifiable by tests conducted in terms of experience or observation and those verifiable by reference to a set of criteria or principles of judgment. A single index called the A/E Ratio may be formed in the following manner:

Analytic/Evaluative Ratio:
$$A/E = (FAC + XPL + SUG + SGX) / (EVL + JUS + OPN + OPJ)$$

2. The diagnostic-prescriptive dimension distinguishes between processes that focus on the analysis and evaluation of the instructional process it-

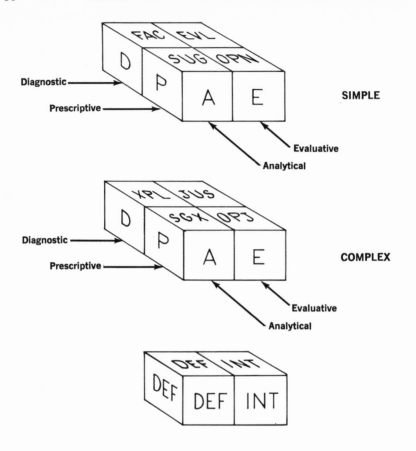

FAC = Fact	XPL = Explanation of FAC	DEF = Definition
EVL = Evaluation	JUS = Justification of EVL	INT = Interpretation
SUG = Suggestion	SGX = Explanation of SUG	
OPN = Opinion	OPJ = Justification of OPN	

FIGURE 4

Diagram of the Substantive-Logical Categories (Logical Analysis)
of M.O.S.A.I.C.S. System

self, past and future, and those which focus on actions and objectives that are recommended or assigned. A single index called the D/P Ratio may be formed in the following manner:

Diagnostic/Prescriptive Ratio:
$$D/P = (FAC + XPL + EVL + JUS) / (SUG + SGX + OPN + OPJ)$$

3. The complex-simple dimension distinguishes between processes that relate statements, facts, evaluations, suggestions, and opinions to other

factors, reasons, generalizations, or principles, and those processes which involve single elements alone. A single index called the C/S Ratio may be formed in the following manner:

Complex/Simple Ratio:
$$C/S = (XPL + JUS + SGX + OPJ) / (FAC + EVL + SUG + OPN)$$

Examples of substantive and substantive-logical meanings:

What's a linkage group?//	T/SOL/SBJ/DEF/1
It's a situation where several genes are located on the same chromosome.//	S/RES/SBJ/DEF/1
Do you mean really make them toe the line?//	T/SOL/SMD/INT/1
I mean exactly that!//	S/RES/SMD/INT/1
Did Jack get that question right?//	O/SOL/SXC/FAC/1
He did./ He even got the lab set up all by himself.//	T/RES/SXC/FAC/2
Why were they so unresponsive?//	S/SOL/SXA/XPL/1
Well, a lot of the lesson consisted of talking/ I didn't give them any other stimuli/ no overheads/ no demonstrations/ no changes of pace.//	T/RES/SXA/XPL/5
That was a pretty good lesson!//	O/STR/SXC/EVL/1
Well, I don't agree.//	T/REA/SXC/–/–/STA/NEG/1
Why do you say that?//	O/SOL/SXC/JUS/1
It's partially because of all the blank stares,/ the doodling in notebooks,/ and a general lack of reaction from them./	T/RES/SXC/JUS/3
We could have them go over this stuff again/ and organize all these observations.//	T/STR/SOC/SUG/2
Or we might jump ahead right into surface tension.//	O/REA/SOC/SUG/1
I'm leery of that/ because they just don't see the whole picture/ of what we've done so far.//	T/REA/SOC/SGX/3
But a change of pace might make these observations more relevant.//	O/REA/SOC/SGX/1
You really should have probed those answers more deeply.//	O/STR/SMC/OPN/1

Why do you say that?//   T/SOL/SMC/OPJ/1
Well, they may have been just parroting
   back your lecture./ They may not have
   really understood.//   O/RES/SMC/OPJ/2

6. Procedural Areas

Bellack included a series of "instructional meanings" or procedural factors in his system. These allowed him to analyze topics
relating to classroom management, assignments, and procedures that
are part of the instructional process but not part of the formal content
of instruction. His system included a total of twelve separate categories (see Appendix E).

The M.O.S.A.I.C.S. system condenses these twelve categories to
four because some categories occurred very rarely in practice, while
others could meaningfully be subsumed under a more general category. The following four categories comprise the procedural areas of
M.O.S.A.I.C.S.:

STA (Statement): References to a particular statement made by a partici-
        pant in the interaction, chiefly regarding the meaning, truth, or
        propriety of that utterance (equal to Bellack's STA).
PRC (Procedures): References to conference procedures, management as-
        signments, and materials (includes Bellack's PRC, ASG, and MAT).
ACT (Action): References to verbal, cognitive, physical, or emotional actions
        (includes Bellack's ACT, ACV, ACC, ACP, and ACE).
PER (Personal): References to participant himself and such personal inter-
        actions as jokes and "small talk" (equal to Bellack's PER).

7. Procedural-Logical Meanings

Procedural-logical meanings describe the ways in which the
procedural areas are treated in verbal discourse. These include those
processes listed under substantive-logical meanings as well as distinctly didactic verbal moves that are involved in positive and negative
ratings and giving instructions.

A. Logical and quasi-logical processes

        DEF: Defining
        INT : Interpreting
        FAC: Fact Stating
        XPL: Explanation

EVL: Evaluation
JUS: Justification for Evaluation
SUG: Suggestion
SGX: Explanation of Suggestion
OPN: Opinion
OPJ: Justification for Opinion

B. Rating (judgments about the truth or falsity, appropriateness or inappropriateness of preceding statements)

POS (Positive): Distinctly affirmative rating.
ADM (Admitting): Mildly accepting or equivocally positive rating, often given with hesitation.
RPT (Repeating): Implicit positive rating in which there is only a repeat, rephrasing, or restatement of a preceding move.
QAL (Qualifying): An indication of a reservation, however mild or oblique.
NAD (Not Admitting): Rating that rejects by stating the contrary rather than by making an explicitly negative comment.
NEG (Negative): A distinctly negative rating.

Positive/Negative Ratio:
$$P/N = (POS + ADM + RPT) / (QAL + NAD + NEG)$$

C. Extra-logical processes

PON (Positive or Negative): A solicitation or response of either a yes-or-no answer or a positive or negative response (equal to Bellack's PON and AON).
PRF (Performance): Solicitations that ask or demand that someone do something. These include imperatives and directives.
NCL: Not clear.

Examples of rating reactions:

POS: Yes. Right. Correct. Good answer. Exactly. Precisely.
ADM: All right. Okay. Uh-huh.
RPT: A simple repetition, rephrasing, or restatement.
QAL: Yes, but . . . however . . . nevertheless . . .
NAD: He did *not* say that. They were *not* working.
NEG: No. Wrong. Uh-uh. That's a terrible answer. Nope.

In general, instructional and associated instructional-logical meanings may occur either alone or as part of a pedagogical move that also contains substantive-logical meanings. In either case, the speaker, pedagogical move, and substantive meaning are always categorized.

Examples of instructional and instructional-logical meanings:

That's a good point!//	O/REA/SXC/–/–/STA/POS/1
I disagree./ You should have followed that question up.//	S/REA/SMC/OPN/1/STA/NEG/1
May I say something?//	T/SOL/SOC/–/–/PRC/PON/1
What should we do next?//	S/SOL/SPR/–/–/PRC/OPN/1
I'm confused!//	T/REA/SXD/–/–/ACT/FAC/1
I'm not very happy with this./ These kids are completely out of control.//	O/REA/SXD/EVL/1/ACT/FAC/1
That's a very nice dress.//	S/REA/GNR/–/–/PER/POS/1
There's a fungus among us.//	T/REA/SXC/–/–/PER/PRF/1 [1]
Will you shut that door please?//	S/SOL/SPR/–/–/ACT/PRF/1

8. Summary of the M.O.S.A.I.C.S. System

Categories:

I. Speaker
>   S: Supervisor
>   T: Teacher who taught specific class being supervised
>   O: Observer also interacting in the supervision

II. Pedagogical Move
>   STR: Structuring, launching or halting move that directs the flow of discourse
>   SOL: Soliciting, asking for a physical or verbal response
>   RES: Responding, answering or fulfilling the expectation of a solicitation
>   REA: Reacting, amplifying, qualifying, or otherwise making an unsolicited reaction to a previous move
>   RSM: Summary reaction, reaction to more than one move or a genuine summary or review

III. Substantive Areas (Content Analysis)
>   A. Instructional
>   1. Generality
>>   S: Specific, pertinent to the specific class being discussed, the "clinical" aspect of supervision
>>   G: General, pertinent to theory, generalizations, past experience, the "methods course" aspect of supervision
>   2. Focus
>>   O: Objectives and content to be taught
>>   M: Methods and materials of instruction, relatively strategic and planned aspects of implementation of objectives
>>   X: Execution, critical incidents, tactical and unexpected interactions

[1] PER/PRF is a convention for a joke; see Appendix G.

    3. Domain
        C: Cognitive, pertaining to knowledge, learning, information, understanding
        A: Affective, pertaining to affective interactions between pupil and subject, such as interest, motivation, attention
        D: Disciplinary and social interactions between teacher-pupil and pupil-pupil

  B. Related
      SBJ: Subject being taught, if discussed in terms of the understanding of conference participants
      SPR: Supervision and teacher-training
      GRL: General topics related to education
      GNR: General topics not related to education

IV. Substantive-Logical Meanings (Logical Analysis)
  A. Processes Relating to the Proposed Use of Language
      DEF: Defining, definitions and verbal equivalents
      INT: Interpretations and rephrasings
  B. Diagnostic Processes
      FAC: Fact stating, accounts, descriptions, or reports
      XPL: Explanations, reasons, or relationships
      EVL: Evaluations
      JUS: Justifications, reasons for evaluations
  C. Prescriptive Processes
      SUG: Suggestions, alternatives, and possible actions
      SGX: Explanations, reasons, and relationships for suggestions
      OPN: Opinions, directives of what should or ought to be done
      OPJ: Justifications for opinions, reasons, support, and criticisms

V. Number of Thought Units Contained in Substantive-Logical Area

VI. Procedural Areas
      STA: Statement, reference to a particular statement, usually with respect to its truth, validity, or propriety
      PRC: Procedures, management, assignments, and materials relating to the supervisory conference
      ACT: Action, references to verbal, cognitive, physical, or emotional actions
      PER: Personal interactions and small talk

VII. Procedural-Logical Meanings
  A. Processes Related to the Proposed Use of Language
      DEF: Defining
      INT: Interpreting
  B. Diagnostic Processes
      FAC: Fact stating
      XPL: Explanations

EVL: Evaluations
JUS: Justifications
C. Prescriptive Processes
SUG: Suggestions
SGX: Explanations of suggestions
OPN: Opinions
OPJ: Justifications for opinions
D. Rating Processes
POS: Positive, distinctly positive or affirmative rating
ADM: Admitting, mildly accepting or equivocally positive rating
RPT: Repeating, implicit positive rating by a repeat or rephrasing of a previous move
QAL: Qualifying, a reservation, however mild
NAD: Not admitting, rejection by a statement of the contrary
NEG: Negative, distinctly negative rating
E. Extra-Logical Processes
PON: Positive or negative, solicitations or responses of either a yes-or-no answer or a positive or negative response
PRF: Performance, solicitations for action
NCL: Not clear

VIII. Number of Thought Units Contained in Procedural Area

IX. Teaching Cycles
1. STR
2. STR SOL
3. STR REA
4. STR REA REA ...
5. STR SOL RES
6. STR SOL RES RES ...
7. STR SOL REA
8. STR SOL REA REA ...
9. STR SOL RES REA
10. STR SOL RES REA REA ...
11. STR SOL RES REA RES ...
12. STR SOL RES REA RES ... REA ...
13. SOL
14. SOL RES
15. SOL RES RES ...
16. SOL REA
17. SOL REA REA ...
18. SOL RES REA
19. SOL RES REA REA ...
20. SOL RES REA RES ...
21. SOL RES REA RES ... REA ...

X. Critical Ratios
  A. Initiatory/Reflexive Ratio:
     $\text{I/R} = (\text{STR} + \text{SOL}) / (\text{RES} + \text{REA} + \text{RSM})$
  B. Participation Index:
     $\text{P.I.} = (\% \text{ moves by participant}) / (\% \text{ membership of participant})$
  C. Analytic/Evaluative Ratio:
     $\text{A/E} = (\text{FAC} + \text{XPL} + \text{SUG} + \text{SGX}) / (\text{EVL} + \text{JUS} + \text{OPN} + \text{OPJ})$
  D. Diagnostic/Prescriptive Ratio:
     $\text{D/P} = (\text{FAC} + \text{XPL} + \text{EVL} + \text{JUS}) / (\text{SUG} + \text{SGX} + \text{OPN} + \text{OPJ})$
  E. Complex/Simple Ratio:
     $\text{C/S} = (\text{XPL} + \text{JUS} + \text{SGX} + \text{OPJ}) / (\text{FAC} + \text{EVL} + \text{SUG} + \text{OPN})$
  F. Positive/Negative Ratio:
     $\text{P/N} = (\text{POS} + \text{ADM} + \text{RPT}) / (\text{QAL} + \text{NAD} + \text{NEG})$

Detailed instructions for making coding decisions appear in Appendix G. Further examples of the categories in M.O.S.A.I.C.S. are found in Appendix H, which contains a completely coded ten-minute protocol of a supervisory conference recorded at the Harvard-Newton Summer School in 1967.

The M.O.S.A.I.C.S. system was tested and modified to its final form in a longitudinal study of five supervisory groups at the Harvard-Newton Summer School. The next section describes the experimental design and the actual procedures developed for analyzing the supervisory tapes.

USING THE SYSTEM

An observational study was conducted by this investigator at the Harvard-Newton Summer School in 1967. The purposes of this study were twofold: to test the reliability, practicality, and potential utility of the M.O.S.A.I.C.S. instrument, and to generate data on supervisory interactions comparable with the data produced by Bellack on instructional interactions.

The Harvard-Newton Summer School in the summer of 1967 was markedly different from previous years. Harvard's Graduate School of Education had developed a two-year Master of Arts in Teaching program, in which the summer school preceded an entire year of academic study and an internship year of approximately four-fifths teaching responsibility in the schools. Most of the interns were scheduled for the internships in the second year, and consequently the pressures of "survival training" for the summer program were greatly reduced.

The focus of the new summer program was on the analysis of instruction, the study of individual pupils, and creative possibilities for curriculum and instruction. The number of actual classes taught each day by the supervisory groups had been reduced from two to one. Although each class was separated into two classroom groups, the actual amount of "practice teaching" by the interns had been cut almost in half.

This reduction permitted each intern to spend a full period every day with a "small group" of four or five pupils. These "small groups" were unstructured, relatively content-free periods designed to enable the intern to understand and relate to the problems, personalities, and personal feelings of individual pupils, particularly with respect to their reactions to the traditional classroom. Many of these pupils were also the subjects of "case studies" done by the interns in conjunction with a course in educational psychology taught during the summer school.

A normal morning generally consisted of five class periods, which were utilized for the planning of instruction, teaching of the two class groups, the analysis of instruction, small group interactions by interns, and observations of other classes and/or analysis of small groups. Afternoons were spent in further planning and analysis, as well as in lectures in educational psychology.

The actual study was performed with the five supervisory groups comprising the science department, of which this investigator was the department chairman. Each group consisted of an experienced supervisor, called a "master teacher," and four to six interns. The master teachers were chosen on the basis of their experience and expertise both as teachers and as supervisors of student teachers (see table 1). None, however, had previously supervised at the Harvard-Newton Summer School.

The intern population consisted of nineteen candidates for the M.A.T. degree in science education, seven candidates for the Ed.M. degree in guidance, and one school administrator participating only in the summer program. Guidance interns were distributed among all the academic departments in the summer school. Since the summer program was designed to focus on broad problems of curriculum and instruction, these interns were distributed to supervisory groups in such a way that each group contained a comparable mix of subject backgrounds and experience. In effect, a given curriculum such as junior high school biology was planned, taught, and analyzed by a group of recent biology, chemistry, physics, and psychology majors (see table 2).

TABLE 1

Background and Experience of Master Teachers (Supervisors)

Supvr. No.	Sex	Degrees	No. Sem. Hours in Science	No. Sem. Hours in Education	No. Years Teaching Exp.	No. Sem. Hours in Supervision	Experience in Pre-Service Supervision	Experience in In-Service Supervision
1	F	B.A. M.A.T.	72	20	6	0	4 Stud. Tchrs.	None
2	F	B.S. M.A.T.	57	24	8	4	5 Stud. Tchrs.	5 years as Elem. Sci. Supvr.
3	M	B.S. M.A.	92	35	10	4	14 Stud. Tchrs.	None
4	M	B.A. M.Ed. M.S.	122	32	15	0	3 Stud. Tchrs.	3 years as Sec. Sci. Supvr.
5	M	B.S. M.Ed. Ed.D.	124	80	11	4	Est. at 90 Stud. Tchrs. (College Supvr.)	None

TABLE 2

Education and Experience of Intern Teachers in Each Supervisory Group

Group	College & Year	Major Field	Experience
1 a	Barnard Coll. '67	Chemistry	1/2 yr. practice teaching
b	M.I.T. '67	Physics	
c	Georgian Court Coll. '67	Biology	7 yrs. teaching, gr. 5 & 7
d	Syracuse U. '67	Biology	
e	U. Calif. (Berkeley) '67	Psychology	
f	Mass. Maritime '54	Social Science	13 yrs. public school
	Boston U. '65 (Ed.M.)		business manager
2 a	E. Texas State U. '67	Biology	1/2 yr. practice teaching
b	Haverford Coll. '67	Biology	
c	Radcliffe Coll. '64	Biology	2 yrs. teaching elem. school
d	U. Minnesota '65	Physics	2 yrs. teaching elem. school in Peace Corps
e	Brandeis U. '67	Psychology	
f	Boston U. '64	Psychology	2 yrs. elem. school guidance counselor
3 a	Brandeis U. '67	Chemistry	
b	Cornell Coll. (Iowa) '67	Chemistry	
c	U. Calif. (Berkeley) '67	Physics/Math	
d	Montclair State Coll. '67	Biology	1/2 yr. practice teaching
e	Harvard U. '65	Social Relations	Exp. as industrial engineer
4 a	Harvard U. '67	Physics	
b	Wellesley Coll. '67	Biology	
c	Amherst Coll. '66	Physics	
	S.U.N.Y. (grad. stud.)	Physics	
d	Smith Coll. '64	Chemistry	
	Harvard U. (grad. stud.)	Chemistry	
5 a	Coll. Mt. St. Vincent '67	Chemistry	
b	M.I.T. '67	Physics	
c	Cornell U. '67	Biology	
d	Mt. Holyoke Coll. '67	Psychology	
e	Harvard Ext. '67	Social Studies	
f	Antioch Coll. '67	Psychology	

Pupils at the Harvard-Newton Summer School were accepted from many of the communities surrounding Harvard University. The school consisted of two parts: an elementary and junior high school section, chiefly an "enrichment" school, held at the Weeks Junior High School in Newton and a high school section, chiefly "remedial," held at the Newton High School. The science department at the Harvard-Newton Summer School was composed of one elementary class (fifth- and sixth-grade physical science), three junior high classes (seventh-grade biological science, eighth-grade physical science, and ninth-grade biological science), and one high school class (eleventh-grade remedial chemistry).

In general, interns were encouraged to observe and even teach on different levels, and several actually changed supervisory groups at midsummer. This was particularly true for guidance interns and some science interns who wished more experience at the elementary or high school levels. The high school chemistry class was in some respects different from the other four. Not only was it a remedial class with definite curriculum restraints, but it began earlier and ran for two full hours. The intern group was composed of the four interns who were scheduled to begin their internship year of high school teaching the following September. No guidance interns were present in this group because none could be found who had had any previous experience in chemistry.

Approximately twenty supervisory conferences were tape-recorded for each group. Taping procedures were designed to minimize the effects of the taping on individual groups. A tape recorder, microphone, and a checksheet for identifying conference participants were given to each master teacher before the conference. The investigator was not present during these conferences. The master teacher was asked to turn the recorder on at the beginning of the conference and off at the end, leaving the checksheet with the recorder to be picked up after the conference.

There are some indications that the participants rapidly came to ignore the presence of the microphone. Interns at Harvard-Newton soon learn to accept or at least to tolerate constant exposure. Several interns remarked that they were tape-recorded, video-recorded, and visited so much that the investigator's microphone practically became part of the woodwork. There are even casual comments on these tapes about the investigator himself, comments indicating that the participants had either forgotten about his "presence" there or else felt relatively unthreatened by the taping procedure.

No special arrangements were made for the placing of microphones other than requesting that they be placed near the center of

TABLE 3

Schedule of Planning (P) and Analysis (A) Conferences Analyzed
for Each Supervisory Group

Day	Group 1	2	3	4	5
7/3					
7/4					
7/5					
7/6					
7/7					
7/10	P			P A	
7/11	A	P	P A	A	
7/12	P	A			P A
7/13	A	P	A	A	
7/14		A		P	P
7/17				P	A
7/18		P	P A		
7/19					P
7/20			P A		A
7/21	P A	A			
7/24					P A
7/25	P A		P A	A	
7/26		P			P
7/27		A	P A	P A	A
7/28					
7/31		P		P A	P A
8/1	P A	P A	P	P A	
8/2		A			
8/3			P A	P A	A
8/4	P A				
8/7	P A	P A			P
8/8		P A		P	
8/9	P A		P A		P
8/10					A
8/11					

the group and away from sources of background noise such as open doors and aquarium pumps. A single microphone was used, generally supported above eye level and cushioned against direct and transmitted shocks. Due to the small size of these groups, recording fidelity was quite adequate and most of the tapes were audible enough to be categorized without difficulty.

An attempt was made to sample two planning and two analysis conferences a week for each group. Wherever possible, the planning and analysis of a single class were recorded. Scheduling difficulties, the absence of other research personnel, and equipment problems prevented completely uniform sampling. No conferences were recorded during the first week when initial confusions and anxieties indicated that the presence of a tape recorder would be very distracting. Eight planning and eight analysis conferences for each group were finally chosen for categorization by the M.O.S.A.I.C.S. instrument (see table 3).

Analysis was performed on ten-minute samples of each of the eighty selected tapes. This data pool of 160 minutes of conference time per supervisory group compares closely with the estimated 170 minutes of teaching time for each of Bellack's instructional groups. This sample of supervisory conferences represents approximately 10% of the total supervisory interaction in the science department during the Harvard-Newton Summer School.

After every other conference, conference participants were asked to fill out a reaction sheet on which they were to (1) estimate the amount of time actually spent on certain content and process areas compared to the amount of time that would have been most appropriate for those areas; (2) give an overall evaluation of the effectiveness or productivity of the conference; and (3) enumerate the specific comments, techniques, or activities that were most helpful, least helpful, and that the participant felt should have occurred but did not occur in the conference. The completion of these questionnaires was optional. They were placed in sealed envelopes and deposited in boxes at the conference sites. The envelopes were not opened until well after the summer had ended. The response rate on these confidential questionnaires was very good, despite their anonymity and the problems of stress and fatigue during the summer. A total of 61 conferences were sampled and 314 questionnaires were actually returned, although some were incomplete.

The conference tapes were also analyzed after the summer school had ended. The analysis procedures differ from those of Bellack, who used the following procedure:

(1) each protocol of a single class session was first coded by one member of the coding team; (2) this initial coding was then reviewed by a second person, who noted his disagreements with the original analysis; (3) finally, these disagreements were arbitrated by two coders, who, whenever possible, were not involved in the initial coding of the protocol. [1966, p. 14]

Lacking other research personnel, and in hopes that a procedure could be developed that would be both reliable and practical with direct coding from tape recordings, the investigator utilized the following analysis procedures:

1. Each selected tape was replayed and notes were taken on the content of the conference. Participants were identified and quotations recorded when possible.

2. A random choice was made for analyzing a ten-minute segment either early or late in the conference.

3. The tape was rewound and replayed until the beginning of a teaching cycle was identified.

4. The tape was replayed from the beginning of this cycle for a minimum of ten minutes, measured by a stopwatch, until the end of the last teaching cycle. Notes were made during this replay of the readings of a tape counter, the total elapsed time, and the substantive area being discussed.

5. The tape was replayed and the speaker and pedagogical moves were recorded, with substantive areas added from the previous replay where possible.

6. The tape was replayed and the substantive meanings, substantive-logical meanings, instructional meanings, and instructional-logical meanings recorded.

7. After this basic analysis, the next tape was analyzed.

8. After a third of the tapes had been analyzed in this manner, the investigator returned to the original tape.

9. The tapes were replayed and the initial codings were reviewed. During this process the investigator also added the number of thought units contained in each move.

10. After the remainder of the tapes had been analyzed in this manner, a stratified random sample of one conference per supervisory group was chosen from the analyzed tapes and this conference was reanalyzed for reliability purposes.

11. The investigator then proceeded to the next third of the analysis and followed the same procedure.

Although this is a long process, it is relatively practical compared with the time and money required to produce, verify, analyze, review, and arbitrate codings of typescripts.

TABLE 4

Comparison of Percent of Inter-Observer Agreement in Bellack's Study with
Percent of Intra-Observer Agreement in Study Using M.O.S.A.I.C.S.

Category	% Agreement for Moves		% Agreement for Lines/Units	
	Bellack	M.O.S.A.I.C.S.	Bellack	M.O.S.A.I.C.S.
Speakers	*	99	*	98
Pedagogical moves	94	95	93	95
Substantive meanings:				
specificity (S or G)	*	99	*	98
Focus (O, M, or X)	*	96	*	97
Domain (C, A, or D)	*	97	*	97
Total	95	94	96	93
Substantive-logical				
meanings	88	92	91	90
Instructional meanings	88	91	91	89
Instructional-logical				
meanings	87	85	84	88

*These categories are used only in the M.O.S.A.I.C.S. instrument

The average time required to perform the analysis with the
M.O.S.A.I.C.S. instrument was about ten minutes of analysis time for
each minute of conference time. In terms of the amount and variety
of output, the time spent in analysis is very efficiently used.

Reliability tests were designed to be comparable with Bellack's
data. Bellack's coding teams used Percent of Observer Agreement
figures for twelve randomly selected five-page samples. Three reliability tests of the same type were performed with the M.O.S.A.I.C.S.
data on samples of comparable size. A comparison of Bellack's reliability figures and the average of these three reliability tests is given
in table 4. This comparison indicates that the Percent of Intra-Observer
Agreement for the M.O.S.A.I.C.S. data is comparable with the Percent of Inter-Observer Agreement for the Bellack data.

Because of the enormous amount of data generated in a short
period by the M.O.S.A.I.C.S. system (approximately 80,000 bits of
data for 13.3 hours of actual supervisory time) and the vast number
of possible category patterns and combinations that might be of interest to the analyst, analysis by hand is out of the question.

This investigator therefore wrote a computer program for the IBM 7094 to perform the basic data analysis. This program changes the letter codings of the M.O.S.A.I.C.S. categorization into a numerical code and performs a series of tabulations and cross-tabulations computed by number and percentage of moves and units for each category and for selected patterns of categories. These are then printed out for each supervisory session, the totals for each group, and the totals for all groups, with subtotals for planning, analysis, early conferences, and late conferences. The analyst punches the basic data on IBM cards and submits these to the computer. The actual computer time used to perform the entire analysis portion of this study was less than five minutes.

The results of this study are briefly presented in the next chapter. The first section is a composite analysis of clinical supervision in science; the second section examines each of the five supervisory groups in order to explore the functioning of individual groups; and the third section compares the "rules of the game" for these five supervisory groups with those of Bellack's fifteen teaching groups.

•4•

A Study of Clinical Supervision in Science at the Harvard-Newton Summer School

The primary purpose of the present chapter is to put flesh and blood onto the bones of the technical research instrument defined in Chapter 3. What meanings may be inferred from these categories about the actual processes of clinical supervision? How do the different ratios and dimensions of M.O.S.A.I.C.S. help the researcher to condense the overwhelming volume of data produced and make it more meaningful? What are the potentialities of the instrument both for describing and understanding complex supervisory interactions and for generating questions and hypotheses for future research? This chapter demonstrates how M.O.S.A.I.C.S. might be a useful instrument for research in three significant areas: research on the processes of clinical supervision as a fundamental element of teacher education, clinical research on the interactions within individual supervisory groups, and research comparing teaching interactions and supervisory interactions.

The study described in Chapter 3 was designed to demonstrate the potentialities and use of this instrument. The design of this study is not ideal for more systematic research purposes because of the small population and the number of uncontrolled variables. On the other hand, the amount of time sampled per group represents a substantial portion of the total time spent in formal group supervision. The sample is also fairly uniformly distributed in time over the experimental period, and planning and analysis conferences are sampled with equal frequency. The literature contains no reports of longitudinal studies, detailed descriptive analyses of clinical supervision either of individuals or of groups, studies of supervisory conferences that are functionally different (such as planning and analysis conferences), or studies of supervision at different grade levels. Therefore, a fairly detailed presentation of this research data is warranted.

Space limitations do not permit a complete analysis of the data. No analysis will be performed on individual conferences and only the salient data summaries and patterns will actually be included in this book. Although the discussion of these data will necessarily be limited, interested researchers may extend the analysis by reference to the tables in this chapter and in Appendix I. The tables contain percentages of pedagogical moves and thought units for each supervisory group and for the mean of all groups. This chapter contains tables of category totals for all supervisory conferences combined, while Appendix I contains tables comparing planning with analysis conferences and early with late conferences.

CLINICAL SUPERVISION IN SCIENCE AT THE HARVARD-NEWTON SUMMER SCHOOL

This section discusses and interprets the M.O.S.A.I.C.S. data totals for all supervisory groups studied. It focuses on the regularities apparent in all groups by separately discussing each of the major subdivisions of the instrument, and concludes with discussions of planning vs. analysis and early vs. late conferences. The tables give percentage totals for pedagogical moves and for thought units. However, the discussion will center primarily on thought units, since these units are more indicative of the relative activity or the relative stress on different dimensions of meaning in the conference.

Tables 49 through 54 in Appendix J present data from the conference questionnaires concerning the amount of difference in emphasis that individual participants felt should have been placed in certain content and process areas for individual conferences. The questionnaires asked the participants to estimate on a five-point scale the amount of time actually spent and the amount of time that should have been spent in these areas. The difference between these two estimates is recorded as the emphasis preference. For example, an emphasis preference of 1.0 means that, on the average, the participants felt that additional time should have been spent in that area in the conference, equal to one unit on an arbitrary five-point scale (*none, little, some, much, all*) or about 25.0% more time. Similarly, an emphasis preference of −.5 indicates that the average participant would have preferred about 12.5% less time or stress on that area.

These values do not generate particularly informative insights into overall reactions to the process of supervision. In the first place, the reactions are based on immediate impressions of specific preceding conferences and thus fluctuate very widely. There is also evident response bias. Many respondents indicated either no desire for different emphasis or at most a one-point increase—desires for decreased emphasis (negative values) were rare, as were very strong preferences (emphasis preferences greater than one). As a result of this moderate rating plus a certain amount of "halo effect," in which participants either noted satisfaction or desired moderate increases in some areas, the preferences tended to be diluted or regressed to a moderately positive value. The relationships are therefore small and only moderately suggestive for purposes of generalization, although they become more revealing for the clinical analysis of individual groups.

1. Pedagogical Moves

The rate of verbal interaction in clinical supervision is fairly high. Table 5 includes the average number of moves/minute and units/minute. On the average, each minute of supervisory discourse contains about seven pedagogical moves and twenty-one thought units. It is interesting that the 2.9-second duration of an average thought unit corresponds almost exactly with the 3-second time interval chosen by Flanders (1965) as his basic unit of analysis.

The data in table 5 are primarily intended to give the reader an overview of the basic frequencies involved in this study and to permit him to examine some of the factors from which the percentages and participation indices in the succeeding tables are derived. Some relationships, however, are more evident in a table of this sort than in the other tables. For example, the ratio of units/move gives an indication of the amount of time and consequently the stress placed on certain categories. This stress can also be determined from the other tables by comparing the percentages for moves and for units in any given category. If these percentages are equal, one may conclude that the moves are of average length. In this study, an average move is about three units long. If, for example, reacting moves account for 50% of all moves and 50% of all units, then it may be concluded that reacting moves are an average of three units long. If soliciting moves account for 18% of all moves but only 9% of all units, then these moves must be only half as long as an average move. In contrast, if summary reactions comprise 1% of the moves and 2% of the units, an average move of this type must be approximately six units long.

It is evident from table 5 that moves are, on the average, longest for supervisors and shortest for observers. While this is potentially significant in itself, an examination of specific groups shows that supervisors 3, 4, and 5 differ in important respects from supervisors 1

TABLE 5

Basic Analysis Data for Supervisory Conferences

Data Category	Supervisory Group					
	1	*2*	*3*	*4*	*5*	*Total*
Number of moves by supervisor	547	292	299	595	309	2042
By teacher	365	377	279	467	307	1795
By observer	679	350	221	258	285	1793
Total moves	1591	1019	799	1320	901	5630
Number of units by supervisor	1330	842	1180	1946	1492	6790
By teacher	1049	1381	1002	995	1170	5597
By observer	1650	1063	718	483	770	4684
Total units	4029	3286	2900	3424	3432	17071
Teaching cycles initiated by supervisor	154	99	135	191	90	669
By teacher	83	87	51	94	68	383
By observer	176	98	59	49	83	465
Total teaching cycles	413	284	245	334	241	1517
Total time analyzed (min.)	161.9	162.7	165.9	163.4	164.4	818.3
Average number of moves/min.	9.8	6.3	4.8	8.1	5.5	6.9
Of units/min.	24.8	19.3	17.8	20.7	20.7	20.9
Of teaching cycles/min.	2.6	1.7	1.4	2.0	1.5	1.9
Average no. of units/move by supervisor	2.4	2.9	3.9	3.3	4.8	3.3
By teacher	2.9	3.7	3.6	2.1	3.8	3.1
By observer	2.4	3.0	3.2	1.9	2.8	2.6
Total	2.5	3.2	3.6	2.6	3.8	3.0
Average no. of units/cycle by supervisor	8.6	11.7	11.0	10.1	16.6	11.1
By teacher	10.1	12.4	10.8	8.4	14.2	11.0
By observer	10.5	10.5	14.2	14.2	11.7	11.6
Total	9.8	11.5	11.8	10.2	14.2	11.2
Average no. of supervisors/conference	1.0	1.0	1.0	1.0	1.0	1.0
Of teachers/conference	1.1	2.4	2.0	1.5	2.1	1.8
Of observers/conference	3.9	3.3	2.9	2.2	3.3	3.1
Total	6.0	6.7	5.9	4.7	6.4	5.9

and 2. In each of the former cases the supervisor's moves are longest, followed by the teacher's and finally by the observer's. In contrast, supervisors 1 and 2 have unusually short moves. Their average moves are, in fact, shorter than those of most of the other participants in their groups. This same grouping of supervisors will be evident in many other sections of the data. Supervisors 1 and 2 are females and supervisors 3, 4, and 5 are males. The differences evident in this study, however, do not appear to be primarily a function of sex. They appear to represent aspects of a nondirective supervisory style that each of these supervisors was consciously attempting to achieve. More will be said about these differences later.

Table 6 presents the percentages for each type of pedagogical move made by conference participants. The first factor to note is the similarity of the total moves and units, or total activity, for each type of participant. On the average, supervisor, teacher, and observer each speak roughly a third of the time. All types of participants in these conferences are thus making comparable contributions to the planning and analysis of instruction. Once again, however, the supervisors occupy the largest portion of the time, followed by the teachers and finally by the observers. Supervisors 1 and 2 characteristically speak less than any of the other supervisors. In group 1 it is the observers who speak most frequently, while in group 2 it is the teachers who are most active.

Examination of the individual pedagogical moves shows that structuring and reacting moves occupy most of the conference time. These two moves comprise almost 73% of the total units. Although the lack of emphasis on solicitations and responses might be surprising to some, this finding is consistent with the concept of clinical supervision expressed in the literature. Proposing observations, hypotheses, suggestions, and opinions for reaction by other participants is a fundamental aspect of the analysis of instruction. It is also consistent with the kind of interaction one expects in the mutual give-and-take of small-group discussions.

As expected, reactions are the most common type of move for all participants and summary reactions are the least common. By comparing lengths of moves, it is evident that both structuring and summary reacting moves tend to be unusually long. These moves are particularly long for supervisors, who thus appear to place more emphasis on those moves which shape and control the flow of discourse. This is done either by launching the discussion in a given direction or by halting it, often with a summary, before directing it into a new area. Once again, supervisors 1 and 2 are dramatically different from

TABLE 6

Percentages of Moves and Units by Supervisory Groups
in Each Pedagogical Move Category: All Conferences

Category by Speaker	% Moves by Group						% Units by Group					
	1	2	3	4	5	$\bar{X}$	1	2	3	4	5	$\bar{X}$
SOL: Supvr.	7.6	8.4	13.9	9.9	7.1	9.1	4.9	4.9	6.6	5.6	5.3	5.4
Tchr.	2.6	4.4	3.5	4.0	4.6	3.7	1.6	2.2	1.3	2.2	2.1	1.9
Obs.	5.3	5.7	4.9	2.8	4.9	4.7	2.5	2.8	2.4	1.6	1.8	2.2
Total	15.5	18.5	22.3	16.7	16.6	17.5	9.0	9.9	10.3	9.4	9.2	9.5
RES: Supvr.	3.2	2.4	3.0	3.9	2.7	3.1	2.8	4.0	3.2	4.2	3.1	3.4
Tchr.	4.0	8.8	11.4	8.6	7.8	7.6	5.3	10.9	12.8	8.2	8.1	8.8
Obs.	6.3	5.6	5.1	2.8	4.6	4.9	5.8	5.5	3.5	1.5	3.0	3.9
Total	13.5	16.8	19.5	15.3	15.1	15.6	13.9	20.4	19.5	13.9	14.2	16.1
STR: Supvr.	3.5	3.1	6.4	6.1	4.4	4.6	4.8	4.9	18.9	16.4	16.7	11.9
Tchr.	3.1	4.7	3.8	4.2	4.6	4.0	6.6	9.0	6.5	5.1	10.1	7.5
Obs.	6.6	4.3	3.6	1.8	5.0	4.4	11.5	6.8	8.0	2.6	5.7	7.1
Total	13.2	12.1	13.8	12.1	14.0	13.0	22.9	20.7	33.4	24.1	32.5	26.5
REA: Supvr.	19.5	14.4	13.4	24.5	19.0	18.8	18.9	11.5	11.0	29.8	16.5	17.8
Tchr.	12.8	18.8	15.9	18.6	17.2	16.4	12.1	19.8	13.5	13.4	13.7	14.4
Obs.	23.9	18.5	13.8	12.1	17.2	17.7	20.5	17.0	10.5	8.4	12.0	14.0
Total	56.2	51.7	43.1	55.2	53.4	52.9	51.5	48.3	35.0	51.6	42.2	46.2
RSM: Supvr.	0.5	0.3	0.8	0.7	1.1	0.6	1.7	0.3	1.0	0.8	1.9	1.2
Tchr.	0.4	0.2	0.4	0.0	0.0	0.2	0.4	0.2	0.5	0.0	0.0	0.2
Obs.	0.4	0.2	0.3	0.0	0.0	0.2	0.6	0.2	0.4	0.0	0.0	0.2
Total	1.3	0.7	1.5	0.7	1.1	1.0	2.7	0.7	1.9	0.8	1.9	1.6
Total: Supvr.	34.3	28.6	37.5	45.1	34.3	36.2	33.1	25.6	40.7	56.8	43.5	39.7
Tchr.	22.9	36.9	35.0	35.4	34.2	31.9	26.0	42.1	34.6	28.9	34.0	32.8
Obs.	42.5	34.3	27.7	19.5	31.7	31.9	40.9	32.3	24.8	14.1	22.5	27.4
I/R: Supvr.	0.48	0.67	1.18	0.55	0.50	0.61	0.41	0.62	1.68	0.63	1.02	0.77
Tchr.	0.33	0.33	0.27	0.30	0.37	0.32	0.46	0.36	0.29	0.34	0.56	0.40
Obs.	0.39	0.41	0.44	0.31	0.45	0.40	0.52	0.42	0.72	0.42	0.50	0.51

SOL = Solicitation
RES = Response
STR = Structuring
REA = Reacting
RSM = Summary reaction
I/R = (STR + SOL) / (RES + REA + RSM)

the others in this respect. They structure less than a third as much as do the other three supervisors.

If structuring moves are unusually long, solicitations are unusually short. Questions tend to be brief and to the point. Table 6 indicates that supervisors ask most of the questions and teachers answer most of them. Since role differences are not as evident for the structuring and reacting moves, the solicitation-response patterns appear to represent that aspect of clinical supervision which deals with the individual teacher's performance rather than with the analysis of instruction in general. Future studies of the logical parameters of each pedagogical move might help elucidate this distinction, which is evidently more complex than this brief analysis indicates.

The initiatory/reflexive ratio is generally highest for the supervisor and lowest for the teacher. In other words, the teachers in these supervisory conferences are proportionally less in control of the direction and flow of the discourse than is either of the other types of participant. Teachers are not only asked more questions, but they themselves tend to structure and solicit less. The role of the teacher in the conference appears to be reflexive.

Role differences become much more evident in the examination of participation indices in table 7. Participation indices permit a direct comparison of the role of a specific participant with the role of a hypothetical "random" participant whose index is 1. The data reveal a surprising regularity, for with few exceptions, a supervisor's P.I. for total moves and units is consistently greater than 2; a teacher's is approximately 1; and an observer's averages about 0.5. Therefore, although their total activity is roughly equal, the activities of individual supervisors, teachers, and observers differ sharply. An individual supervisor speaks approximately twice as much as an individual teacher and four times as much as an observer.

These role differences come into sharper focus when individual pedagogical moves are examined. The supervisors' principal role appears to be to control the flow of discourse. In terms of thought units, supervisors have unusually high participation indices for structuring (2.66) and soliciting (3.36), with a correspondingly high initiatory total of 2.84. Their indices for responding are relatively low (1.25), indicating that they resemble other participants in terms of answering questions. Supervisors' reactions average 2.28, which approximates their participation index for all moves. Summary reactions, at 4.07, are almost exclusively the province of the supervisors. The summary reaction, although a reflexive move, may be considered an important mechanism for controlling discourse because it often effectively limits discussion in preparation for a new structuring move or solicitation.

TABLE 7

Participation Index of Moves and Units by Supervisory Groups
in Each Pedagogical Move Category: All Conferences

Category by Speaker	P.I. for Moves by Group						P.I. for Units by Group					
	1	2	3	4	5	$\overline{X}$	1	2	3	4	5	$\overline{X}$
SOL: Supvr.	2.94	3.02	3.69	2.81	2.71	3.08	3.26	3.30	3.79	2.82	3.65	3.36
Tchr.	0.89	0.65	0.47	0.73	0.85	0.68	0.95	0.61	0.38	0.71	0.70	0.65
Obs.	0.54	0.64	0.44	0.36	0.57	0.51	0.43	0.58	0.47	0.37	0.38	0.44
RES: Supvr.	1.41	0.95	0.91	1.21	1.13	1.18	1.20	1.31	0.97	1.43	1.38	1.25
Tchr.	1.56	1.43	1.74	1.71	1.58	1.57	2.03	1.46	1.95	1.79	1.75	1.76
Obs.	0.72	0.69	0.53	0.40	0.59	0.60	0.65	0.56	0.36	0.23	0.41	0.46
STR: Supvr.	1.59	1.71	2.75	2.39	1.99	2.09	1.26	1.58	3.35	3.22	3.25	2.66
Tchr.	1.25	1.06	0.82	1.05	1.00	0.99	1.53	1.19	0.58	0.64	0.95	0.91
Obs.	0.77	0.73	0.53	0.32	0.69	0.65	0.78	0.68	0.48	0.23	0.34	0.51
REA: Supvr.	2.08	1.86	1.84	2.10	2.25	2.10	2.20	1.59	1.87	2.73	2.47	2.28
Tchr.	1.21	1.00	1.10	1.02	0.99	1.00	1.25	1.12	1.15	0.79	0.99	1.01
Obs.	0.66	0.74	0.65	0.48	0.63	0.64	0.62	0.73	0.61	0.35	0.55	0.58
RSM: Supvr.	2.30	2.86	3.16	4.74	6.33	3.55	3.76	2.87	3.12	4.74	6.33	4.07
Tchr.	1.64	0.78	0.79	0.00	0.00	0.65	0.79	0.78	0.78	0.00	0.00	0.40
Obs.	0.48	0.59	0.40	0.00	0.00	0.38	0.34	0.59	0.43	0.00	0.00	0.24
Total: Supvr.	2.05	1.91	2.22	2.14	2.17	2.14	1.98	1.71	2.41	2.69	2.78	2.35
Tchr.	1.22	1.01	1.04	1.08	1.05	1.03	1.38	1.15	1.03	0.88	1.03	1.06
Obs.	0.66	0.71	0.56	0.42	0.62	0.61	0.63	0.67	0.50	0.31	0.44	0.53
Init.: Supvr.	2.31	2.51	3.33	2.64	2.38	2.66	1.82	2.14	3.46	2.94	3.34	2.84
Tchr.	1.05	0.81	0.60	0.87	0.92	0.81	1.37	1.00	0.53	0.66	0.90	0.84
Obs.	0.64	0.67	0.48	0.35	0.63	0.57	0.68	0.65	0.48	0.27	0.35	0.50
Refl.: Supvr.	1.95	1.65	1.59	1.94	2.07	1.92	2.06	1.52	1.60	2.49	2.33	2.07
Tchr.	1.28	1.10	1.29	1.16	1.10	1.12	1.39	1.22	1.42	0.99	1.14	1.18
Obs.	0.67	0.72	0.61	0.45	0.61	0.63	0.61	0.68	0.52	0.32	0.50	0.54

SOL = Solicitation
RES = Response
STR = Structuring
REA = Reacting
RSM = Summary reaction
Init. = STR + SOL
Refl. = RES + REA + RSM
Participation Index (P.I.) = (% Moves or units by speaker) /
(% Participation in conference)

Teachers, on the other hand, have relatively low participation indices for soliciting (0.65) and high indices for responding (1.76). Teachers tend to answer many more questions than they ask. Their structuring moves (0.91) and reacting moves (1.01) are close to their averages for all moves, and their general reflexive role in the conference is demonstrated by a reflexive total of 1.18, compared with an initiatory total of 0.84.

The role differentiation for observers is not well defined. With the exception of summary reactions, which are unusually low at 0.24, their participation indices fall in a narrow range from 0.44 to 0.58. Their initiatory total (0.50) and reflexive total (0.54) are almost identical. All of these figures are averages for the five supervisory groups. Considerable variation is evident, and these differences will be discussed in the later section of this chapter that examines individual supervisory groups.

Table 54 in Appendix J presents information from conference participants about the amount of initiation from supervisors, teachers, and observers they would have preferred. It is immediately obvious that most participants, including the supervisors themselves, felt that supervisors should have initiated less in the conferences. Only in group 1 did the students wish for greater supervisor initiation, and the percentage of her initiatory moves was the lowest of any supervisor. Except for the elementary group 2, in which the students felt that the teachers initiated too much, most participants would have desired more initiation by both teachers and observers.

In general, the most extreme preferences in most categories are usually taken by the supervisors and the least extreme preferences by the teachers whose instruction or planning is the focus of supervision. One might hypothesize several possible explanations for this, but a major factor is probably perspective—the supervisors are least concerned with immediate personal problems in teaching and are thus better able to conceptualize and analyze the ongoing processes of supervision. The observers can afford to be more emotionally detached than the teachers, whose preferences are probably in a small number of particular areas that are of most concern to the immediate class being analyzed.

2. Teaching Cycles

From table 5 it can be seen that approximately two teaching cycles occur each minute. Since the supervisor primarily controls the flow of discourse, it might be expected that a cycle initiated by him would be taken more seriously and extended farther by the other participants. In other words, one would expect that teaching cycles initiated by the supervisor would be longer than cycles initiated by the other participants. This is not, however, the case. Although the number of units/cycle is consistently close to eleven, in three out of five cases the longest cycles (and presumably those most emphasized in the discussion), are initiated by the observers. In only one case is either the supervisor's or the teacher's average cycle the longest.

Table 8 gives a breakdown of the major cycles found in this study, and while only eight of the twenty-one cycles are actually reported in the table, these eight cycles represent 87.9% of the total units in this discourse. The percentages in this table are computed somewhat differently from the other percentages in the study. Table 8 presents the percentages for given cycles based on the total number of cycles initiated by each participant. For example, 6.5% of all the cycles initiated by supervisor 1 were of type 3 (STR–REA). This computation indicates the differences, if any, among the patterns of cycle initiation for different participants.

In terms of units, three teaching cycles account for almost two-thirds of the discourse. These are all cycles that include a large number of reactions: 4 (STR–REA–REA . . .), 19 (SOL–RES–REA–REA . . .), and 10 (STR–SOL–RES–REA–REA . . .). Differences are evident when percentages of cycles are compared with percentages of units. Cycle 14 (SOL–RES) ranks second in total frequency but ranks only sixth in total units. These cycles tend to be unusually short and chiefly represent simple questions and answers about observations, plans, and interpretations. On the other hand, cycle 10 (STR–SOL–RES–REA–REA . . .) contains the greatest number of units per cycle. Although these cycles occur infrequently, they represent a substantial percentage of the total discourse.

Table 8 shows that cycle 4 (STR–REA–REA . . .) is the predominant teaching cycle and accounts for over a third of all supervisory discourse. In other words, over 37% of the interaction consists of a structuring move that is subsequently amplified, qualified, or contradicted by more than one of the other participants. This is twice the activity of cycle 19 (SOL–RES–REA–REA . . .), in which a response to one participant's question produces a series of reactions and over four times the activity of cycle 10 (STR–SOL–RES–REA–REA . . .), in which a statement or proposition is followed by a question, an answer, and a series of reactions. The high incidence of multiple reactions indicates that supervisory discourse is characterized by a relatively free give-and-take among participants, particularly when it is recalled that supervisors, teachers, and observing interns are approximately equally active in the reacting move.

TABLE 8

Percentage* of Each Initiator's Cycles and Units
for Major Teaching Cycle Types: All Conferences

Cycle Types by Initiator	% Cycles by Group						% Units by Group					
	1	2	3	4	5	$\bar{X}$	1	2	3	4	5	$\bar{X}$
Type 3: Supvr.	6.5	4.0	6.7	2.6	3.3	4.6	2.8	3.4	8.8	2.7	4.0	4.3
Tchr.	8.4	10.3	15.7	14.9	16.2	12.8	5.0	10.9	15.8	10.1	17.8	11.8
Obs.	10.8	9.2	13.6	8.2	12.0	10.8	6.5	7.0	15.8	4.6	9.4	8.3
$\bar{X}$	8.7	7.7	10.2	6.9	10.0	8.6	5.0	7.0	12.2	4.8	9.4	7.5
Type 4: Supvr.	19.5	19.2	13.3	23.6	23.3	19.9	30.3	29.5	26.8	34.8	32.8	31.1
Tchr.	32.5	28.7	17.6	23.4	22.1	25.6	53.0	36.9	27.8	34.6	27.5	36.3
Obs.	39.8	25.5	20.3	26.5	37.3	32.5	58.4	40.7	26.2	38.6	51.5	46.2
$\bar{X}$	30.8	24.3	15.9	24.0	27.8	25.2	48.0	35.5	26.8	35.6	36.6	37.2
Type 5: Supvr.	2.6	3.0	6.7	6.8	4.4	4.9	1.4	6.8	9.8	4.7	5.0	5.5
Tchr.	2.4	3.4	7.8	2.1	10.3	4.7	2.0	3.8	7.8	1.4	12.9	5.6
Obs.	1.7	1.0	6.8	6.1	1.2	2.6	1.5	0.6	4.4	7.9	1.2	2.5
$\bar{X}$	2.2	2.5	6.9	5.4	5.0	4.2	1.5	3.9	7.9	4.6	6.2	4.6
Type 9: Supvr.	1.3	1.0	2.2	2.1	3.3	1.9	1.1	1.8	4.0	2.3	5.0	2.9
Tchr.	4.8	3.4	5.9	2.1	2.9	3.7	4.0	6.5	7.8	1.6	2.3	4.3
Obs.	0.6	2.0	1.7	0.0	0.0	0.9	0.2	2.8	2.0	0.0	0.0	0.9
$\bar{X}$	1.7	2.1	2.9	1.8	2.1	2.0	1.3	3.7	4.2	1.7	2.8	2.6
Type 10: Supvr.	3.9	2.0	4.4	3.1	5.6	3.7	7.4	2.8	8.5	6.4	8.0	6.8
Tchr.	7.2	3.4	7.8	9.6	7.4	7.0	16.5	3.2	13.2	22.9	8.2	12.0
Obs.	4.0	3.1	5.1	6.1	1.2	3.7	6.1	4.9	12.3	7.3	1.1	6.1
$\bar{X}$	4.6	2.8	5.3	5.4	4.6	4.5	8.7	3.6	10.5	10.4	6.1	7.9
Type 14: Supvr.	19.5	19.2	21.5	16.8	17.8	18.8	10.5	9.3	8.4	5.4	9.3	8.3
Tchr.	14.5	16.1	15.7	21.3	13.2	16.4	4.8	5.4	8.5	9.5	4.6	6.2
Obs.	12.5	16.3	16.9	12.2	24.1	15.9	3.8	6.5	7.6	3.3	8.5	5.7
$\bar{X}$	15.5	17.3	19.2	17.4	18.7	17.3	6.2	7.1	8.2	5.9	7.7	7.0
Type 18: Supvr.	14.9	20.2	11.9	15.2	11.1	14.6	12.7	14.8	7.0	11.8	5.4	10.2
Tchr.	9.6	5.7	9.8	5.3	10.3	7.8	5.1	4.3	4.9	2.9	6.8	4.8
Obs.	5.7	9.2	8.5	6.1	8.4	7.3	2.8	8.8	6.0	2.0	7.1	5.1
$\bar{X}$	9.9	12.0	10.6	11.1	10.0	10.7	6.5	9.5	6.3	7.7	6.3	7.3
Type 19: Supvr.	18.8	22.2	10.4	15.7	13.3	16.0	27.3	29.1	13.9	20.6	15.0	20.6
Tchr.	9.6	20.7	7.8	10.6	13.2	12.8	6.7	20.9	6.4	9.8	16.8	13.1
Obs.	16.5	15.3	20.3	24.5	12.0	16.8	18.6	18.1	23.1	30.3	17.9	20.6
$\bar{X}$	16.0	19.4	12.2	15.6	12.9	15.4	19.0	22.9	15.1	20.1	16.3	18.8

Type 3 = STR-REA
Type 4 = STR-REA-REA...
Type 5 = STR-SOL-RES
Type 9 = STR-SOL-RES-REA

Type 10 = STR-SOL-RES-REA-REA...
Type 14 = SOL-RES
Type 18 = SOL-RES-REA
Type 19 = SOL-RES-REA-REA...

*Percentages are based on 100% for each initiator.

Table 8 reveals some interesting differences between participants. Comparisons between cycle 3 (STR–REA) and cycle 4 (STR–REA–REA . . .) indicate that structuring moves are treated differently, depending on the initiator. Cycle 3 represents a structuring move that receives a single reaction and is then essentially dropped. In four out of five groups, the teachers initiate an unusually high proportion of these cycles, and in all cases the supervisors initiate the least. Thus, structuring moves by teachers frequently generate very limited discussion, while similar moves by supervisors rarely do so. Cycle 4 represents a structuring move that produces multiple reactions or extended discussion. In almost all cases it is the observers who initiate the highest proportion of these cycles and the supervisors who initiate the least. This is surprising, since it might be expected that structuring moves by the supervisor, not the observers, would more frequently generate extended discussions.

Cycles 5, 9, and 10 are initiated by STR followed by SOL. In other words, a statement or proposition is followed by a question that is related to it. In some cases a single individual will state the proposition and follow this by a question directed at another participant; in other cases the participant who makes the structuring move is questioned by someone else. Cycles 5, 9, and 10 may be considered relatively directive if both initiatory moves are made by the same participant. For example, if a participant states a proposition and then asks a specific question relating to it, the other participants have little immediate opportunity to alter either the content or the logic of the discussion. This type of cycle is primarily the province of the supervisor. On the other hand, if the solicitation comes from a different participant, a more open style of interaction is indicated: the structuring move is often being questioned or challenged. Most STR–SOL . . . cycles in supervision are of the latter type.

For all three cycle types, teachers tend to initiate the largest proportion and observers the least. This may indicate either more extensive challenging of teachers' propositions or more careful attention to the clarity of those propositions. The fact that supervisors rank higher than observers may be a result of a greater incidence of the cycle variety in which the same participant makes both initiatory moves.

Cycles 14 (SOL–RES), 18 (SOL–RES–REA), and 19 (SOL–RES–REA–REA . . .) may also be compared in this manner. These are all solicitation-response cycles and differ only in the number of reactions directed to the elicited response. Supervisors have consistently higher percentages of all of these cycles. Thus, questioning cycles are a more significant role feature for the supervisor than for the other participants.

Since these cycles generate more responses and reactions, they appear to be taken more seriously when initiated by the supervisor. In contrast, such cycles initiated by the teachers tend to generate the fewest responses and reactions.

This type of comparison may be more evident in the data in table 9, which presents total percentages and participation indices for teaching cycles arranged by patterns of initiatory moves. Compared with their average participation indices, supervisors initiate an unusually high proportion of solicitation cycles (SOL . . .), and teachers initiate a correspondingly low proportion of these cycles. On the other hand, supervisors and observers tend to have relatively high indices for structuring cycles (STR . . .), while the teachers' indices for STR–SOL . . . cycles are particularly high. In other words, when supervisors or observers state a proposition or offer a suggestion, a discussion is likely to follow; when teachers do so, a question is more likely to follow. In general, supervisors and observers have higher participation indices for teaching cycles than they have for pedagogical moves. This is consistent with the finding that these participants make more initiatory moves and generate longer discussions. The indices for teachers are comparably lower for teaching cycles because teachers initiate less than they respond or react.

3. Substantive Areas

Table 10 presents the basic data for the substantive areas or Content Analysis System of M.O.S.A.I.C.S. Much of this data is consistent with the literature on clinical supervision. Over 93.0% of the units in these conferences directly involves the analysis of instruction. In fact, over 99.7% of the total conference time is actually spent on the analysis of instruction, the subject matter, or discussions of the process of supervision.

Only 7.5% of the units are classified as "general," or concerned primarily with generalizations, learning theory, and past experience. The "curriculum and methods course" component of clinical supervision is thus given very little emphasis in these groups. The analysis of instruction in the specific class, on the other hand, accounts for about 86.0% of the total supervisory time. Clinical supervision is indeed clinical in the groups studied; it focuses almost entirely on the specific class being taught by the group. In general, these supervisory groups spend relatively little time talking "about teaching" and concentrate most of their energy on basic clinical analysis.

Table 51 in Appendix J indicates some preference by most participants for more emphasis on generalizations, although this fluctuates widely and appears to bear little relationship to the actual amount of

TABLE 9

Percentages and Participation Indices for Teaching Cycles
According to Initiatory Pattern of Cycle: All Conferences

Pattern by Initiator	% Cycles by Group						% Units by Group					
	1	2	3	4	5	$\overline{X}$	1	2	3	4	5	$\overline{X}$
STR... : Supvr.	9.9	8.5	11.8	16.8	10.3	11.5	11.2	11.9	19.9	23.8	19.5	17.1
Tchr.	8.4	12.4	7.4	12.6	10.8	10.3	12.2	16.0	8.6	11.0	12.8	12.2
Obs.	21.5	12.7	8.2	5.1	17.0	13.4	29.9	15.5	12.2	8.8	17.3	17.3
Total	39.8	33.6	27.4	34.5	38.1	35.2	53.3	43.4	40.7	43.6	49.6	46.6
STR-SOL... : Supvr.	3.9	2.5	9.2	7.4	6.4	5.5	4.1	4.1	13.0	8.0	9.8	7.5
Tchr.	3.6	4.4	4.9	3.8	6.3	4.2	4.9	6.5	6.0	6.0	7.3	6.1
Obs.	3.8	3.0	3.7	2.1	1.7	3.0	4.0	3.6	6.0	3.5	1.1	3.7
Total	11.3	9.9	17.8	13.3	14.4	12.7	13.0	14.2	25.0	17.5	18.2	17.3
SOL... : Supvr.	23.5	23.9	34.1	33.0	20.6	27.1	17.7	19.5	19.0	24.6	14.2	18.9
Tchr.	8.1	13.8	8.5	11.7	11.1	10.7	3.8	10.5	4.5	6.2	8.1	6.5
Obs.	17.3	18.8	12.2	7.5	15.7	14.3	12.2	12.4	10.9	8.1	9.9	10.7
Total	48.9	56.5	54.8	52.2	47.4	52.1	33.7	42.4	34.4	38.9	32.2	36.1
Total: Supvr.	37.3	34.9	55.1	57.2	37.3	44.1	33.0	35.5	51.9	56.4	43.5	43.5
Tchr.	20.1	30.6	20.8	28.1	28.2	25.1	20.9	33.0	19.1	23.2	28.2	24.8
Obs.	42.6	34.5	24.1	14.7	34.4	30.7	46.1	31.5	29.1	20.4	28.3	31.7

Pattern by Initiator	Participation Index: Cycles						Participation Index: Units					
	1	2	3	4	5	$\overline{X}$	1	2	3	4	5	$\overline{X}$
STR... : Supvr.	1.48	1.69	2.55	2.31	1.71	1.94	1.26	1.84	2.89	2.59	2.49	2.12
Tchr.	1.12	1.01	0.80	1.11	0.87	0.95	1.22	1.01	0.63	0.77	0.79	0.83
Obs.	0.83	0.78	0.60	0.32	0.87	0.73	0.87	0.74	0.61	0.44	0.68	0.70
STR-SOL... : Supvr.	2.06	1.68	3.06	2.64	2.82	2.56	1.88	1.92	3.08	2.17	3.41	2.56
Tchr.	1.69	1.22	0.82	0.87	1.34	1.07	2.00	1.25	0.72	1.04	1.22	1.14
Obs.	0.52	0.62	0.42	0.34	0.23	0.45	0.47	0.52	0.49	0.44	0.12	0.41
SOL...: Supvr.	2.88	2.92	3.69	3.00	2.75	3.08	3.14	3.08	3.27	3.00	2.79	3.10
Tchr.	0.88	0.67	0.46	0.68	0.72	0.66	0.60	0.68	0.39	0.48	0.77	0.58
Obs.	0.55	0.69	0.45	0.31	0.64	0.52	0.56	0.60	0.64	0.45	0.60	0.57
Total: Supvr.	2.23	2.33	3.26	2.71	2.36	2.63	1.98	2.37	3.07	2.67	2.75	2.59
Tchr.	1.07	0.84	0.62	0.85	0.86	0.81	1.11	0.90	0.57	0.71	0.86	0.80
Obs.	0.66	0.71	0.49	0.32	0.67	0.59	0.71	0.65	0.59	0.44	0.55	0.61

STR... = Teaching cycles 1, 3, 4
STR-SOL... = Teaching cycles 2, 5, 6, 7, 8, 9, 10, 11, 12
SOL... = Teaching cycles 13, 14, 15, 16, 17, 18, 19, 20, 21
Participation Indices (P.I.) = (% Cycles or units by initiator) /
                               (% Participation in conference)

TABLE 10

Percentage of Moves and Units by Supervisory Groups
in Each Substantive Area and Dimension: All Conferences

Category	% Moves by Group						% Units by Group					
	1	2	3	4	5	$\overline{X}$	1	2	3	4	5	$\overline{X}$
SOC	21.2	9.4	11.6	15.8	17.4	15.8	23.0	9.9	10.3	13.8	23.7	16.6
SOA	1.1	0.2	4.4	1.0	1.3	1.4	1.4	0.2	4.5	0.8	1.2	1.5
SOD	0.1	0.8	4.8	0.0	0.0	0.9	1.2	1.1	5.2	0.0	0.0	1.1
SMC	32.0	23.5	25.3	42.1	28.1	31.2	27.4	21.3	20.2	42.5	25.7	27.7
SMA	2.5	3.0	7.8	0.5	2.1	2.8	2.8	2.1	9.9	0.5	1.7	3.2
SMD	1.4	2.9	7.4	0.5	0.0	2.1	1.2	2.5	8.7	0.8	0.0	2.4
SXC	19.6	16.9	11.6	13.3	23.4	17.1	20.8	19.2	9.9	12.8	19.8	16.9
SXA	6.7	7.9	14.1	0.8	14.9	7.9	6.6	8.4	13.0	1.3	13.4	8.3
SXD	7.0	19.6	5.1	1.7	0.3	6.7	8.2	23.3	7.1	2.0	0.1	8.1
GOC	0.0	0.2	1.5	0.5	0.6	0.4	0.0	0.3	1.9	0.7	0.8	0.7
GOA	0.0	0.0	0.4	0.1	0.0	0.1	0.0	0.0	0.3	0.1	0.0	0.1
GOD	0.0	0.0	0.0	0.2	0.0	0.0	0.0	0.0	0.0	0.1	0.0	0.0
GMC	0.3	0.5	1.5	0.8	2.3	0.9	0.5	0.4	4.1	2.1	2.2	1.8
GMA	0.1	2.0	0.0	0.2	0.0	0.4	0.4	1.3	0.0	0.2	0.0	0.4
GMD	0.6	0.3	0.3	2.8	0.0	0.9	0.7	0.2	1.0	7.8	0.0	1.9
GXC	0.3	3.0	0.4	1.3	1.8	1.3	0.9	3.5	0.9	1.2	2.4	1.7
GXA	0.2	0.0	0.1	0.1	0.0	0.1	0.6	0.0	0.2	0.1	0.0	0.2
GXD	0.0	1.3	0.3	0.9	0.0	0.5	0.0	1.2	0.2	2.0	0.0	0.7
O	22.4	10.6	22.7	17.4	19.3	18.7	24.6	11.5	22.2	15.4	25.7	20.0
M	36.8	32.3	42.2	46.9	32.5	38.4	33.0	27.7	43.9	53.9	29.6	37.3
X	33.8	48.8	31.7	18.1	40.4	33.6	37.2	55.5	31.3	19.5	35.7	35.9
C	73.4	53.5	51.9	73.7	73.6	66.8	72.6	54.5	47.3	73.1	74.6	65.3
A	10.6	13.2	26.8	2.7	18.3	12.7	11.8	12.0	27.9	2.9	16.3	13.7
D	9.1	24.9	17.8	6.1	0.3	11.1	10.3	28.2	22.2	12.8	0.1	14.2
S	91.7	84.4	92.1	75.7	87.6	86.0	91.6	87.9	88.8	74.5	85.6	85.8
G	1.4	7.3	4.4	6.7	4.7	4.7	3.2	6.8	8.6	14.3	5.4	7.5
Instr. total	93.1	91.7	96.5	82.4	92.2	90.7	94.8	94.7	97.4	88.8	91.0	93.3
SBJ	3.5	1.7	3.5	14.1	3.0	5.6	2.5	1.5	2.6	8.9	2.3	3.6
SPR	2.7	6.0	0.0	2.7	4.2	3.1	2.3	3.5	0.0	1.9	6.4	2.9
GRL	0.1	0.0	0.0	0.4	0.6	0.2	0.1	0.0	0.0	0.2	0.3	0.1
GNR	0.6	0.7	0.0	0.5	0.0	0.4	0.3	0.2	0.0	0.2	0.0	0.2
Rel. total	6.9	8.3	3.5	17.7	7.8	9.3	5.2	5.2	2.6	11.2	9.0	6.8

O = Objectives   C = Cognitive   S = Specific   SBJ = Subject
M = Methods   A = Affective   G = General   SPR = Supervision
X = Execution   D = Social   GRL = Related
                                              GNR = Nonrelated

time spent in this area by different groups. Strongest preferences were commonly shown by the supervisors, who were probably more concerned with generalization and transfer than the students, who were more involved with the immediacy of the situation. The teachers and observers desired moderately increased emphasis in both specific and general areas.

The instructional focus is primarily divided between methods and materials ($M = 37.3\%$) and instructional interactions ($X = 35.9\%$). Objectives and content comprise only 20.0% of the conference discussions. The moderately high stress on methodology is to be expected in the supervision of novice teachers, but this average value is probably lower than many educators would have expected. Instructional supervision often appears to consist mainly of criticisms and prescriptions of methods and materials, but these clinical supervisors place approximately equal stress on the analysis of instructional interactions with children. These are all average values, however, and the considerable variation that is evident will be discussed under individual groups.

The low emphasis on objectives and content will be disturbing to many, particularly since much of this discussion actually involves the subject matter or content involved in a particular class. A more detailed discussion of the interactions in this area will be presented in the next section because logical treatments give an indication of how these content areas are actually discussed in the conference. In general, objectives do not generate much heated discussion in these groups. Individual groups show considerable variation but probably for different reasons. Group 2, for example, may have minimized objectives because of the supervisor's philosophical orientation toward curriculum in which specific content objectives for elementary school pupils are given minor stress. Group 4 may have shown the same tendency for an entirely different reason: the curricular restraints of the remedial-credit course were very great in this group, and the content and sequencing were relatively inflexible.

The different percentages for instructional foci are also evident in the participants' emphasis preferences. There is very little desire, if any, for further stress on objectives and content, while there was a desire for as much or more emphasis on the analysis of specific classroom interactions than on methodology. Again, this appears to contradict the commonly held opinion that student teachers primarily desire assistance with problems in methodology.

The instructional domains reveal a heavy emphasis on discussion of learning factors. The cognitive domain encompasses fully 65.3% of conference time, whereas the affective domain ($A = 13.7\%$) and the social-disciplinary domain (D = 14.2%) appear to be somewhat equally neglected. The variance between groups in these latter two domains is very great: the affective domain ranges from 2.9% to 27.9% of conference time, while the social-disciplinary domain shows a range of 0.1% to 28.2%.

Emphasis preferences again bear out these relationships. There is a strong positive preference for more emphasis on the cognitive domain by all types of participants, especially the supervisors. The affective and social-disciplinary domains both receive comparably smaller ratings. Surprisingly, there is some tendency for observers to desire more emphasis on both domains than the teachers, whom one might expect to be more immediately concerned with these affect-loaded areas.

In the instructional domains, as in the instructional foci, the average values are probably less important than differences among individual groups. While the relative proportions of stress in these areas may prove to be useful in comparing different types of supervision or supervisors, these proportions are particularly useful for clinical analysis of particular groups. As the next section will show, logical analyses reveal striking differences among the ways in which groups treat these individual dimensions. The differing stresses found in the comparison of planning vs. analysis and early vs. late conferences permit the researcher to study the functioning of clinical supervision and of individual groups in considerable depth. These differences will be discussed in another section of this chapter.

Analysis of individual substantive areas reveals that 61.2% of the total discourse is concentrated in three specific cognitive areas: Specific Objectives Cognitive (SOC = 16.6%), Specific Methods Cognitive (SMC = 27.7%), and Specific eXecution Cognitive (SXC = 16.9%). It might be expected that this same relative stress on objectives, methods, and execution would also be apparent in the other instructional domains. However, when specific categories in the cognitive domain are compared with those in the affective and social-disciplinary domains, an interesting anomaly appears. In the cognitive domain the following approximate ratios of activity are found: O:M:X (Objectives: Methods:eXecution) = 1:2:1. In the affective domain these ratios become: O:M:X = 1:2:5, and in the social-disciplinary domain they become: O:M:X = 1:2:7. These same factors may be viewed in another way by comparing ratios for instructional foci: for Objectives, C:A:D (Cognitive:Affective:Disciplinary) = 13:1:1; for Methods, C:A:D = 10:1:1; and for eXecution, C:A:D = 2:1:1.

Why is 49% of the discussion on instructional interactions (executions) concerned with attitudinal and social factors while objectives and methods are treated in an overwhelmingly cognitive manner? The explanation for this is not at all clear. It is reasonable to assume that much of this discussion concerns motivational and disciplinary *problems*. Are the supervisory groups treating these primarily as learning problems? Are problems in these areas so touchy and anxiety-producing that they are approached indirectly, through cognitive factors? Or do these supervisory groups have such a strong cognitive bias that these problems simply do not receive treatment? Group 3 appears to be an exception to this situation. The explanation of this anomaly is probably complex and appears to warrant considerable further research.

Discussion of the related substantive areas is in these groups very limited, a fact which appears to be in contrast to some of the descriptive research on general instructional supervision discussed in Chapter 2. General factors related to education (GRL) and general factors not related to education (GNR) both comprise a very insignificant proportion of supervisory time. No group spends more than 0.4% of the conference time in these two areas. Discussion of supervision (SPR) averages less than 3% of conference time and is moderately important (at 6.4%) only in the case of a supervisor who had actually written his doctoral thesis on a study of supervision. Discussion of the subject matter for the purpose of understanding by the conference participants (SBJ) is important only for the group teaching high school chemistry in which several of the teachers had had little background in chemistry. It is particularly low at 1.5% for the elementary group, which might be expected both from the level of difficulty of the subject and from the type of curriculum being used by this group.

4. Substantive-Logical Meanings

The substantive-logical meanings or logical analysis categories are presented in table 11. In all groups, without exception, the discussion is more analytical than evaluative ($A/E = 1.85$), more diagnostic than prescriptive ($D/P = 2.02$), and more complex than simple ($C/S = 1.89$). Clinical supervision in these groups may be well characterized as the complex analysis and diagnosis of instruction.

These consistencies are even more remarkable when ranges and means are examined for individual dimensions. The three major dimensions and the three minor dimensions are almost identical on both measures: analytical (range 45.4% to 63.4%, mean 53.3%), diagnostic (range 44.5% to 63.0%, mean 54.9%), complex (range 45.8% to 64.8%, mean 53.7%), evaluative (range 22.5% to 37.3%, mean 28.8%), prescriptive (range 22.3% to 33.5%, mean 27.2%), simple (range 17.9% to 33.5%, mean 28.4%). These dimensions thus appear to be a very useful measure of characteristic operations in supervision,

TABLE 11

Percentage of Moves and Units by Supervisory Groups in Each
Substantive-Logical Category and Dimension: All Conferences

Category	% Moves by Group						% Units by Group					
	1	2	3	4	5	$\bar{X}$	1	2	3	4	5	$\bar{X}$
DEF	0.0	0.4	0.3	0.0	0.9	0.2	0.0	0.2	0.1	0.0	0.5	0.1
INT	3.7	4.3	7.1	4.4	5.7	4.8	3.2	2.0	2.9	2.2	2.1	2.5
FAC	25.8	25.0	17.6	25.1	23.6	24.0	20.9	19.7	10.4	17.8	19.5	18.0
XPL	12.3	21.7	20.4	14.7	17.6	16.6	18.4	29.3	25.8	20.3	26.1	23.7
SUG	5.5	4.6	3.5	4.2	7.0	5.0	5.0	3.4	3.8	4.1	8.5	5.0
SGX	5.3	4.5	3.4	4.5	6.0	4.8	6.4	5.7	5.4	6.2	9.3	6.6
EVL	7.0	4.2	3.9	4.5	4.7	5.1	4.5	2.2	1.6	2.2	2.4	2.7
JUS	7.4	5.9	9.0	3.3	6.2	6.2	10.9	11.8	15.2	4.2	11.0	10.5
OPN	3.9	3.0	2.5	4.2	2.7	3.4	3.1	2.1	2.1	4.2	2.0	2.7
OPJ	5.4	6.0	7.1	6.7	5.2	6.0	10.1	11.1	18.4	19.0	7.1	12.9
FAC + XPL	38.1	46.7	38.0	39.8	41.2	40.6	39.3	49.0	36.2	38.1	45.6	41.7
EVL + JUS	14.4	10.1	12.9	7.8	10.9	11.3	15.4	14.0	16.8	6.4	13.4	13.2
SUG + SGX	10.8	9.1	6.9	8.7	13.0	9.8	11.4	9.1	9.2	10.3	17.8	11.6
OPN + OPJ	9.3	9.0	9.6	10.9	7.9	9.4	13.2	13.2	20.5	23.2	9.1	15.6
Anal.	48.9	55.8	44.9	48.5	54.2	50.4	50.7	58.1	45.4	48.4	63.4	53.3
Eval.	23.7	19.1	22.5	18.7	18.8	20.7	28.6	27.2	37.3	29.6	22.5	28.8
A/E	2.06	2.92	1.99	2.60	2.88	2.43	1.77	2.14	1.22	1.63	2.82	1.85
Diagn.	52.5	56.8	50.9	49.6	52.1	51.9	54.7	63.0	53.0	44.5	59.0	54.9
Presc.	20.1	18.1	16.5	19.6	20.9	19.2	24.6	22.3	29.7	33.5	26.9	27.2
D/P	2.56	3.14	3.08	2.53	2.49	2.70	2.26	2.82	1.78	1.33	2.19	2.02
Complex	30.4	38.1	39.9	29.2	35.0	33.6	45.8	57.9	64.8	49.7	53.5	53.7
Simple	42.2	56.8	27.5	38.0	38.0	37.5	33.5	27.4	17.9	28.3	32.4	28.4
C/S	0.72	0.67	1.45	0.77	0.92	0.90	1.37	2.11	3.62	1.76	1.65	1.89

Anal. / Eval. = A/E = (FAC + XPL + SUG + SGX) / (EVL + JUS + OPN + OPJ)
Diag. / Presc. = D/P = (FAC + XPL + EVL + JUS) / (SUG + SGX + OPN + OPJ)
Complex/Simple = C/S = (XPL + SGX + JUS + OPJ) / (FAC + EVL + SUG + OPN)

and the results warrant verification in other studies of supervisory interaction.

In this study, 41.7% of the discourse involves facts and explanations. This is almost as much time as all the other categories combined. Together with their associated complex categories, the totals for evaluations (13.2%), suggestions (11.6%), and opinions (15.6%) are roughly equal.

There are differences in length of moves for substantive-logical meanings. Many of these differences may be explained by the fact that complex categories, which involve relationships to other factors in the discussion, naturally consume more time than simple categories. With one minor exception, every supervisory group places greater stress on the complex categories than on their simple analogues.

Some of these differences, however, are not as easy to explain. It can be seen that the complex evaluative categories, particularly opinions, take considerably more time than their analytical counterparts. Participants in supervision tend to dwell on these evaluative meanings, possibly in order to qualify or justify them fully. Because discourse with evaluative overtones tends to be threatening, participants may draw out evaluative discussions in order to prevent misunderstandings or defensive reactions.

The emphasis preferences in table 54 in Appendix J show a strong preference for analysis over evaluation by the supervisors and the observers, but not for the teachers. While supervisors and observers are generally either negative or neutral about evaluations, teachers are almost universally somewhat positive. This may be a reflection of the often noted desire of novice teachers for "constructive criticism" and a notion of "how am I doing?"

Similar relationships are seen in comparing diagnostic with prescriptive categories. Diagnosis tends to be overwhelmingly analytical, with FAC + XPL exceeding EVL + JUS by a factor greater than three. Prescription, however, tends to be predominately evaluative, with OPN + OPJ at 15.6% exceeding SUG + SGX at 11.6%. It appears to be much easier for conference participants to be analytical or "academic" when talking about instruction; feelings tend to be much stronger when they recommend specific courses of action.

The emphasis preferences of most participants show that they would have preferred greater stress on the prescriptive areas than on the diagnostic areas. While this may be partially due to the fact that the prescriptive areas received much less actual stress than the diagnostic areas, it is surprising that the preferences did not actually change the priorities of the conferences (the amount of prescription actually decreased over the summer). The participants may have been wishing for more prescriptions "that actually work," and thus concentrated their time on diagnosis to find out "why."

One of the major advantages of a multidimensional instrument is the ability to examine relationships between two or more of the individual dimensions. Table 12 presents the logical ratios produced by the supervisory groups within each major substantive area and permits analysis of the ways in which different content areas are treated in supervisory discourse. The advantages of category ratios for reducing the volume of data are evident in this table. This type of interdimensional analysis would require six 18 $\times$ 10 data matrices, or 1,080 separate data points, to include all of the pertinent individual categories in the substantive areas and substantive-logical meanings. By combining factors and using ratios, this unmanageable volume of data is reduced to a workable size. Table 12 contains most of the useful information for this comparison, but requires only 162 data points to do so.

Logical treatments might be expected to differ with differing content. Table 12 indicates that this is indeed the case. Some very consistent differences are evident when the complex/simple ratio is examined: executions are treated in a more complex manner than methods, with objectives receiving the simplest treatment. Thus, not only are objectives discussed proportionately less than other instructional foci, but they are also discussed more simply. Objectives do not appear to generate much heated discussion in these groups.

Similarly, in almost every case the social-disciplinary domain is treated in a more complex manner than the affective domain, with the cognitive domain receiving the simplest analysis. Although cognitive concerns consume the greatest amount of conference time, discussion in this domain tends to be more straightforward, possibly because it produces fewer strong personal overtones for the conference participants. In this same light it is evident that the social-disciplinary domain generates particularly strong emotional overtones.

The analytical-evaluative dimension is less consistent, but differences are again evident. Executions are treated analytically, while methods and objectives tend to have a high evaluative component. This finding is consistent with the relationships discussed earlier. Classroom interactions are ordinarily discussed on the basis of questions such as: "What happened?" and "Why did it happen?" Methods, on the other hand, tend to be discussed in terms of questions like: "What would be a better way of doing it?" or "How could you do this more effectively?" The evaluative overtones of objectives commonly occur when participants discuss the importance and rationale of different objectives for pupils.

TABLE 12

Logical Treatment of Content Units by Supervisory Groups:
Logical Ratios in Each Major Content Area for All Conferences

Complex/Simple (C/S Ratio)

Group	O	M	X	C	A	D	S	G	Total
1	1.25	1.31	1.66	1.22	1.59	4.42	1.36	8.75	1.43
2	1.68	2.49	2.02	1.82	2.99	2.46	2.10	2.02	2.09
3	2.79	3.73	5.00	2.56	4.70	8.75	3.81	3.81	3.81
4	0.59	2.45	2.06	1.57	3.26	3.87	1.49	6.30	1.82
5	0.92	1.37	2.56	1.51	1.60	*	1.44	5.50	1.53
$\bar{X}$	1.22	2.09	2.25	1.57	2.51	3.75	1.78	4.52	1.90

Analytic/Evaluative (A/E Ratio)

Group	O	M	X	C	A	D	S	G	Total
1	1.16	1.59	2.43	1.63	2.01	2.30	1.71	3.18	1.74
2	0.99	1.35	3.20	2.04	1.34	2.66	2.10	2.02	2.09
3	1.00	0.87	2.05	1.42	1.17	0.79	1.22	0.74	1.17
4	2.24	0.88	6.53	1.63	3.50	0.75	1.73	0.71	1.46
5	3.61	2.32	2.21	2.44	3.29	*	2.96	0.36	2.57
$\bar{X}$	1.62	1.22	2.73	1.82	1.76	1.45	1.87	0.90	1.75

Diagnostic/Prescriptive (D/P Ratio)

Group	O	M	X	C	A	D	S	G	Total
1	1.01	0.66	**	3.45	2.53	6.90	2.09	2.34	2.11
2	0.87	0.40	**	1.73	4.00	8.73	2.62	8.10	2.77
3	1.45	0.65	**	1.82	1.79	1.43	1.87	0.82	1.74
4	1.75	0.50	**	1.27	2.68	0.53	1.33	0.53	1.13
5	1.41	0.49	**	1.64	7.10	*	2.07	1.29	2.01
$\bar{X}$	1.27	0.54	**	1.62	2.92	2.46	1.98	1.08	1.98

Complex/Simple = C/S = (XPL+SGX+JUS+OPJ) / (FAC+EVL+SUG+OPN)
Anal. / Eval. = A/E = (FAC+XPL+SUG+SGX) / (EVL+JUS+OPN+OPJ)
Diag. / Presc. = D/P = (FAC+XPL+EVL+JUS) / (SUG+SGX+OPN+OPJ)

*Not enough data is available in this particular supervisory group.
**By definition, prescriptive operations do not apply to X (execution). Such operations may always be considered O (objectives) or M (methods).

The analytic/evaluative ratio for instructional domains shows wide fluctuations. On the average, the cognitive domain is treated analytically and the social-disciplinary domain evaluatively. This is consistent with the notion that disciplinary problems produce greater anxieties and more defensive reactions in novices. General categories are treated more evaluatively than are specific categories. The reason for this is unclear. Discussion may shift to general topics during evaluative discussions in an effort to reduce the impression that the individual rather than the enterprise itself is being evaluated.

The diagnostic-prescriptive dimension does not apply to executions because prescriptive processes in this area may all be treated as either objectives or methods. As expected, methods are treated much more prescriptively than objectives. Although objectives are frequently evaluated, there is rarely much discussion of alternatives, and strong opinions are uncommon.

It might be expected that the social-disciplinary domain would be treated prescriptively while discussion in the cognitive domain would be primarily diagnostic. Although individual groups differ widely, the reverse is generally the case. For some reason, possibly an attempt to be indirect about sensitive areas in the conference, the affective and social-disciplinary domains are treated diagnostically. The fluctuations in these domains are extremely wide, and are probably best discussed in the context of individual groups.

On the average, discussion of specific classes tends to be diagnostic while more general discussions tend to be prescriptive. This may be an attempt either to avoid an "authoritarian atmosphere" in the conference or to reduce the pressure on individual teachers. It is possible, for example, to offer a suggestion or an opinion to a particular teacher by inference, using such statements as "I think teachers should . . ." or "Generally, most teachers are much too. . . ." This feature is seen with all the logical ratios: general discussions tend to be unusually complex, evaluative, and prescriptive.

5. Procedural and Procedural-Logical Categories

Table 13 presents data for the procedural and procedural-logical categories of M.O.S.A.I.C.S. Procedural categories comprise 23.8% of all conference moves, but these moves account for only 15.3% of all units. Procedural moves thus tend to be brief and simple.

Almost half of the procedural units fall in the category STA (statements). This category refers to statements previously made in the discourse and provides a focus for positive or negative ratings of these statements. Roughly 7% of the average conference thus consists

TABLE 13

Percentage of Moves and Units by Supervisory Groups in Each
Procedural and Procedural-Logical Category: All Conferences

Category	% Moves by Group						% Units by Group					
	1	2	3	4	5	$\overline{X}$	1	2	3	4	5	$\overline{X}$
STA	9.9	7.6	9.8	13.3	10.3	10.3	7.8	5.8	5.7	9.6	6.1	7.1
ACT	5.8	6.1	9.9	8.9	5.5	7.1	4.1	3.1	4.4	5.5	2.3	3.9
PRC	5.7	3.8	2.4	3.1	3.1	3.9	4.6	2.6	3.5	3.2	2.6	3.3
PER	2.1	2.8	3.1	3.1	1.4	2.5	0.9	1.0	0.9	1.5	0.5	1.0
Proc. total	23.5	20.3	25.2	28.4	20.3	23.8	17.4	12.5	14.5	19.8	11.5	15.3
POS	2.1	1.1	1.3	1.1	2.1	1.6	1.5	0.8	0.7	1.0	0.9	1.0
ADM	4.2	4.5	6.4	9.4	6.1	6.1	3.8	3.3	3.4	6.4	3.7	4.1
RPT	1.8	0.6	0.8	1.5	0.4	1.2	0.9	0.3	0.2	0.9	0.3	0.5
QAL	1.3	1.0	1.1	1.0	1.4	1.2	0.9	0.9	1.0	1.0	0.8	0.9
NAD	0.4	0.4	0.3	0.2	0.1	0.3	0.7	0.3	0.4	0.3	0.3	0.4
NEG	0.1	0.0	0.0	0.0	0.0	0.0	0.0	0.1	0.0	0.0	0.0	0.0
Pos. sum	8.1	6.2	8.5	12.0	8.6	8.9	6.2	4.4	4.3	8.3	4.9	5.6
Neg. sum	1.8	1.4	1.4	1.2	1.5	1.5	1.6	1.3	1.4	1.3	1.1	1.3
P/N	4.5	4.4	6.1	10.0	5.7	6.0	3.9	3.4	3.1	6.4	4.5	4.3
DEF	0.0	0.0	0.0	0.0	0.0	0.0	0.0	0.0	0.0	0.0	0.0	0.0
INT	0.5	0.5	1.1	0.5	0.0	0.5	0.3	0.2	0.5	0.2	0.0	0.3
FAC	5.7	5.5	3.9	8.1	4.7	5.8	4.6	2.8	2.9	5.7	2.5	3.8
SUG	0.4	0.5	0.3	0.4	0.6	0.4	0.3	0.5	0.1	0.2	0.5	0.3
XPL	1.1	0.5	0.8	0.9	0.9	0.8	1.0	0.4	1.9	0.9	0.6	1.0
SGX	0.3	0.5	0.0	0.5	0.4	0.4	0.3	0.4	0.2	0.8	0.3	0.4
EVL	0.1	0.0	0.0	0.1	0.0	0.1	0.0	0.0	0.0	0.0	0.0	0.0
OPN	0.3	0.2	0.4	0.3	0.1	0.2	0.3	0.1	0.1	0.1	0.1	0.1
JUS	0.0	0.0	0.0	0.0	0.0	0.0	0.0	0.0	0.0	0.0	0.0	0.0
OPJ	0.3	0.3	0.0	0.3	0.1	0.2	0.4	0.3	0.0	0.4	0.1	0.2
PRF	1.6	0.9	3.1	0.9	1.2	1.5	0.9	0.5	1.2	0.4	0.5	0.7
PON	0.4	0.2	0.8	0.0	0.0	0.3	0.1	0.1	0.2	0.0	0.0	0.1

Pos. sum = POS + ADM + RPT
Neg. sum = QAL + NAD + NEG
P/N = (Pos. sum) / (Neg. sum)

of interpersonal ratings, which may be considered an explicit form of positive or negative reinforcement.

The rating reactions themselves are predominantly positive. The P/N ratio, or ratio of all positive ratings to all negative ratings, has a range of 3.1 to 6.4 and a mean of 4.3. In all cases, therefore, positive ratings or explicit positive reinforcements are at least three times as frequent as negative ratings. An examination of individual rating categories shows that extreme ratings are rare and explicitly negative ratings, such as "You're wrong" or "Definitely no," are practically non-existent. Distinctly positive ratings such as "You're absolutely right" barely reach 1% of the total discourse, and are almost equaled by qualifying ratings such as "Yes, but. . . ." By far the most common ratings are admitting reactions (ADM), which offer a mildly positive acceptance of prior statements. Such reactions are often used as a stylistic device for encouraging participants to continue or to expand on their own statements. Some supervisors, noticeably supervisor 4, use this reaction very frequently. In general, the rating of previous statements is common in supervision and tends to be both positive and moderate.

Categories relating to conference procedures (PRC) and physical, mental, or emotional actions (ACT) each account for less than 4% of conference discourse. Most of the logical categories refer to these areas. The most common logical categories are facts (FAC) and explanations (XPL). Personal categories (PER) such as jokes and small talk account for about 1% of conference activity. The supervisory groups show very few differences on these categories.

The overall evaluations of the conferences (see table 54, Appendix J) are based on a four-point scale of effectiveness (0 = ineffective, 1 = moderately ineffective, 2 = moderately effective, 3 = effective). Most evaluations are slightly greater than 2, or moderately effective. Supervisors tend to be somewhat more pessimistic about conferences, while observers tend to be somewhat optimistic. While it might be surprising to some, the two highest evaluations were for two groups that had very directive supervisors, while the lowest overall evaluation of effectiveness was received by the group with the least directive supervisor. One could speculate at length about novice teacher expectations, immediate and delayed reinforcement, etc., but this certainly points up the danger of premature or simplistic generalizations about the process of supervision. The most that probably can be said is that supervision is a very complex process that cannot be understood on the basis of simple global differences.

6. Comparisons Between Planning and Analysis Conferences

Comparisons between planning and analysis conferences may be made from the tables in Appendix I. Differences in content and logic might be expected, since these conference types do not have the same function, but differences in the other areas would probably not be expected. Analysis follows soon after planning, the same individuals commonly participate in both conferences, and many of the conference pairs focus on planning and analysis of the same teaching episode. In actuality, reasonably consistent differences are evident in almost all of the major dimensions of meaning analyzed by M.O.S.A.I.C.S. These differences often help to illuminate subtle factors in the process of clinical supervision.

Planning conferences provide the major opportunity for the participants to engage in decision-making for future classes. With very few exceptions, planning conferences contain more solicitations, more responses, and fewer reactions as participants question objectives and proposed methodology for the approaching class. Analysis conferences contain more structuring and reacting moves as participants state propositions and react to one another's observations of the previous class. Initiatory/reflexive ratios are generally lower in analysis conferences, indicating that they are somewhat less structured than planning conferences.

Some role differences are also evident. Supervisors and teachers both talk more in planning than in analysis. Supervisors tend to ask and answer more questions, structure and summarize more often, and have consistently higher I/R ratios. Teachers ask more questions, answer considerably more, and also have higher I/R ratios in planning. Observers become much more active in analysis, with percentages of total units increasing from 22.5% to 32.3%. Most of this increase occurs in the structuring and reacting moves. In both types of conferences, however, it is the supervisor who usually solicits and the teacher who responds. Most of the increase in structuring and reacting in analysis may be attributed to activity by the observers. Apparently, decisions in planning are made primarily by the teachers and the supervisors, while the observers mainly discuss teaching in the less structured analysis conferences. The emphasis preferences (table 52 in Appendix J) indicate relatively strong negative reactions to the high percentage of supervisor initiation in planning. This is somewhat reduced in analysis.

Differences in teaching cycles between planning and analysis reflect the differences evident in pedagogical moves. Analysis conferences show a 10% increase in the freely reacting (STR . . .) cycles, much of which may be attributed to initiation by the observers. The more structured (STR–SOL . . .) cycles become less frequent in analysis, a decrease almost entirely attributable to the supervisors, all of whom show considerably less initiative for this type of cycle in analysis. It may be inferred that the reduction occurs primarily in that variety of cycle in which the supervisor states a point and then questions another participant (usually the teacher) about it. Solicitation cycles also become less frequent in analysis, a decline to which both supervisors and teachers contribute. These differences are evident both in percentages and in participation indices.

Differences in substantive areas between planning and analysis are greater than differences for any other category group. Planning conferences concentrate on objectives and methods with relatively few references to past classroom interactions or expectations of future interactions. Consequently, in the average planning conference about 31% of the units focus on objectives and content, 49% on methods and materials, and only 13% on execution. The variance of these values is very great, and there are striking differences among individual groups.

On the other hand, these percentages are markedly different for analysis conferences, and the variance is even greater. In analysis, discussion of objectives drops from 31.3% to 9.1% and methodology decreases from 49.0% to 26.0%. Units for instructional interactions increase almost fivefold, from 12.7% to 58.5%. These differences hold, without exception, for every supervisory group. In general, planning conferences concentrate on methodology and to a lesser extent on objectives, with relatively few specific references to classroom interactions; analysis concentrates heavily on the analysis of classroom interactions, with moderate stress on methodology and few references to objectives. The emphasis preferences indicate that the participants in planning conferences are relatively neutral about objectives while wishing even more stress on methodology and considerably more stress on execution (expectations or predictions of future classroom interactions).

Differences in length of moves are also evident. Not only are objectives discussed more frequently in planning conferences, but they are also discussed at greater length. Objectives appear to be "taken care of" in planning and are given scant attention in analysis. This is in accord with what some supervisors have proposed: that the planning conference is the optimal time to challenge the substance and rationale of objectives, since doing this in analysis makes subsequent discussion of methods and execution more difficult. "If I shouldn't have taught that material in the first place, why even discuss what actually happened?"

Methodology is discussed less frequently in analysis than in planning. When it is discussed in analysis, however, the higher percentage of units indicates that the discussions are more extended. These discussions generally concern "What you might have done" or "What you could do in the future." It is possible that such suggestions and opinions are taken more seriously in analysis after the teacher has actually been "on the firing line."

Striking differences are also evident in the instructional domains. An inordinate amount of time (79.5% of the total) is spent in the cognitive domain in planning, contrasting with only 4.4% in the affective domain and 8.9% for social-disciplinary factors. In analysis, however, cognitive factors decrease to 51.6%, while the affective domain increases by a factor of five to 22.7% and the social-disciplinary domain more than doubles to 19.4%. Since these are reactions to what happened in the class, why do they not assume comparable importance in planning? It is interesting that with one very minor exception all supervisory groups show these same differences in all instructional domains. These data seem to indicate that planning conferences are much less responsive to the realities of actual teaching than are analysis conferences. The heavy stress on cognitive factors in planning is particularly disturbing when it is recalled that the affective and social-disciplinary stresses in analysis are primarily reactions to persistent and indicative problems that have arisen in the classroom. The emphasis preferences reflect the high stress on cognitive factors in planning by indicating a desire for even greater emphasis, particularly on the part of the teachers. All participants, however, also show an average preference for more emphasis on the affective and social-disciplinary domains in planning.

Not only does the content differ in these conferences, but there are major differences in the ways in which content is treated. For example, the complex/simple ratio nearly doubles in analysis conferences for all supervisory groups. In every case this represents both a substantial increase in complex categories and a comparable decrease in simple categories. Reasons for this change are not obvious. It may be caused by the immediacy of the situation. It is difficult for novices to spend much time on complex relationships, rationales, and justifications in planning conferences when the teaching appears to be "off in the future" and problems of "What can I do?" and "How can I do it?" are paramount. Planning also requires time to reflect, amplify, and qualify one's ideas, and much of this probably occurs informally after the conference. In analysis, however, conference participants carry immediate impressions and strong emotional reactions to what has just happened. In such a situation, discussion naturally centers on questions of "Why?" and "Why not?"

Planning sessions also tend to be considerably more prescriptive, as participants examine suggestions and opinions of what to do in the approaching class. Analysis conferences, as one might expect, predominate in diagnostic analysis. The diagnostic total increases from 46.8% to 62.6% and the prescriptive total decreases from 32.4% to 22.2% in analysis. In three of the five supervisory groups, the diagnostic/prescriptive ratio nearly triples from planning to analysis.

Compared with analysis, the participants would have preferred somewhat more diagnosis in planning, but their desire for more stress on prescription was high in both types of conferences. The analytic focus of these conferences is in sharp contrast to a commonly held view of instructional supervision as *ex post facto* evaluations and opinions: "What you *should* have done is. . . ." This appears to be one of the major advantages of clinical supervision. Discussion of what should have been done in a previous class is minimized and is replaced by constructive planning for the future, based on past learning and past mistakes.

There is an unmistakable tendency for analysis to be more evaluative than planning. The average analytic/evaluative ratio drops from 2.31 to 1.53, and with only one minor exception each supervisory group both increases evaluative factors and decreases analytic factors. Analysis conferences are intimately related to the immediacy and stresses of real teaching, and these emphases may be partially understood in terms of the emotional overtones that are carried from the classroom. This may also be interpreted in another light: planning conferences may not be emotionally involving enough. Evaluative emphases and significant stress on affective and social-disciplinary factors in analysis contrast sharply with the rather academic focus on analytic and cognitive factors in planning.

There are few major differences in the procedural areas between planning and analysis. It should be noted, however, that the activity in procedural categories decreases for every supervisory group in analysis conferences. STA (reactions to prior statements) is the only category showing an increase. In other words, there is more interpersonal rating and less personal interaction in analysis conferences. Participants "stick to the point" more and spend less time discussing procedures.

Another difference is evident in analysis: as rating reactions increase, they also tend to become more negative. Four of the five groups show a net decrease in the positive/negative ratio in analysis. Although the amount of this decrease is not particularly large, it does indicate a tendency for the participants to disagree more and to be less concerned with positive reinforcement in analysis conferences.

7. Comparisons Between Early and Late Conferences

Comparisons between early and late conferences may also be made from the tables in Appendix I. Differences are evident in almost all major category groups, but these differences are generally smaller than those between planning and analysis. Overall percentages for each type of pedagogical move remain relatively constant, with the single exception that structuring becomes somewhat less frequent toward the end of the summer. Reflexive moves as a whole become more common as the summer progresses and initiatory/reflexive ratios tend to decline. It is interesting that three of the five supervisors, including the relatively nondirective supervisors 1 and 2, increase their initiatory/reflexive ratios over the summer as well as the number of their structuring moves. In general, the overall distribution of pedagogical moves changes little over the summer, but the changes that are evident seem to indicate that the discussion is becoming less directive.

One major change in roles is evident: the teachers appear to gain more confidence and talk more frequently as the summer progresses. This increase is apparent for almost every type of move, particularly for the reflexive moves. I/R ratios for teachers, with only one exception, show moderate declines. Observers, in contrast, show a net decrease in activity over the summer that approximately equals the amount of increase for teachers. This decline in observer activity is particularly noticeable for structuring and reacting moves. The amount of supervisor discourse remains relatively constant. These are averages for all supervisory groups, and intergroup differences are common.

As noted previously, structuring moves become less frequent over the course of the summer but solicitations remain approximately constant. A possible interpretation is that the discussion is becoming less directive. Teaching cycles reflect these changes in an unexpected way, for STR . . . cycles remain approximately constant while SOL . . . cycles increase. Although this may appear contradictory, it can be accounted for by a decrease in STR–SOL . . . cycles. Interestingly, almost all of this change is caused by a decrease in the supervisors' initiation of these cycles. If this decrease occurs in the first variety of cycle, in which the speaker makes both initiatory moves, this would also indicate a decrease in directiveness over the course of the summer. In general, an increase in the amount of the teacher's activity and a corresponding decrease in activity for the observers is also evident in their teaching cycle initiation.

In the substantive areas, instructional foci do not change much over the summer. Emphasis on objectives remains relatively constant at about 20%. The stress on methodology increases while the stress on classroom interactions shows a moderate decline. These data might be disturbing to many clinical supervisors who view supervision primarily as the objective analysis of teacher-pupil-curriculum interactions with the intent of rational understanding. One might expect a growing emphasis on the execution focus as the participants become more perceptive and their understandings become more complex. The increasing emphasis on methodology is understandable in terms of the immediate concerns of novice teachers. As their perceptions and understandings become more complex, the discontinuity between their expectations of pupil achievement and interest and what actually occurs in the classroom tends to become greater. Such a discontinuity is often taken personally, and novices naturally turn to such questions of technique as "What can I do?" and "Why didn't it work?"

Over the course of the summer discussion in the cognitive domain increases moderately, but the affective domain shows a substantial increase from 10.7% to 16.5%. This may be evidence of the interns' growing awareness of the difficulties encountered in motivating pupils. It does not take novices long to realize that the content and methods that were motivating to them do not necessarily motivate their pupils. On the other hand, social and disciplinary factors drop from 18.7% to 10.0%. This is very hard to explain when one considers that discipline problems commonly increased during the summer. It may be that the supervisory groups come to recognize the affective and cognitive bases of these problems and accordingly turn their attention toward these domains. This shift may also be designed to reduce tension and anxiety in the group. Motivational problems place the onus on the content and the pupils; disciplinary problems are more often taken as a personal failure or a personal affront.

In the related substantive areas, SBJ (discussions of the subject matter for the purpose of comprehension by conference participants) increases from 1.8% to 5.2% toward the end of the summer. Were the interns beginning to recognize their own lack of understanding of their disciplines? Discussion of supervision, on the other hand, drops from 4.7% to 1.2% as the conference participants learn the "rules of the game" of clinical supervision and require less formal discussion and direction.

Changes over the summer in the substantive-logical meanings are generally smaller than the differences noted between planning and analysis. The complex/simple ratio declines toward the end of the summer in four of the five supervisory groups. This change in C/S is evident in most of the individual categories: the averages for all of the complex categories decrease and all of the simple categories increase except for OPN (opinions). Most of these changes are very small, with the exception of the category FAC (facts), which shows a 30% increase. Since the discussion of classroom interactions decreases over the summer, it may be inferred that the increase in FAC probably occurs in the discussion of objectives and methods. A possible interpretation is that the intern teachers are recognizing the importance of explicitly stated objectives and carefully formulated methodology, particularly in planning conferences.

In most cases the diagnostic/prescriptive ratio increases over the summer, indicating an increase in the objective analysis of instruction and a reduction in the "what to do and how to do it" focus of supervision. The major factor in this change is a reduction in the prescriptive categories. Although suggestions show a slight increase, the categories for opinions decline by almost a third. This change in the number of opinions may be interpreted to mean that the participants begin to avoid prescriptions of what should or ought to be done in class as they come to appreciate the complexities of instructional interactions. The analytic/evaluative ratio also increases over the summer. The percentage of evaluations and justifications remains approximately constant, and most of the change in the A/E ratio may be attributed to the decline in the number of opinions.

As with most categories, differences among individual groups are common and there appear to be very few changes that are consistent for all groups. For example, while the frequency of opinions declines for most groups, group 3 produces more than twice as many opinions later in the summer. There is not a single dimension in which the change from early to late conferences is in the same direction for all supervisory groups. In fact, there is not one logical category in which net changes are uniform for all groups. Clinical supervision is obviously a much more complicated and idiosyncratic process than group summaries or averages would indicate.

All groups increase their percentages in the procedural areas over the summer. In general, rating reactions (STA) and personal interactions increase. This may demonstrate that the conference participants gradually feel freer to interact personally. Both positive and negative ratings tend to increase, but most of the P/N ratios show a net decline. Thus, while the interaction becomes freer, the participants apparently feel freer to react negatively.

The emphasis preferences for early and late conferences may be found in tables 50 and 53 in Appendix J. Very few overall differences are evident in the course of the summer—early and late preferences rarely differ by more than a tenth of a point, although there are differences in individual groups. Some small changes are evident: some desire for greater stress on execution, and a moderate desire for increased supervisor initiation coupled with a reduction in the desire for increased teacher initiation. The students tended to give the later conferences a somewhat lower evaluation while the supervisors tended to rate them higher. In general, there are few strong differences either in the nature of the conferences or in the desires of the participants for change over the course of the summer.

The discussion in the preceding section focuses on the totals from all the supervisory groups in this study and gives a composite picture of clinical supervision as interpreted through M.O.S.A.I.C.S. output. In many instances these groups show considerable individual variation. The next section discusses the groups individually and very briefly examines the interactions within each group. The reader who is interested in exploring these individual case studies in greater depth may refer to Appendix J, which contains tables of participants' emphasis preferences for selected conference categories and overall conference evaluations.

CLINICAL PROFILES OF FIVE SUPERVISORY GROUPS

1. Supervisory Group 1 (Seventh-Grade Biological Science)

This group clearly demonstrates how the supervisor's style can influence the style of interaction of the entire group. Supervisor 1 tends to speak in a rapid, to-the-point manner. Both her moves and the cycles she initiates contain the smallest number of units of any supervisor. Teachers and observers in the group show the same tendency: they all rate next to lowest on these factors when compared with the other groups. In general, group 1 shows the highest rate of verbal interaction, the greatest number of moves, units, and cycles per minute.

Teachers in group 1 take more initiative than teachers in any other group. Their participation indices are highest of all groups for structuring, soliciting, reacting, and summarizing, and lowest for responding. Observers also take considerable initiative, particularly in structuring and responding. In contrast, supervisor 1 is herself one of the least directive supervisors. She has the lowest participation index for structuring of any supervisor, the lowest initiatory/reflexive ratio, and the next-to-lowest activity for total moves, solicitations, and responses.

This same pattern is evident in the figures for teaching cycles. Both teachers and observers have the highest participation indices of any group for the initiation of teaching cycles. The supervisor has the lowest. The freely reacting STR ... cycle types comprise 53.3% of all cycles in this group, and both teachers and observers initiate an unusually high proportion of them. No other group has as low a percentage as 13.0% for the more directive STR–SOL ... cycles. In general, this group abounds in extremes, most of which indicate a lack of explicit directiveness. The group as a whole produces an unusually small percentage of soliciting, responding, and structuring moves and an unusually large percentage of reacting and summarizing moves.

In the substantive areas, this group concentrates on the analysis of instruction almost exclusively (94.8%) and in a highly specific manner (S = 91.6%, G = 3.2%). The analysis in question focuses mainly on the cognitive domain, with moderately low emphasis on the affective and social-disciplinary domains. Percentage distributions for objectives, methods, and execution are roughly comparable to the average of all groups, with objectives and executions receiving somewhat greater stress.

In terms of substantive-logical meanings, discussion in group 1 is moderately analytical and diagnostic but considerably less complex than that in any other group. The latter factor may be partially explained by the rapidity of the interaction and the unusually high value for FAC, which often indicates a stress on observation and objective feedback. A high percentage in the factual category may also indicate that objectives and methodology are carefully and explicitly stated and elaborated in the conference.

In planning conferences, unusual initiative is taken by the teachers for most types of moves. High stress is placed on objectives and moderately high stress on methodology, with cognitive factors emphasized and social-disciplinary factors practically neglected. Logical meanings differ little from the average of all groups: the discussion is strongly analytical, moderately prescriptive, and unusually simple.

In analysis conferences, the observers take over initiative from the teachers and the supervisor becomes even less directive. Analysis concentrates heavily on execution, with large increases in both the affective and the social-disciplinary domains. General patterns of interaction shift toward an even stronger emphasis on structuring and reacting.

Over the course of the summer, the supervisor becomes somewhat more directive, increasing in SOL, STR, RSM, and I/R. Teachers and observers become correspondingly less directive. Contrary to the average trend, stress on objectives increases while that on methods decreases over the summer. Emphasis on the cognitive domain also decreases, while the affective domain assumes an unusually high stress toward the end. It is possible that many of these content changes are the result of increased supervisory participation.

Virtually all changes in substantive-logical categories are in the direction of the average changes for all groups. Discussion becomes more analytical and diagnostic, with sharp decreases in evaluative and prescriptive meanings. Discourse also becomes less complex over the summer, presumably because of an increase in descriptive and factual feedback or increasingly explicit statements of objectives and methodology.

This group shows distinctive changes in the procedural areas over the course of the summer. Early conferences contain an unusually high percentage of rating reactions, particularly negative ratings. Group 1 shows twice as many units in the qualifying, not-admitting, and negative categories as any other. The negative sum is twice as high as any other group's, and the positive/negative ratio is unusually small early in the summer. In late conferences, however, the negative sum becomes the lowest of all groups. All other groups increase activity in most negative categories over the summer. The reasons for these changes are unclear. It is possible that the early stress on negative ratings is evidence of an open, honest interaction in which the participants feel free to disagree with one another. This type of interaction may have developed earlier in this group than in the others. The reduction in negative ratings toward the end of the summer may indicate another stage in the development of group interactions in which the participants begin to understand one another's points of view and become honestly supportive of different orientations and interpretations.

2. Supervisory Group 2 (Fifth- and Sixth-Grade Physical Science)

Group 2 places greatest stress on solicitations and responses, particularly on extended responses, in contrast to the first group's emphasis on reacting moves. Structuring is a significantly rare move in this group. As in the previous group, however, the supervisor interacts minimally and nondirectly. Her participation indices for total moves, reactions, and summary reactions are the lowest of any supervisor's.

Observers in this group take major responsibility for practically every type of move, particularly for reflexive moves. All initiatory/reflexive ratios in this group are low, and those for the supervisor and the observers are particularly low. Although teachers have only average participation indices for most moves, their percentage of initiatory moves tends to be somewhat higher than average. These same trends are evident in teaching cycles. Observers and teachers initiate disproportionately large numbers of cycles and the supervisor a contrastingly small number. The directive STR–SOL ... cycles are infrequent, while SOL ... cycles, at 42.4%, are more frequent than in any other group.

The substantive areas or content categories show distinctive emphases in this group, which may be largely attributed to the fact that an elementary school class is being supervised. Stress on classroom executions and interactions is the highest of any group. This may result from the supervisor's attempts to increase the novices' perceptions and understandings of elementary school children. This factor, plus the choice of an open-ended E.S.S. (Elementary Science Study) unit, may account for the relatively low emphasis on content objectives and methodology. In the same vein, the cognitive domain receives relatively low stress while the social-disciplinary domain (in this group, positive social factors are emphasized) receives unusual stress.

The substantive-logical meanings also reflect these findings. The analytic/evaluative ratio and the complex/simple ratio are both unusually high, and the diagnostic/prescriptive ratio is the least prescriptive of any group. In essence, this group focuses intensely on complex analytic diagnoses of instructional interactions with children.

As in the previous group, supervisor 2 reduces her involvement in analysis sessions, particularly for initiatory moves. Contrary to the previous group, however, observers make proportionately fewer moves in the analysis sessions, while the teachers take more initiative. In general, the pattern of discourse tends to shift from SOL–RES in planning to greater emphasis on STR–REA in analysis.

In planning conferences, this group minimizes methodology, moderately stresses objectives, and places almost three times the average stress on classroom interactions. Fully 36% of the discussion in planning involves analysis of past instructional interactions. Treatment of these substantive areas tends to be strongly analytical, diagnostic, and complex.

On the other hand, almost three-quarters of the analysis conference is spent in the direct analysis of classroom interactions. This discussion is more analytic and more diagnostic than that of any other group. The complex/simple ratio is fairly low, indicating a stress on description, observation, and factual feedback. A distinct tendency toward positive reinforcement is also evident in analysis conferences, with the positive/negative ratio almost doubling from planning to analysis.

Over the course of the summer, teachers assume considerably more initiative and observers comparably less. This is evident in practically every pedagogical move category. Basic patterns of interaction shift from SOL–RES patterns to STR–REA patterns, presumably because fewer questions are required to keep the discussions moving along.

Discussion of content and objectives is relatively infrequent early in the summer and drops still lower toward the end. In contrast, methodology begins very low and increases to an average percentage. Discussion of execution remains on a very high level, and dramatic changes are evident in the instructional domains. A strong early emphasis on the social-disciplinary domain drops off considerably, being replaced by an increase in the cognitive domain and a sevenfold increase in the affective domain.

As in most other groups, discussion tends to get more analytical toward the end of the summer. In the other logical areas, however, group 2 tends to reverse the average trend: discussion gets more prescriptive and less complex. This tendency toward simple and prescriptive reactions later in the summer may be the result of some disenchantment with the open-ended curriculum and an evident desire for more direction on the part of the elementary pupils. An interesting concomitant is the fact that the positive/negative ratio also decreases over the summer.

3. Supervisory Group 3 (Eighth-Grade Physical Science)

Supervisor 3 would probably be called one of the more directive of the supervisors because of his stress on initiatory pedagogical moves. Interestingly enough, he does not dominate the discourse in terms of total time; with 40.7% of the total talk and a participation index of 2.41, he falls midway between the other supervisors on these factors. However, his P.I.'s of 3.79 for soliciting and 3.35 for structuring are unusually high, greater than those of any other supervisor. In contrast, his reflexive moves, particularly for responding, are unusually low. His initiatory/reflexive ratio of 1.68 is more than twice as high as that of most other supervisors.

In contrast to the supervisor, teachers in this group show little initiative, having participation indices for structuring and soliciting that are smaller than those in any other group. The teaching cycles

reflect this situation. Compared with other groups, participation indices for cycle initiation are highest for the supervisor, lowest for the
teacher, and intermediate for the observers. STR–SOL . . . cycles are
relatively frequent, while STR . . . cycles are rare—another indication of a rather directive form of interaction.

One may infer that other elements of the discourse, such as content and logic, reflect certain predispositions of this supervisor because
of his initiatory style of supervision. For example, this group concentrates more than any other on the analysis of instruction; related topics
account for only 2.6% of the discourse. Also, this analysis tends to be
highly specific, with only 8.6% of the units being devoted to generalizations and theoretical analyses. In contrast to other groups, very
little time is spent on the cognitive domain. The affective domain at
27.9% and the social-disciplinary domain at 22.2% are both unusually
high.

It may be inferred that these factors are related. Supervisor 3
reasoned that the interns should develop and teach their own units
very early in the summer. The motivational and disciplinary problems
that soon arose, particularly in one of the two teaching groups, may
be attributed to the interns' inexperience in teaching and curriculum
development. The supervisor's initiation of discussion in the affective
and social-disciplinary domains appears to be a response to some of
the problems that developed in these groups.

The analytic/evaluative ratio is the lowest of any group, indicating strong evaluative overtones in the discourse. The diagnostic/
prescriptive ratio is also moderately low, demonstrating an abundance
of suggestions and opinions, often of an evaluative nature. The com-
plex/simple ratio is the highest of any group.

The procedural areas and procedural-logical meanings seem to
bear out some of these patterns. Rating reactions to statements (STA)
are unusually rare, in keeping with the relatively long moves and low
rate of interaction. However, the positive/negative ratio of 3.1 is the
lowest of any group, indicating a low frequency of positive reinforcement. It can be seen, for example, that qualifying reactions are very
common, while positive reactions are infrequent.

As is commonly found in other groups, the supervisor and teachers take major initiative in planning sessions while the observers predominate in analysis. Analysis sessions also tend to be less structured,
with lower percentages for STR, SOL, and RSM, and comparably
higher percentages for RES and REA.

Certain substantive areas seem particularly characteristic of this
group. Objectives are given equal and major stress in both planning
and analysis, a factor that is not even approximated in other groups.
The cognitive domain is given very little attention in both types of

conferences, while the affective and social-disciplinary domains get comparably high attention in both. The value of 42.5% for the affective domain in analysis is inordinately high, showing a preoccupation with the analysis of how pupils actually react to subject matter in terms of motivation and involvement. This appears to be a direct reaction to the problems that developed in class.

Logical treatments also show extremes in this group. The analytic/evaluative ratio is lowest of all groups in both planning and analysis, but in analysis this ratio drops to the unusually low value of 1.00. This indicates that equal stress is placed on both analytic and evaluative factors. Planning conferences are relatively prescriptive, but this changes in analysis to a highly diagnostic focus. The complex/simple ratio is highest of all groups for both types of conferences, but in analysis conferences it reaches a value of 5.12, fully twice as high as any other group's. The positive/negative ratio also makes a dramatic shift: from 5.0 in planning, which is the most positive of any group, to 2.1 in analysis, which is the most negative. Optimism and positive reinforcement in planning shift abruptly in analysis conferences.

Changes over the summer are equally dramatic. While most supervisors reduce their influence as the teachers and observers increase theirs, the reverse occurs in this group. The supervisor increases in every category except SOL, with an unusually large increase in structuring moves. Teachers decrease in activity for every move except SOL and RES. As the supervisor's I/R ratio increases, these ratios for the other participants decrease. Once again, the effects of classroom difficulties are evident in these data.

Stress on objectives, methods, and execution remains remarkably constant over the summer. However, changes in instructional domain are dramatic and unexpected. The cognitive domain receives little stress early in the summer but this stress increases sharply toward the end. In contrast, the affective and social-disciplinary domains begin inordinately high and drop to average levels later in the summer.

The substantive-logical meanings also change in unusual ways. Toward the end of the summer, discussion becomes less analytical and more evaluative, less diagnostic and more prescriptive. Even the positive/negative ratio drops sharply, indicating an increase in negative reinforcement over the summer. Many of these changes are probably related both to the difficulties being experienced by the interns and the assumption of more control by the supervisor.

4. Supervisory Group 4 (Eleventh-Grade Remedial Chemistry)

Group 4 probably approximates "actual supervision" in the schools more closely than do the other groups. Faced with a remedial chemistry class and the need to cover a great deal of material in a short period of time, this group had more curricular restraints than any other. The pupil population was also different. Most had previously failed chemistry, and they would receive no credit if they failed the summer course as well.

Supervisory discourse is rapid, and moves and cycles tend to be relatively short. Approximately a quarter of the discussion consists of short questions and answers, another quarter involves structuring moves, and the rest consists of reactions. Much of the discourse tends to be reflexive, and all initiatory/reflexive ratios are small.

The supervisor clearly predominates in this group, accounting for 56.8% of all thought units. Supervisor 4 speaks more, answers more questions, and reacts more than any other supervisor. He accounts for over two-thirds of all structuring moves and virtually all summary reactions. His major role appears to be that of a "reflexive authority figure" who states propositions, answers questions, qualifies and expands previous moves, and summarizes the ongoing discussion.

Both teachers and observers are relatively inactive, with the lowest participation indices for total moves of any group. Observers are particularly inactive. Their participation indices average only 0.31, and without exception are lower than any other group for all types of pedagogical moves. Most of the discourse, therefore, takes place between supervisor and teacher. STR–SOL . . . is the only teaching cycle type for which the teacher's participation index is greater than 1. These are primarily cycles in which the teacher's propositions are questioned by the supervisor.

The substantive areas are also different from those of the other supervisory groups. A great deal of time is spent in related areas, particularly in discussion of the subject matter, and no other group places as much stress on general categories in the analysis of instruction. The group, therefore, spends considerable time on the "curriculum and methods course" aspect of supervision. The "clinical" aspect accounts for about three-quarters of the whole.

In terms of content, methods and materials of instruction alone account for over half of the total discussion, while objectives are rarely examined and classroom execution is less emphasized than in any other group. Discussion is largely cognitive (73.1%), with affective or motivational factors accounting for only 2.9% of the total. The basic supervisory question thus appears to be "How do we get them to learn this material?" a question that is somewhat understandable in terms of the curricular restraints and the pupil population. Emphasis on curriculum rationale and pupil motivation is very low.

The substantive-logical meanings give additional insight into this interaction. This group has a larger prescriptive component than any other ($D/P = 1.33$), in keeping with its stress on problems of methodology. An unusually high evaluative component ($A/E = 1.63$) is also evident, and this is largely accounted for by high values in the two opinion categories. Thus, a great deal of time is spent on what should or ought to be done, in keeping with the stress both on methodology and authority. The complex/simple ratio is a moderate 1.76.

High values are found for most of the procedural areas. It is evident that rating reactions are very common and that positive ratings are the rule. In general, interaction is rapid, rating of previous statements is common, and positive reinforcement is the norm. This latter factor, together with a high value for personal (PER) areas, indicates a warm, positive interaction in the discussion.

As in other groups, the teachers reduce their activity considerably in analysis, and the observers increase theirs. The observers, however, remain less active than those in any other group. Discourse changes from SOL . . . patterns in planning to STR . . . patterns in analysis. It may therefore be inferred that probing questions and answers in planning give way to more open reactions in analysis.

In terms of content, few major changes are obvious: objectives are rarely discussed in planning conferences, while methodology occupies fully 64% of the discussion. Affective elements fail even to reach 1% of planning and reach only 5.6% of analysis. Logical meanings follow the general pattern found in most other groups: discussion becomes more evaluative, more prescriptive, and more complex in analysis.

The supervisor reduces his activity and his initiatory/reflexive ratio over the course of the summer, and the other participants increase theirs. Questions, answers, and reactions assume much more importance later in the summer, while structuring decreases in importance. Instructional foci remain relatively constant; but an early extreme stress on the cognitive domain (80.6%) declines somewhat, while stress on the social-disciplinary domain nearly doubles. Could the increase in disciplinary problems be a function of the unusually low stress throughout on the affective domain? As in most other groups, the discussion becomes more analytical, more diagnostic, and more simple over the course of the summer. The positive/negative ratio also decreases as the participants begin to disagree with one another more freely.

5. Supervisory Group 5 (Ninth-Grade Biological Science)

Group 5 is generally characterized by relatively long moves. Extended monologues are common both for the supervisor and the teachers, both of whom have the longest average moves and teaching cycles of any group. This group shows a remarkable consistency when comparisons are made between the supervisor, the teachers, and the observers for different categories. The supervisor scores highest and the observers score lowest on all the basic dimensions: number of moves, number of units, number of teaching cycles, length of moves, and length of teaching cycles.

This same consistency holds for soliciting, structuring, reacting, summarizing, and initiatory/reflexive ratios. The only difference occurs in responding moves: the supervisor answers fewer questions than do the teachers. Once again, the observers answer least of all. This supervisor's percentages of moves are not particularly high when compared with other supervisors. However, when participation indices are compared, thus taking the size of the group into account, it can be seen that the supervisor clearly predominates on all types of moves. His indices are higher than at least three-quarters of the other supervisors on every type of move. Supervisor 5 structures, solicits, and summarizes more than all other members of the group combined. Virtually no other participants summarize in this group.

In the substantive areas, group 5 places a very strong emphasis on content and objectives and a moderately weak emphasis on methodology. The instructional domains show an unusual distribution. Nearly three-quarters of all units are in the cognitive domain, higher than in any other group, while almost none are in the social-disciplinary domain. A total of only three thought units out of well over three thousand are in this domain. It is possible that sampling errors account for part of this, and it is also possible that discipline problems were chiefly discussed in private conferences with individual teachers. However, discipline problems were common in the class, and the absence of an open examination of those problems is surprising. Possibly because of the supervisor's experience, a great deal of time (6.4%) was spent discussing supervision.

In the logical areas, discussion in group 5 is unusually analytical with an A/E ratio of 2.82. This value is considerably higher than that for any other group. Suggestions are very common, whereas opinions are rare. Consequently, the diagnostic/prescriptive ratio is of only average size. The complex/simple ratio is comparatively low, indicating a relatively simple interaction despite the length of the pedagogical moves. Procedural and procedural/logical categories are infrequent. Generally, negative reactions are infrequent and the positive/negative ratio is relatively high, indicating a high proportion of positive reinforcement.

As is often found, the supervisor and teachers reduce their activity from planning to analysis, while the observers increase theirs. Analysis tends to be considerably more reactive than planning. Changes in instructional foci parallel those in other groups, although high values for objectives in planning drop considerably in analysis and totals for execution in planning are unusually low.

Striking differences are evident in the instructional domains. Planning tends to be exceedingly lopsided, with 89.3% cognitive, 1.3% affective, and 0.0% social-disciplinary. In analysis, the cognitive domain drops to 61.3% and the affective domain increases almost twenty-threefold to 29.8%. This difference in the affective domain is as difficult to explain as is the virtual absence of social-disciplinary factors in either planning or analysis.

Changes in the logical areas parallel those in most other groups, but the magnitudes of these changes are relatively large. Discussion in analysis becomes considerably more evaluative (A/E drops from 4.90 to 1.91), more diagnostic (D/P increases from 1.29 to 3.94), and more complex (C/S increases from 1.17 to 2.30). The positive/negative ratio drops almost in half in analysis, particularly because of increasing negative ratings.

Changes are also evident over the summer. Supervisor 5 shows an unusual decrease in activity from early to late conferences, particularly for initiatory moves, while the teachers almost double their activity. All I/R ratios decrease as the discussion becomes freer and more reactive. Almost all content areas reverse the trends seen in other groups. Discussions of objectives and executions increase, while methodology decreases; the affective and social domains increase while the cognitive domain decreases; and specific areas increase over the general areas.

Changes in logical areas parallel those in other groups but are greater in magnitude. Discussion becomes more analytical, more diagnostic, and less complex. Discussion of related areas decreases sharply, partially because of a decrease in the discussion of supervision. Apparently Supervisor 5 spent an unusual amount of time discussing supervision in the early weeks to establish his own "rules of the game," and reduced this as these rules became known.

The preceding analyses of individual supervisory groups are little more than "thumbnail sketches." They serve the dual purpose of indicating the diversity of supervisory interactions that occurred in this supposedly homogeneous environment and demonstrating the potentiality of the M.O.S.A.I.C.S. instrument for examining these individual differences. The next section of this chapter compares these supervisory groups with Bellack's teaching groups in order to demonstrate the use of M.O.S.A.I.C.S. in comparative studies.

COMPARISONS OF THE "RULES OF THE GAME" FOR SUPERVISORY GROUPS AND TEACHING GROUPS

Most studies of teaching, including Bellack's, examine interactions in relatively large groups. This is a reasonable approach for preliminary research, since most formal instruction is presently carried on in such groups. One might expect, however, that group size alone could be an important determinant of the nature of instructional interactions. As an extreme example, a one-to-one tutorial session will obviously differ in many respects from a large public lecture. The nature and extent of these instructional differences are practically unknown. Many of the differences that appear in the comparison of Bellack's study with the M.O.S.A.I.C.S. study of supervision may actually be only a function of group size.

The analysis in this section compares groups that are dissimilar in a great many respects. Bellack's study focuses on fifteen teachers who are instructing high school students in a specific four-day unit on international trade. An average of twenty-three students participated in each class. The study of clinical supervision at the Harvard-Newton Summer School focuses on five supervisors whose primary experience in teaching varies from elementary school to graduate school. Supervision focuses upon extremely broad and poorly defined problem areas in education. There is an average of five supervisees in each group, all of whom are graduate students. The pupils, mostly from Boston suburbs, range in age from ten to about eighteen. Any comparisons between teaching groups and supervisory groups must therefore be considered extremely tentative, and no attempts will be made to generalize from this comparison.

With these distinctions in mind, it appears that verbal behavior in small-group supervision is very different from that in large-group instruction. Tables 14 and 15 present basic data for comparisons of pedagogical moves. In terms of percentages of moves, the results for the two groups are almost exactly reversed. Teachers speak one-and-a-half times as many moves as all their pupils combined, while the supervisees speak one-and-a-half times as many moves as their supervisors.

These differences become even more dramatic when percentages of lines and units are compared, thus comparing total time spent in verbal interaction. Teachers in Bellack's study speak almost three times as many lines as their pupils, with a range of 60.3% to 92.8% for total lines. The situation for supervisory groups changes little from the 2:3 ratio seen for percentages of moves: supervisors speak about two-thirds as many units as supervisees, with a percentage range of 25.6% to

TABLE 14

Comparison of Percentages of Moves in Each Pedagogical Move Category
Between Teaching Groups (Bellack) and Supervisory Groups (Weller)

Teaching Group	% Teacher Moves						% Pupil Moves					
	SOL	RES	STR	REA	RSM	Total	SOL	RES	STR	REA	RSM	Total
1	29.9	1.4	2.5	25.3	0.9	60.6	1.7	30.0	0.4	3.4	0.0	39.4
2	29.9	1.2	4.8	20.8	1.6	59.0	2.6	26.6	0.7	7.5	0.2	41.0
3	36.6	2.1	7.0	18.8	1.2	65.8	3.1	24.4	0.0	3.7	0.0	34.2
4	29.6	2.8	4.1	23.5	1.3	61.4	3.1	24.6	0.0	8.6	0.0	38.6
5	24.5	5.8	5.2	20.4	1.6	58.3	9.4	17.9	0.4	9.0	0.1	41.7
6	33.7	3.3	3.7	20.7	2.8	64.5	2.7	27.5	0.2	2.5	0.0	35.5
7	25.7	5.8	7.8	22.5	1.1	63.7	6.6	21.4	1.7	4.9	0.0	36.3
8	27.6	4.4	3.7	23.5	1.7	61.7	4.7	22.9	0.4	8.0	0.0	38.3
9	29.0	1.7	13.2	25.8	2.2	72.1	1.5	22.5	0.0	2.8	0.0	27.9
10	28.3	2.4	5.5	23.4	2.1	62.3	3.1	25.3	0.1	5.5	0.0	37.7
11	32.9	2.1	8.6	20.7	2.2	66.9	2.6	26.7	0.4	1.3	0.0	33.1
12	21.5	5.8	7.3	21.3	1.1	58.3	8.0	18.6	0.1	11.2	0.0	41.7
13	30.1	3.7	1.2	22.0	2.3	60.1	4.2	30.1	0.4	3.9	0.0	39.9
14	29.8	2.7	4.5	25.9	2.5	66.4	2.7	25.2	0.0	1.5	0.0	33.5
15	24.6	5.3	3.6	23.0	1.2	57.8	7.3	22.9	0.4	9.2	0.0	41.3
$\bar{X}$	28.8	3.5	4.8	22.6	1.7	61.7	4.4	25.0	0.4	5.7	0.0	38.3

Supervisory Group	% Supervisor Moves						% Supervisee Moves					
	SOL	RES	STR	REA	RSM	Total	SOL	RES	STR	REA	RSM	Total
1	7.6	3.2	3.5	19.5	0.5	34.4	7.9	10.3	9.7	36.7	0.8	65.6
2	8.4	2.4	3.1	14.4	0.3	28.7	10.1	14.4	9.0	37.3	0.4	71.3
3	13.9	3.0	6.4	13.4	0.8	37.4	8.4	16.5	7.4	29.7	0.7	62.6
4	9.9	3.9	6.1	24.5	0.7	45.1	6.8	11.4	6.0	30.7	0.0	55.9
5	7.1	2.7	4.4	19.0	1.1	34.3	9.5	12.4	9.6	34.4	0.0	65.7
$\bar{X}$	9.1	3.1	4.6	18.8	0.6	36.3	8.4	12.5	8.4	34.1	0.4	63.7

56.8%. Teachers in Bellack's study not only produce about twice as many moves as supervisors, but these moves are also longer.

Most of the moves in teaching groups are solicitations and responses. Teachers and pupils contribute roughly equal numbers of these moves, which constitute almost 62% of the total. As expected, teachers do most of the soliciting and pupils mainly respond. These moves, however, tend to be short, and over 50% of the total lines spoken are in structuring or reacting categories. Teachers clearly predominate in these categories. Discourse in supervisory groups, on the

TABLE 15

Comparison of Percentages of Lines/Units in Each Pedagogical
Move Category Between Teaching Groups (Bellack) and
Supervisory Groups (Weller)

Teaching Group	% Teacher Lines						% Pupil Lines					
	SOL	RES	STR	REA	RSM	Total	SOL	RES	STR	REA	RSM	Total
1	27.5	1.4	7.2	36.9	3.1	76.3	1.2	18.0	0.4	2.3	0.0	23.7
2	20.1	1.0	11.2	25.5	3.4	61.5	1.6	23.9	0.8	10.2	0.4	38.5
3	30.1	3.7	10.1	22.9	3.3	70.2	2.1	18.2	0.0	2.5	0.0	29.8
4	20.7	3.7	5.9	26.7	3.3	60.3	1.8	24.8	0.6	7.0	0.0	39.7
5	15.5	9.4	15.5	17.3	3.4	61.3	5.4	14.4	0.5	10.7	0.2	38.7
6	20.2	5.9	16.2	25.5	14.4	82.2	1.1	14.3	0.0	1.6	0.0	17.8
7	15.5	7.5	24.0	22.2	2.4	72.0	4.2	13.5	2.4	4.1	0.0	28.0
8	20.4	8.8	8.8	30.5	4.5	73.5	2.9	15.0	0.3	7.3	0.0	26.5
9	12.8	0.9	46.6	29.5	2.8	92.8	0.3	5.8	0.0	0.9	0.0	7.2
10	12.0	5.3	19.7	34.7	9.4	81.2	1.2	10.6	0.0	5.9	0.0	18.8
11	23.2	2.8	22.4	18.2	6.8	73.7	0.9	13.4	0.5	1.2	0.0	26.3
12	16.0	6.2	22.0	25.3	3.3	73.4	1.4	10.0	0.1	7.9	0.0	26.6
13	28.9	6.1	1.7	27.5	6.6	70.9	3.0	21.4	0.7	3.3	0.0	29.1
14	23.8	3.5	8.0	28.3	8.5	72.6	1.3	13.0	0.0	0.6	0.0	20.3
15	14.7	9.1	8.7	24.2	4.0	60.8	5.5	15.6	0.2	10.8	0.0	36.2
X	20.3	5.0	14.5	26.7	5.3	72.1	2.5	15.6	0.4	5.1	0.0	27.2

Supervisory Group	% Supervisor Units						% Supervisee Units					
	SOL	RES	STR	REA	RSM	Total	SOL	RES	STR	REA	RSM	Total
1	4.9	2.8	4.8	18.9	1.7	33.0	4.1	11.1	18.1	32.6	1.0	67.0
2	4.9	4.0	4.9	11.5	0.3	25.6	5.0	16.4	15.8	36.8	0.4	73.4
3	6.6	3.2	18.9	11.0	1.0	40.7	3.7	16.3	14.5	24.0	0.9	59.3
4	5.6	4.2	16.4	29.8	0.8	56.8	3.8	9.7	7.7	21.8	0.0	43.2
5	5.3	3.1	16.7	16.5	1.9	43.5	3.9	11.1	15.8	25.7	0.0	56.5
X	5.4	3.4	11.9	17.8	1.2	39.8	4.1	12.7	14.6	28.4	0.4	60.2

other hand, consists mainly of structuring and reacting. Approximately
two-thirds of all moves and three-quarters of all units are in these categories. On the average, supervisees contribute almost twice as many
of these moves as the supervisors, but the supervisors' moves are
proportionately longer. Supervisees also contribute about twice as many
moves as supervisors in the solicitation-response categories. Like the
teaching groups, supervisors primarily solicit whereas supervisees pri-

marily respond. In general, teachers in Bellack's study have higher activity than their pupils for every category except RES; supervisors have higher activity only for SOL and RSM.

Pedagogical roles are more evident in comparisons of a different sort. Table 16 takes individual pedagogical moves and compares percentage distributions and participation indices for each participant in these categories. Teachers in Bellack's study clearly dominate almost all moves. They produce 89.0% of all solicitations, 97.3% of all structuring moves, 84.0% of all reactions, and 99.1% of all summary reactions. Teachers' participation indices for these moves are all greater than 20.

Pupils, on the other hand, have a very limited role to play. They dominate only in the responding move and seldom solicit. Their participation indices for structuring and summarizing are only .03 and .01, respectively, when compared with a hypothetical "random participant" at 1.00. Their reactions, although more frequent than their solicitations, form a very minor part of classroom discourse.

The situation is quite different in the supervisory groups. Supervisors produce only 56.8% of all solicitations, 44.9% of all structuring moves, 38.5% of all reactions, and 75.0% of all summary reactions. Most of these values are considerably lower than comparable figures for Bellack's teachers. Although supervisors have higher participation indices than supervisees for every type of pedagogical move, the differences are all much smaller than those in teaching groups. Supervisors and supervisees are actually very similar in the responding move.

TABLE 16

Percentages and Participation Indices for Lines/Units for Each Pedagogical Move by Participants in Teaching (Bellack) and Supervision (Weller)

Category	Teachers		Pupils		Supervisors		Supervisees	
	%	P.I.	%	P.I.	%	P.I.	%	P.I.
SOL	89.0	21.4	11.0	0.1	56.8	3.3	43.2	0.5
RES	24.3	5.8	75.7	0.8	21.1	1.2	78.9	1.0
STR	97.3	23.3	2.7	0.03	44.9	2.6	55.1	0.6
REA	84.0	20.1	16.0	0.2	38.5	2.3	61.5	0.7
RSM	99.1	23.8	0.9	0.01	75.0	4.4	25.0	0.3
Total lines/units	72.1	17.3	27.2	0.3	39.8	2.3	60.2	0.7

In terms of percentages, supervisees actually dominate the structuring and reacting moves as well as the responding move.

Table 17 presents these data in a different way by examining the distribution of pedagogical moves for each participant. In terms of moves, Bellack's teachers primarily solicit and react. Structuring moves, by virtue of their length, comprise a significant portion of teaching time or total lines spoken. Emphasis is roughly evenly divided between STR + REA and SOL + RES for moves, whereas STR + REA involves a higher percentage of lines or total time spent in verbal behavior.

Pupils, on the other hand, are primarily responders of relatively short answers. When they do structure (1.8% of their moves), they tend to do so at length. Their initiatory/reflexive ratios are very low, indicating that they serve primarily a reflexive role in the classroom. Teachers are very much in control of the flow of discourse in these classrooms.

In contrast, the supervisors and supervisees are surprisingly similar in the distribution of their pedagogical moves. Only in SOL and RES is there any major difference, and these differences are much smaller than those found in teaching groups. It may be said, then, that while individual supervisees are less active than supervisors, they tend to participate in much the same way except that they solicit less and

TABLE 17

Percentages of Moves and Line/Units for Each Participant: Comparisons of Pedagogical Roles for Teaching Groups and Supervisory Groups

Category	Teachers		Pupils		Supervisors		Supervisees	
	Moves	Lines	Moves	Lines	Moves	Lines	Moves	Lines
STR	7.7	20.1	1.8	11.1	12.8	30.0	13.2	24.4
REA	39.2	44.7	15.1	19.1	53.7	47.8	54.0	47.8
STR + REA	46.9	64.8	16.9	30.2	66.5	77.8	67.2	72.2
SOL	46.6	28.0	11.3	8.7	24.9	13.6	13.2	6.6
RES	5.5	6.8	65.4	57.5	8.6	8.6	19.6	21.2
SOL + RES	52.1	34.8	76.7	66.2	33.5	22.2	32.8	27.8
I/R	1.21	0.94	0.16	0.14	0.61	0.77	0.36	0.45
Total	99.0	99.6	93.6	96.4	100.0	100.0	100.0	100.0

respond more. The roles of supervisor and supervisee for pedagogical moves appear to be distinguished primarily on the basis of relative activity, not on the distribution of pedagogical functions in the conference.

Teaching cycles are presented in table 18. Five cycle types account for approximately three-quarters of all cycles for both groups. For Bellack's teaching groups, cycles 13, 14, 18, 19, and 21 comprise 74.0% of all cycles. Without exception, these cycles all begin with a single soliciting move. SOL–RES is clearly the basic pattern in these teaching groups. The percent of teacher-initiated cycles is 84.5%, so it must be concluded that the teacher not only dominates the amount and type of verbal discourse but also essentially determines the pedagogical patterns of that discourse.

The situation is different in the study of clinical supervision. Supervisors initiate only 44.1% of all teaching cycles. Cycles of types 3, 4, 14, 18, and 19 comprise 77.2% of all cycles initiated in these groups. Two of these types (3 and 4) are initiated by single structuring moves while the other three are SOL–RES cycles. In supervision, therefore, STR–REA cycles form an important pattern of discourse. These patterns are very rare in teaching groups. STR–REA and STR–REA–REA . . . cycles account for 33.8% of all cycles in supervision but only 2.2% in teaching. On the other hand, cycles in which a solicitation elicits multiple responses and reactions (SOL–RES–REA–RES . . . and SOL–RES–REA–RES . . . REA . . .) account for 9.5% of the discourse in teaching groups but are virtually nonexistent in supervision (0.1% of the total).

Table 19 presents teaching cycles in a way that permits analysis of initiatory and reflexive patterns. Cycles initiated by SOL . . . account for almost 80% of all cycles in teaching groups. Patterns are more varied in supervision, with 51.9% in SOL . . . cycles and 35.3% in STR . . . cycles. Both types of groups place comparable emphasis on STR–SOL . . . cycles.

Striking differences between these groups are evident in reflexive patterns, particularly for multiple reactions and responses. Supervisory groups produce three times as many simple reactions and almost nineteen times as many multiple reactions as teaching groups. Multiple reactions actually form the commonest reflexive patterns for supervision, whereas they are extremely rare in teaching. In contrast, multiple responses which are reacted to by other participants are common in teaching but very rare in supervision. It may be inferred that most of these patterns in teaching represent the teacher's reaction to a pupil's response, while in supervision all participants react to one

TABLE 18

Comparison of Percentages of Each Teaching Cycle Type Between
Teaching Groups (Bellack) and Supervisory Groups (Weller)

Teaching Group	% Cycle Type											
	1	2	3	4	5	6	7	8	9	10	11	12
1	0.4	0.6	0.6	0.4	1.7	0.0	0.0	0.0	3.6	0.2	0.6	1.3
2	1.4	1.1	0.4	1.4	3.6	0.4	0.0	0.0	3.9	2.1	0.0	3.9
3	1.3	3.3	3.0	1.3	3.7	0.3	0.3	0.0	6.3	0.7	0.7	1.0
4	1.5	1.5	0.4	0.4	1.5	0.4	0.4	0.0	5.6	1.1	0.7	3.7
5	1.8	2.5	4.3	0.7	5.0	0.4	0.4	0.0	6.8	0.0	0.7	2.4
6	2.5	0.5	0.5	0.0	2.0	0.0	0.0	0.0	3.9	0.5	0.0	1.5
7	5.3	1.1	3.4	1.5	9.1	0.0	0.4	0.0	9.1	2.3	0.0	1.9
8	0.3	1.3	0.6	1.3	3.8	0.0	0.0	0.0	3.8	1.9	0.3	1.3
9	11.5	2.0	0.0	2.0	3.4	0.0	2.0	0.0	17.6	1.4	0.0	0.0
10	2.1	0.4	0.4	0.9	4.3	0.0	0.4	1.3	8.1	0.4	0.0	0.4
11	2.1	4.2	0.3	0.0	4.5	0.3	0.3	0.0	13.9	0.7	1.4	0.7
12	1.6	3.2	0.8	1.6	4.0	0.0	0.4	0.0	9.7	2.0	0.0	4.9
13	0.3	0.6	0.3	0.2	0.8	0.0	0.0	0.0	1.0	0.0	0.3	1.1
14	2.3	2.0	2.0	0.0	2.3	0.0	0.4	0.0	5.8	0.4	0.0	2.7
15	1.5	3.9	3.2	2.0	2.0	0.2	0.2	0.0	2.0	0.2	0.2	1.5
$\overline{X}$	1.9	1.8	1.4	0.8	3.1	0.1	0.3	0.1	5.7	0.8	0.4	1.8

Supervisory Group	% Cycle Type											
	1	2	3	4	5	6	7	8	9	10	11	12
1	0.5	1.9	8.7	30.8	2.2	0.2	0.2	0.0	1.7	4.6	0.0	0.0
2	1.4	1.4	7.7	24.3	2.5	0.4	0.4	0.4	2.1	2.8	0.0	0.4
3	1.2	1.2	10.2	15.9	6.9	0.0	0.4	0.0	2.9	5.3	0.4	0.4
4	3.6	0.6	6.9	24.0	5.4	0.0	0.0	0.3	1.8	5.4	0.0	0.0
5	0.4	1.2	10.0	27.8	5.0	0.0	0.0	0.4	2.1	4.6	0.0	0.8
$\overline{X}$	1.5	1.3	8.6	25.2	4.2	0.1	0.2	0.2	2.0	4.5	0.1	0.3

Type 1 = STR
Type 2 = STR-SOL
Type 3 = STR-REA
Type 4 = STR-REA-REA...
Type 5 = STR-SOL-RES
Type 6 = STR-SOL-RES-RES...

Type 7 = STR-SOL-REA
Type 8 = STR-SOL-REA-REA...
Type 9 = STR-SOL-RES-REA
Type 10 = STR-SOL-RES-REA-REA...
Type 11 = STR-SOL-RES-REA-RES...
Type 12 = STR-SOL-RES-REA-RES...REA...

TABLE 18
(cont.)

Comparison of Percentages of Each Teaching Cycle Type Between
Teaching Groups (Bellack) and Supervisory Groups (Weller)

Teaching Group	% Cycle Type									% Initiation	
	13	*14*	*15*	*16*	*17*	*18*	*19*	*20*	*21*	*Tchr.*	*Pupil*
1	6.1	20.8	0.8	0.8	0.6	39.7	7.6	3.4	7.4	93.1	3.5
2	11.1	24.0	1.1	1.1	0.0	19.6	7.5	4.3	9.6	90.0	6.4
3	20.3	23.0	0.7	2.7	0.3	18.7	6.7	1.7	2.0	89.3	8.7
4	12.4	20.2	0.4	1.9	0.4	22.5	10.9	3.7	8.6	88.0	10.1
5	11.5	19.7	0.4	2.2	2.5	13.6	10.0	2.2	8.6	61.2	34.5
6	6.9	35.5	0.5	0.5	1.0	28.0	8.4	1.5	3.4	92.1	5.9
7	2.8	18.9	0.0	0.7	0.0	25.6	9.4	1.9	4.5	77.4	20.3
8	7.3	22.4	0.6	0.0	0.0	30.7	14.4	1.9	5.4	82.4	15.0
9	4.7	7.4	0.0	6.1	0.0	30.4	6.1	0.0	4.7	96.6	2.7
10	4.7	25.5	0.0	0.9	0.0	26.4	10.6	2.1	8.5	88.5	8.9
11	9.7	17.7	0.7	0.7	0.3	33.0	5.2	0.3	2.1	92.4	5.9
12	9.7	22.7	1.6	1.2	0.0	14.2	11.7	1.6	4.9	72.7	23.9
13	13.7	28.2	1.9	1.0	0.5	26.0	8.8	4.3	10.2	87.4	11.6
14	9.3	15.2	0.0	2.3	0.8	31.5	6.2	1.6	12.1	83.8	13.1
15	8.6	23.4	1.5	2.5	1.0	23.2	10.6	2.5	7.1	75.1	22.2
$\overline{\text{X}}$	9.7	22.3	0.8	1.5	0.5	26.0	9.0	2.5	7.0	84.5	13.0*

Supervisory Group	% Cycle Type									% Initiation	
	13	*14*	*15*	*16*	*17*	*18*	*19*	*20*	*21*	*Supvr.*	*Supvee.*
1	5.1	15.5	1.0	1.0	0.7	9.9	16.0	0.0	0.0	37.3	62.7
2	4.6	17.3	0.7	0.7	1.4	12.0	19.4	0.4	0.0	34.9	65.1
3	8.2	19.2	2.0	1.2	1.2	10.6	12.2	0.4	0.0	55.1	44.9
4	3.3	17.4	1.8	1.2	1.8	11.1	15.6	0.0	0.0	57.2	42.8
5	4.1	18.7	0.8	1.2	0.0	10.0	12.9	0.0	0.0	37.3	62.7
$\overline{\text{X}}$	4.9	17.3	1.3	1.1	1.1	10.7	15.4	0.1	0.0	44.1	55.9

Type 13 = SOL
Type 14 = SOL-RES
Type 15 = SOL-RES-RES...
Type 16 = SOL-REA
Type 17 = SOL-REA-REA...

Type 18 = SOL-RES-REA
Type 19 = SOL-RES-REA-REA...
Type 20 = SOL-RES-REA-RES...
Type 21 = SOL-RES-REA-RES...REA...

*Note: Some of the Bellack data in this and other tables differs from 100% for
totals because of his use of NOC (Noncodable) in certain indistinct recordings.

TABLE 19

Comparison of Percentages of Teaching Cycles by Cycle Patterns
Between Teaching Groups (Bellack) and Supervisory Groups (Weller)

Teaching Groups

Initiatory Patterns	*Reflexive Patterns*									Total
	No Reflex. Pattern	RES	RES RES...	REA	REA REA...	RES REA	RES REA REA...	RES REA RES...	RES REA RES... REA...	
STR	1.9	*	*	1.4	0.8	*	*	*	*	4.1
SOL	9.7	22.3	0.8	1.5	0.5	26.0	9.0	2.5	7.0	79.3
STR-SOL	1.8	3.1	0.1	0.3	0.1	5.7	0.8	0.4	1.8	14.1
Total	13.4	25.4	0.9	3.2	1.4	31.7	9.8	2.9	8.8	97.5

Supervisory Groups

Initiatory Patterns	*Reflexive Patterns*									Total
	No Reflex. Pattern	RES	RES RES...	REA	REA REA...	RES REA	RES REA REA...	RES REA RES...	RES REA RES... REA...	
STR	1.5	*	*	8.6	25.2	*	*	*	*	35.3
SOL	4.9	17.3	1.3	1.1	1.1	10.7	15.4	0.1	0.0	51.9
STR-SOL	1.3	4.2	0.1	0.2	0.2	2.0	4.5	0.1	0.3	12.8
Total	7.7	21.5	1.4	9.9	26.5	12.7	19.9	0.2	0.3	100.0

*No reflexive pattern starting with RES is possible after an initiatory move of STR.

another. In general, cycles for teaching and group supervision are very distinctive and indicate sharp differences in both activity and initiative by different participants.

Substantive meanings cannot be compared for these two groups, but the substantive-logical meanings have enough in common to permit direct comparisons (see tables 20 and 21). The teaching groups emphasize definitions far more than the supervisory groups, a factor

TABLE 20

Comparison of Percentages of Moves for Logical Categories Between
Teaching Groups (Bellack) and Supervisory Groups (Weller)

Teaching Group	*% Moves in Logical Categories*										
	DEF	*INT*	*FAC*	*XPL*	*EVL*	*JUS*	*SUG*	*SGX*	*OPN*	*OPJ*	*Total*
1	8.3	1.7	32.9	19.7	2.3	1.4	*	*	*	*	66.3
2	4.7	0.7	15.2	30.1	2.7	4.0					57.4
3	4.6	1.2	17.7	26.0	1.0	2.0					52.5
4	9.4	0.9	16.5	26.7	1.1	1.9					56.6
5	7.8	1.8	10.3	23.0	2.9	5.9					51.7
6	8.5	2.2	13.8	41.8	1.8	0.8					68.9
7	7.7	0.7	27.8	26.5	1.5	1.5					65.7
8	4.1	0.7	25.0	32.5	3.0	3.1					68.5
9	11.9	0.0	16.7	50.7	0.9	2.4					82.6
10	6.6	0.0	19.6	40.8	1.4	1.9					70.4
11	9.3	0.2	27.1	25.8	4.5	2.4					69.4
12	3.9	0.0	24.4	28.9	5.5	1.6					64.6
13	6.5	0.1	30.4	23.4	0.8	0.2					61.6
14	9.6	1.9	11.1	37.4	1.2	0.9					62.2
15	5.1	0.6	20.0	29.0	1.9	2.2					59.2
$\bar{X}$	6.9	0.8	22.0	28.8	2.1**	2.1**					62.9

Supervisory Group	*DEF*	*INT*	*FAC*	*XPL*	*EVL*	*JUS*	*SUG*	*SGX*	*OPN*	*OPJ*	*Total*
1	0.0	3.7	25.8	12.3	7.0	7.4	5.5	5.3	3.9	5.4	76.4
2	0.4	4.3	25.0	21.7	4.2	5.9	4.6	4.5	3.0	6.0	79.7
3	0.3	7.1	17.6	20.4	3.9	9.0	3.5	3.4	2.5	7.1	74.8
4	0.0	4.4	25.1	14.7	4.5	3.3	4.2	4.5	4.2	6.7	71.6
5	0.9	5.7	23.6	17.6	4.7	6.2	7.0	6.0	2.7	5.2	79.6
$\bar{X}$	0.2	4.8	24.0	16.6	5.1	6.2	5.0	4.8	3.4	6.0	76.1

*No categories exist in the Bellack system for SUG, SGX, OPN, and OPJ.

**In the Bellack system, EVL includes OPN, and JUS includes OPJ. These are
separately scored in the M.O.S.A.I.C.S. system.

probably related both to the specificity and the lack of familiarity of
the content. Most of the definitions in supervision occur during discussions of subject matter. The more frequent use of interpretations in
supervision is probably related to the actual process of discussion.
Interpretations commonly consist of a reaction or solicitation which is

TABLE 21

Comparison of Percentages of Lines/Units for Logical Categories Between
Teaching Groups (Bellack) and Supervisory Groups (Weller)

Teaching Group	% Lines/Units in Logical Categories										
	DEF	INT	FAC	XPL	EVL	JUS	SUG	SGX	OPN	OPJ	Total
1	6.1	1.8	23.1	33.6	2.2	4.0	*	*	*	*	70.8
2	3.4	1.5	9.8	36.7	2.7	7.8					61.9
3	3.5	0.03	10.5	43.6	0.7	4.1					62.4
4	8.3	1.8	12.3	42.3	0.8	4.7					70.2
5	6.8	1.1	6.9	37.9	1.5	12.9					67.1
6	3.4	1.4	6.3	59.9	1.4	5.3					77.7
7	5.0	0.4	20.8	41.3	1.4	4.1					73.0
8	2.9	0.5	17.8	43.6	3.0	8.8					76.6
9	7.0	0.0	6.7	63.3	0.2	11.3					88.5
10	2.9	0.0	9.4	63.7	0.8	5.3					82.1
11	4.9	0.1	16.3	44.0	3.1	7.5					75.9
12	3.7	0.0	15.6	47.5	4.2	2.9					74.0
13	5.0	0.1	25.1	38.8	0.9	0.7					70.7
14	7.4	1.4	5.7	51.5	0.7	1.3					68.0
15	3.6	0.6	12.9	42.4	1.2	8.7					69.6
$\overline{X}$	4.9	0.7	13.6	45.9	1.6**	5.9**					72.8

Supervisory Group	DEF	INT	FAC	XPL	EVL	JUS	SUG	SGX	OPN	OPJ	Total
1	0.0	3.2	20.9	18.4	4.5	10.9	5.0	6.4	3.1	10.1	82.6
2	0.2	2.0	19.7	29.3	2.2	11.8	3.4	5.7	2.1	11.1	87.5
3	0.1	2.9	10.4	25.8	1.6	15.2	3.8	5.4	2.1	18.4	85.5
4	0.0	2.2	17.8	20.3	2.2	4.2	4.1	6.2	4.2	19.0	80.1
5	0.5	2.1	19.5	26.1	2.4	11.0	8.5	9.3	2.0	7.1	88.6
$\overline{X}$	0.1	2.5	18.0	23.7	2.7	10.5	5.0	6.6	2.7	12.9	84.7

*No categories exist in the Bellack system for SUG, SGX, OPN, and OPJ.

**In the Bellack system, EVL includes OPN, and JUS includes OPJ. These are
separately scored in the M.O.S.A.I.C.S. system.

intended to clarify another participant's statement. Such interpretations
are often used either to encourage a participant to examine his own
statements or to establish a basis of understanding upon which a
discussion can be built. Supervisors often use this as a stylistic device

to encourage participation. Interpretations are more frequent in all of the supervisory groups than in any of the teaching groups.

The other substantive-logical meanings in the M.O.S.A.I.C.S. system are all somewhat different from Bellack's categories. Nevertheless, it is possible to compare them on the basis of more general logical parameters. In the first place, supervisors spend more time in substantive areas and less time in procedural areas than teachers do. Fully 84.7% of the supervisory conferences concentrate on substantive areas, while on the average only 72.8% of the discourse in the teaching groups focuses on teaching content. Only two of the fifteen teachers fall within the substantive range of the supervisors.

It is evident that supervisory conferences contain considerably more evaluative meanings than do teaching groups. Evaluative meanings comprise 28.8% of supervisory conferences, and the analytic/evaluative ratio is a relatively low 1.8; these meanings comprise only 7.5% of teaching sessions, with an A/E ratio of 7.9. Problems in teaching have much stronger emotional overtones for intern teachers than problems in international trade have for high school pupils. It is interesting to speculate on the kind of interactions that might have ensued with these pupils had the content been more relevant and emotionally involving. Although it cannot be demonstrated with the present data, one might hypothesize that questions of relevance, commitment, involvement, and evaluation are intimately related and that evaluative meanings might be a useful measure of these factors.

Discussion in Bellack's teaching groups is characterized by relatively high complex/simple ratios, which average 3.4 in the classes he studied. The majority of this complex total is accounted for by empirical relationships or explanations (XPL). The supervisory groups have a somewhat higher complex total (53.8% compared with 51.8% for teaching groups) but the total of the simple categories is considerably higher and the complex/simple ratio averages only 1.9. Before examining the differences between supervisory and teaching groups in these logical areas, a distinction must be made between complex categories, which indicate only that explicit relationships are made between and among factors and principles, and complex analysis, which involves much more subtle and undefinable parameters of perception and understanding. The substantive-logical meanings and the complex/simple ratio are measures of the degree to which explicit relationships are stated in discourse, but they do not necessarily measure the complexity of the actual discussion.

One way to examine these differences is to combine FAC + SUG, XPL + SGX, EVL + OPN, and JUS + OPJ for supervisory groups. These combined categories compare closely with Bellack's definitions

for FAC, XPL, EVL, and JUS, particularly for the evaluative categories
(see Appendix E). When teaching (FAC = 13.6%, XPL = 45.9%) is
compared with supervision (FAC + SUG = 23.0%, XPL + SGX =
30.3%) for lines or units spoken, it is evident that empirical statements
are treated in greater complexity in teaching groups than in supervision.

A suggested explanation is that the content of supervision has real
and immediate relevance and produces a greater amount of observational and factual data. However, since the supervisor is not an absolute
authority for the explanation of instructional interactions (presumably,
Bellack's teachers knew much more about relationships in international
trade than did their pupils), explanations are often left to empirical
test and future observations.

When lines and units for evaluative categories are compared,
Bellack's teaching groups (EVL = 1.6%, JUS = 5.9%) show considerably less activity than do the supervisory groups (EVL + OPN =
5.4%, JUS + OPJ = 23.4%). Evaluative discussions produce a higher
proportion of complex categories in both groups than do empirical
discussions. It is possible that participants feel freer to argue when
another participant makes a value judgment or expresses an opinion.
The complex/simple ratio for teaching groups does not change much
from empirical to evaluative discussions, presumably because the
teacher has both more information and more control. The complex/
simple ratio in supervisory groups, however, increases from about 1.3
for empirical meanings to 4.3 for evaluative meanings. A suggested
explanation is that the participants feel greater commitment and freedom to react at length in evaluative discussions.

Table 22 presents the procedural areas discussed in both types of
group. As mentioned earlier, teaching groups spend considerably more
time in these areas than do supervisory groups. The two groups are
roughly comparable in terms of rating reactions to statements of participants (STA). Teaching groups spend more time in the action category (ACT) and place almost three times as much emphasis on
procedures (PRC). The supervisory groups, on the other hand, spend
much more time on personal interactions. These results may be interpreted on the basis of group size. The small size of supervisory groups
encourages personal interactions between all members, and the relatively undefined content focus of supervision permits the group to
proceed without need for much conscious procedural control.

The procedural-logical meanings in Tables 23 and 24 show that
teaching and supervisory groups are roughly comparable on most dimensions. Positive/negative ratios average about 4.0 for both groups,
although considerable variance exists in both teaching and supervision

TABLE 22

Comparison of Percentages of Moves and Lines/Units in Each Procedural
Category Between Teaching Groups (Bellack) and Supervisory Groups (Weller)

Teaching Group	% Procedural Moves					% Procedural Lines/Units				
	STA	ACT	PRC	PER	Total	STA	ACT	PRC	PER	Total
1	22.9	15.4	5.5	0.3	44.1	11.7	8.2	7.2	0.2	27.3
2	20.0	16.7	12.3	0.1	49.1	19.4	6.5	9.9	0.1	35.9
3	14.9	17.8	22.3	2.7	57.7	6.5	8.5	20.2	1.2	36.4
4	23.1	16.7	11.1	1.1	52.0	10.3	7.6	10.7	0.5	29.1
5	24.4	16.5	10.9	0.7	52.5	10.0	9.4	11.7	0.2	31.3
6	19.7	12.4	8.3	1.2	41.6	6.8	3.5	10.7	0.3	21.3
7	22.9	12.0	14.6	0.0	49.5	10.1	5.6	10.5	0.0	26.2
8	24.9	13.9	5.1	0.5	44.4	10.2	5.7	5.9	0.3	22.1
9	21.7	6.8	7.6	0.4	36.5	4.0	1.4	6.1	0.1	11.6
10	22.2	9.0	7.4	0.6	39.2	7.0	2.6	6.9	0.2	16.7
11	18.6	15.3	11.0	0.0	44.9	6.5	6.0	10.8	0.0	23.3
12	19.1	12.0	7.8	0.6	39.5	8.1	6.6	4.6	0.3	19.6
13	21.7	17.5	4.1	0.3	43.6	12.4	10.6	5.4	0.2	28.6
14	24.5	11.6	13.5	0.2	49.8	9.1	4.2	16.7	0.1	30.1
15	23.3	16.3	9.3	0.1	49.0	11.8	8.2	9.8	0.1	29.9
$\overline{X}$	21.9	15.2	9.3	0.5	46.9	9.7	6.5	9.6	0.2	26.0

Supervisory Group	STA	ACT	PRC	PER	Total	STA	ACT	PRC	PER	Total
1	17.8	7.5	6.5	2.1	33.9	7.8	4.1	4.6	0.9	17.4
2	16.5	7.3	4.1	2.8	30.7	5.8	3.1	2.6	1.0	12.5
3	17.0	11.0	5.1	3.3	36.4	5.7	4.4	3.5	0.9	14.5
4	23.7	10.2	4.0	3.2	41.1	9.6	5.5	3.2	1.5	19.9
5	20.9	7.0	4.0	1.4	33.3	6.1	2.3	2.6	0.5	11.4
$\overline{X}$	19.4	8.5	4.9	2.6	35.4	7.1	3.9	3.3	1.0	15.3

STA = Bellack's STA
ACT = Bellack's ACT, ACV, ACC, ACP, ACE, LOG, and LAM
PRC = Bellack's PRC, ASG, and MAT
PER = Bellack's PER

(the range in teaching is 1.3 to 12.1, while it is 2.9 to 6.4 in supervision). Generally, extreme ratings are rarer in supervision than they are in teaching. This is particularly noticeable for POS and NEG ratings. RPT reactions, in which a participant implicitly accepts a statement by repeating it, are much more common in teaching and are primarily part of the teacher's role. The low incidence of performance

TABLE 23

Comparison of Percentages of Moves for Procedural-Logical Categories
Between Teaching Groups (Bellack) and Supervisory Groups (Weller)

Teaching Group	% Procedural-Logical Moves									Total	P/N
	POS	ADM	RPT	QAL	NAD	NEG	PRF	Logical	Other		
1	5.5	4.5	12.6	1.6	0.6	1.4	4.4	11.3	0.4	42.3	6.3
2	3.9	8.2	5.1	2.5	0.5	0.7	7.9	17.4	0.5	46.7	4.7
3	3.4	1.9	6.1	1.0	0.4	0.3	9.8	30.4	1.0	54.5	6.7
4	7.0	7.9	4.5	2.0	1.1	0.8	10.6	16.5	0.7	51.1	5.0
5	8.5	6.6	1.4	4.4	0.9	1.8	12.0	19.0	1.5	56.1	2.3
6	1.3	3.8	9.3	2.2	1.3	1.0	5.8	14.8	0.3	39.7	3.2
7	5.5	4.8	8.6	2.3	0.7	1.4	6.9	15.6	0.0	45.8	4.3
8	5.9	5.7	4.6	5.1	0.9	1.2	6.6	12.8	0.6	43.4	2.3
9	5.8	11.7	2.6	1.7	0.7	0.7	3.7	9.3	0.2	36.4	6.5
10	4.7	3.4	5.6	4.9	1.6	1.4	4.5	12.7	0.0	38.8	1.7
11	4.5	2.5	9.9	1.8	0.4	0.5	3.9	17.7	0.4	41.6	6.3
12	5.8	2.2	7.8	3.0	1.8	0.6	6.2	14.0	0.3	41.7	2.9
13	5.5	4.2	12.6	2.4	0.8	1.0	7.5	8.9	0.2	43.1	5.3
14	4.8	8.5	4.5	4.2	0.6	1.4	8.7	13.6	0.2	46.5	2.9
15	7.2	5.3	5.5	3.7	1.2	0.4	7.1	17.3	0.4	48.1	3.4
$\overline{X}$	5.5	5.2	7.3	2.9	0.9	1.0	7.2	14.9	0.4	45.3	3.8

Supervisory Group	POS	ADM	RPT	QAL	NAD	NEG	PRF	Logical	Other	Total	P/N
1	3.1	8.8	2.0	2.5	1.5	0.6	1.6	11.1	3.5	34.0	3.4
2	2.2	9.7	0.8	2.6	0.9	0.4	0.9	9.4	3.9	30.6	3.3
3	2.1	10.1	0.8	2.9	1.0	0.1	3.1	10.4	5.9	36.4	3.3
4	2.2	15.9	2.3	2.5	0.8	0.0	0.9	13.3	3.3	41.1	6.2
5	2.8	13.6	0.9	2.9	0.7	0.1	1.2	9.1	2.1	33.3	4.7
$\overline{X}$	2.5	11.6	1.5	2.6	1.0	0.1	1.5	10.9	3.6	35.4	4.2

Other = PON and NCL in the M.O.S.A.I.C.S. system, as well as AON and DIR in
    the Bellack system.
P/N = (Positive total) / (Negative total) = (POS + ADM + RPT) / (QAL + NAD + NEG)

(PRF) meanings in supervision may be correlated with the low incidence of ACT and PRC. Participants in supervision rarely ask others
to do anything concrete.

In general, teaching groups and supervisory groups differ considerably on almost all dimensions recorded by these instruments.

TABLE 24

Comparison of Percentages of Lines/Units for Procedural-Logical Categories
Between Teaching Groups (Bellack) and Supervisory Groups (Weller)

Teaching Group	% Procedural-Logical Lines/Units										
	POS	ADM	RPT	QAL	NAD	NEG	PRF	Logical	Other	Total	P/N
1	2.9	2.2	6.2	0.8	0.3	0.7	4.9	9.0	0.2	27.2	6.3
2	12.6	3.3	2.2	1.0	0.2	0.3	4.0	12.4	0.1	36.1	12.1
3	1.4	0.6	2.3	0.3	0.1	0.1	10.9	19.2	0.3	36.2	8.6
4	3.3	3.1	1.8	1.0	0.6	0.4	7.4	11.4	0.4	29.4	4.1
5	3.5	2.4	0.6	1.8	0.3	0.7	6.3	14.7	0.9	31.2	2.3
6	0.3	1.1	3.0	1.1	0.7	0.3	3.6	11.3	0.1	21.5	2.1
7	2.4	2.0	3.8	1.0	0.3	0.6	3.5	12.5	0.0	26.1	4.3
8	2.3	2.2	1.8	2.2	0.6	0.4	3.7	8.6	0.3	22.1	2.0
9	1.1	2.1	0.6	0.3	0.2	0.1	1.2	6.0	0.0	11.6	6.3
10	1.3	1.0	1.4	1.8	0.7	0.4	1.6	8.5	0.0	16.7	1.3
11	1.4	0.9	3.2	0.7	0.1	0.1	2.7	14.0	0.1	23.2	6.1
12	2.6	0.9	3.2	1.2	0.7	0.3	2.9	7.7	0.1	19.6	3.0
13	3.1	2.3	7.0	1.4	0.5	0.5	7.6	6.1	0.1	28.6	5.2
14	1.7	2.6	1.8	1.5	0.2	0.7	10.7	10.7	0.1	30.0	2.5
15	3.7	2.3	2.5	1.7	0.8	0.2	4.5	13.9	0.3	29.9	3.1
$\overline{X}$	2.9	2.0	2.9	1.2	0.4	0.4	5.1	11.0	0.1	26.0	3.9

Supervisory Group	POS	ADM	RPT	QAL	NAD	NEG	PRF	Logical	Other	Total	P/N
1	1.5	3.8	0.9	0.9	0.7	0.0	0.9	7.3	1.4	17.4	3.9
2	0.8	3.3	0.3	0.9	0.3	0.1	0.5	4.9	1.4	12.5	3.4
3	0.7	3.4	0.2	1.0	0.4	0.1	1.2	5.7	1.8	14.5	2.9
4	1.0	6.4	0.9	1.0	0.3	0.0	0.4	8.3	1.6	19.9	6.4
5	0.9	3.8	0.3	0.8	0.3	0.1	0.5	4.0	0.7	11.4	4.2
$\overline{X}$	1.0	4.1	0.5	0.9	0.4	0.1	0.7	6.2	1.4	15.3	4.0

Other = PON and NCL in the M.O.S.A.I.C.S. system, as well as AON and DIR in
        the Bellack system.
P/N = (Positive total) / (Negative total) = (POS + ADM + RPT) / (QAL + NAD + NEG)

Many of these differences appear to be a function of group size alone. The groups studied differ in so many respects that no generalizations are possible from comparisons in this study. This type of analysis, however, appears to be a potentially fruitful way of generating research hypotheses relating to both areas.

•5•

Summary

This study developed from an awareness of the vagueness and uncertainties surrounding instructional supervision. These uncertainties conflict sharply with the importance that many teacher educators have ascribed to the supervisory process. Numerous writers have theorized about supervision; others have proposed methodologies, guidelines, and techniques for use by supervisors; and still others have decried the lack of systematic research on supervision and teacher education. Yet the fact remains that the supervision of teachers is rarely observed and almost never studied, and consequently the nature of the supervisory process as it is actually carried out is virtually unknown.

Some research in this area has been performed, but most studies have been unsystematic, globally evaluative or prescriptive, and unrelated or unrelatable to other studies. Very little research has actually focused on the supervisory process itself. Consequently, scholars who are attempting to develop theories of supervision have been forced to rely on information from related fields, since the "natural history" basis for theory development in instructional supervision does not exist at present.

One of the major problems facing supervisory research is the lack of valid, reliable, and practical research instruments. Research that investigates the implementation of theoretical approaches to supervision has been unable to document the extent of theory implementation or the nature of the changes that occur over a period of time with different supervisors and supervisees; research investigating specific supervisory techniques has been unable to specify the ways in which these techniques are actually used or the effects of interaction between supervisor, technique, and supervisee; and status studies of supervisory

134

practices have had to resort to subjective ratings and participant recall which are both unreliable and ungeneralizable to other situations.

Because of the diversity and uncertainties in most types of supervision, this study focuses on a particular type of supervision that is operationally defined, well-exemplified in practice, and considered by many educators to meet the criterion of "best existing practice." Clinical supervision as practiced at the Harvard-Newton Summer School may be defined as the improvement of instruction through systematic and continuing cycles of planning, observation, and intensive intellectual analysis and evaluation.

A comprehensive observational instrument was developed that focuses specifically on the objectives and practices of clinical supervision. This instrument is called M.O.S.A.I.C.S.: *M*ultidimensional *O*bservational *S*ystem for the *A*nalysis of *I*nteractions in *C*linical Supervision. Although developed primarily for the study of group supervision of student teachers, it is applicable to both individual and group supervision of teachers of diverse experience, subject areas, grade levels, and teaching situations.

M.O.S.A.I.C.S. is based on several fundamental assumptions. Clinical supervision is assumed to be essentially a teaching process carried out primarily through verbal interaction between supervisor and supervisee. The "content" focus of clinical supervision is the instructional process itself: the interaction between teacher, pupils, and subject matter or curriculum. The "methodology" of clinical supervision is primarily the intellectual analysis and evaluation of the instructional process as well as the diagnosis and prescription of teaching content and methodology.

M.O.S.A.I.C.S. uses Arno Bellack's instrument for research on teaching as a basic framework. This instrument was chosen for many reasons. First of all, it is comprehensive and multidimensional and has proven to be of significant value in analyzing the instructional process. Furthermore, it is system-oriented, focusing on spontaneous aspects of instruction that occur irrespective of the persons involved and that are generated by the functioning of the process itself. It focuses on the different but complementary roles of each participant in the interaction, and it permits the analysis of patterns of interaction that appear to be as germane to instructional supervision as they are to instruction itself.

M.O.S.A.I.C.S. retains Bellack's "pedagogical moves" or fundamental units of communication and also his "teaching cycles" or basic patterns of these moves. The basic structure of M.O.S.A.I.C.S. parallels Bellack's structure with separate category groups for speakers, pedagogical moves, substantive areas or content foci, substantive-logical meanings or logical treatments of content, procedural areas relating to conference management, and procedural-logical meanings that analyze logical and rating treatments of the procedural areas. Many of the categories in these dimensions of meaning have been altered to make the system more pertinent to supervision, and several changes have been made to make the system easier to use.

Data reduction and analysis within and among category groups are facilitated by dimensional breakdowns in several areas. Substantive areas dealing with the analysis of instruction are arranged in a three-dimensional mosaic according to instructional generality (specific and general), focus (objectives and content, methods and materials, and executions), and domain (cognitive, affective, and social-disciplinary). Substantive-logical meanings also permit a mosaic analysis according to complex-simple, analytic-evaluative, and diagnostic-prescriptive dimensions. The system contains twenty-one teaching cycle patterns, five ratios facilitating data reduction, and one index permitting the direct comparison of roles for different supervisory participants. The substitution of "thought units" for Bellack's "4½-inch line of elite typescript" permits direct analysis from tape recordings, avoiding the expensive and time-consuming process of producing typescripts. Computer analysis provides fast, error-free data tabulation.

M.O.S.A.I.C.S. was tested and revised many times in the analysis of individual and group supervisory conferences as problems of reliability, practicality, and inclusiveness became evident. It was tested in its final form in a longitudinal study of five supervisory groups in the science department of the Harvard-Newton Summer School. Ten-minute samples from eight planning and eight analysis conferences were analyzed for each supervisory group over the summer. Tests of intra-rater reliability with M.O.S.A.I.C.S. were comparable to similar tests of inter-rater reliability with Bellack's instrument.

This study was designed to demonstrate the use of M.O.S.A.I.C.S. categories and to make these categories, dimensions, and ratios more meaningful through interpretation in a real supervisory situation. It was also designed to demonstrate the potentialities of this system for three different research functions: research on the processes of clinical supervision as a functioning enterprise, clinical research on the interactions over a period of time within individual supervisory groups, and research comparing interactions in clinical supervision with interactions in large group instruction.

Although designed primarily to demonstrate the use and potentialities of the research instrument, this study is one of the most comprehensive ever made of the process of instructional supervision. The time sampled per group represents a substantial portion of the total time spent in supervision; the sample is uniformly distributed in time over the period of supervision; and planning and analysis conferences are sampled with equal frequency. Since the literature contains no reports of longitudinal studies, studies of different types of supervisory conferences, or detailed descriptive studies of group supervision in different grade levels, most of the important data summaries are presented and briefly discussed in the book. The data summaries will permit other investigators to extend the analysis and make use of the study in related research.

Clinical supervision as practiced in the science department of the Harvard-Newton Summer School compares closely with the recommendations and descriptions found in the literature. All interns participate actively in the discussions whether they are functioning as teachers or as observers of the class being supervised. Although the total activity for each type of participant is approximately the same, supervisors speak almost twice as much as individual teachers and four times as much as individual observers.

Discussions in clinical supervision tend to proceed at a rapid rate. Three-quarters of the discourse consists of structuring and reacting moves as the participants propose and react to observations, hypotheses, opinions, and suggestions. The supervisor commonly assumes an initiatory role in the conference with high percentages for structuring, soliciting, and summarizing moves. Teachers tend to assume a reflexive role, asking few questions but answering many. Observers have a relatively neutral role with comparable activity for all major types of pedagogical moves.

Planning conferences contain frequent solicitations and responses and tend to be somewhat more directive than analysis. Supervisors and teachers predominate in planning and take major responsibility for the decision-making process for future classes. Analysis conferences are characterized by frequent structuring and reacting moves as participants discuss their observations of the preceding class. Observers become more active in these analysis conferences, particularly in the structuring and reacting moves. Discussion generally becomes freer and more reactive toward the end of the summer, and teachers tend to take over initiative from observers in the later conferences.

Two-thirds of all discourse falls into three teaching cycle patterns: STR–REA–REA . . . , SOL–RES–REA–REA . . . , and STR–SOL–RES–REA–REA . . . . In general, cycles that contain multiple reactions, indicating an open give-and-take in discussion, are very common in clinical supervision. Distributions among teaching cycles reflect the differences evident in pedagogical moves and help to illuminate the interpersonal dynamics that are evident in these moves.

The substantive areas reveal that over 93% of the conference time involves the analysis of instruction, and almost 100% focuses on instruction, supervision, or the subject matter involved in teaching. Clinical supervision thus tends to be very intense, with little time spent in related or nonpertinent areas of discussion. Instructional analysis is primarily clinical, with only about 7% of conference time being devoted to general topics or the "curriculum and methods course" component of supervision.

Instructional foci are evenly divided between methods and materials (37.3%) and instructional interactions (35.9%), while objectives and content receive only 20% of the stress. Objectives do not generate much extended discussion in these groups, and methodology is less emphasized than it appears to be in much instructional supervision. The stress on the analysis of instructional interactions is a distinguishing characteristic of clinical supervision, particularly in analysis conferences. Planning conferences concentrate mainly on objectives and methodology. Over the course of the summer, discussions of methodology tend to become more common, while instructional interactions decrease in emphasis.

Over two-thirds of the discussions in clinical supervision concentrate on the cognitive domain. The affective and social-disciplinary domains are somewhat neglected, each accounting for only about 14% of the discourse. Planning conferences tend to be overwhelmingly cognitive, while analysis conferences show twice as much activity in the social-disciplinary domain and four times as much activity in the affective domain. It appears that analysis is much more responsive to actual problems of classroom motivation and control than is planning. Late conferences show an increase in the affective domain and a corresponding decrease in the social-disciplinary domain, while the cognitive domain remains relatively unchanged.

The substantive-logical meanings reveal that clinical supervision is unmistakably complex, analytical, and diagnostic. In most cases the totals for simple, evaluative, and prescriptive categories are small. Planning tends to be relatively prescriptive, whereas analysis conferences contain a higher percentage of complex and evaluative categories. Over the course of the summer supervisory discourse becomes less evaluative, less prescriptive, and less complex.

Analysis reveals that the various content foci are treated differently in clinical supervision. Objectives are discussed in a diagnostic and simple manner, while methodology receives a more complex and prescriptive treatment. Both objectives and methods tend to be discussed primarily in terms of cognitive factors. Classroom interactions, on the other hand, generate complex analytic discussions in which considerably more emphasis is placed on the affective and social-disciplinary domains. In other words, objectives and methods receive an academic and cognitive emphasis, and this is not in accord with the complex analysis of motivational and control problems upon which these objectives and methods should be based. This lack of correspondence between objectives, methods, and execution is disturbing and indicates a need for considerable further research.

The procedural areas account for approximately 15% of the total units in supervision. Almost half of these units are ratings of previous statements. These ratings are primarily positive and extremes are rare for both positive and negative ratings. Ratings tend to be more frequent and more negative in analysis and in late conferences.

In general, clinical supervision in the science department of the Harvard-Newton Summer School is definitely not a one-sided affair in which the supervisor transmits information and advice to novice teachers. Rather it is an intense intellectual analysis and evaluation of complex instructional issues in which all participants are actively engaged. Both the dynamics and the effects of clinical supervision appear to warrant extensive further study.

Considerable variation is evident among the five supervisory groups in this study. For example, the elementary group (group 2) and the high school group (group 4) are strikingly dissimilar on most of the basic measures of M.O.S.A.I.C.S. The overall distributions of pedagogical moves in these two groups are similar, but the roles of individual participants are very different. Compared with the elementary supervisor, the high school supervisor speaks more than twice as much and produces almost three times as many structuring moves, reactions, and summary reactions. Teachers and observers in the elementary group both make significantly greater contributions to the discussion.

Differences are also evident in the other dimensions of meaning. The high school group spends 53.9% of the time on methodology and only 19.5% on classroom interactions. The elementary group spends only 27.7% on methodology and 55.5% on classroom interactions. The high school group places the following emphases on the instructional domains: cognitive domain, 73.1%; affective domain, 2.9%; social-disciplinary domain, 12.8%. The elementary group shows a very different distribution of emphasis: cognitive domain, 54.5%; affective domain, 12.0%; social-disciplinary domain, 28.2%. Discussion of the subject matter *per se* is a significant part of the discourse in the high school group but a minor part in the elementary group.

In the logical areas, discussion in the elementary group is relatively analytical, diagnostic, and complex, whereas discussion in the high school group is relatively evaluative, prescriptive, and simple. Rating reactions in the high school group are both more common and more positive than those in the elementary group.

The reasons for these differences are undoubtedly complex and are probably based on such factors as individual personalities, curriculum differences, and pupil ages. These two supervisors appear to be using very distinct supervisory styles, which are too complex to be subsumed under such simple rubrics as "nondirective vs. directive" or "child-centered vs. subject-centered." It is important to note that M.O.S.A.I.C.S. is able to detect striking differences in many different dimensions and that these differences may be interpreted in meaningful ways and partially explained on the basis of the situation and the individuals involved. The potentialities of such clinical analyses for future research appear to be significant.

Comparisons between the supervisory groups and Bellack's teaching groups also reveal striking differences. These differences may be more a function of group size and composition than of group function. Although there are many fewer supervisees in each group than there are pupils in Bellack's groups, these supervisees speak over 60% of all the units spoken while the pupils speak only 27% of the teaching lines. Discourse in teaching groups is evenly divided between soliciting-responding and structuring-reacting, while in the supervisory groups three-quarters of all moves are in the structuring and reacting categories.

Pedagogical roles are much more sharply defined in the teaching groups than in supervision. Teachers in Bellack's groups clearly dominate the structuring, soliciting, reacting, and summarizing moves, while pupils are active primarily in the responding move. In supervision, the supervisees dominate the structuring and reacting moves as well as the responding move. When the distribution of pedagogical moves for each participant is examined, it is seen that these relationships still hold for teaching groups. In supervisory groups, however, all participants are remarkably similar in the distribution of their pedagogical moves. Only for solicitations and responses is there any major difference, and this difference is not large. Although individual supervisees are less active than supervisors, they tend to participate in much the same way except that they solicit less and respond more.

Teaching cycles also show strong differences between teaching and supervision. Teachers initiate over 84% of all cycles in Bellack's teaching groups while supervisors initiate 44%. SOL ... cycles account for almost 80% of all cycles in teaching groups and STR ... cycles account for only 2%; in supervision, SOL ... cycles account for 52% and STR ... cycles are a significant aspect of the discourse at

34%. In general, teaching consists primarily of relatively structured SOL ... and STR–SOL ... cycles while supervision consists primarily of cycles generating multiple reactions among participants.

Discussion in teaching groups is more analytical and somewhat more complex than discussions in supervisory groups, but less time is spent on the substantive areas in teaching. Rating reactions tend to be similar in both groups, with positive ratings the norm and extreme ratings rare in both cases.

In general, M.O.S.A.I.C.S. appears to be a significantly useful instrument for research on supervision. The number of subjects involved in this study is not great, and the data analysis presented in this book is far from exhaustive, but the potentialities inherent in this instrument are evident from the discussion in Chapter 4. The data reveal definite consistencies in clinical supervision as well as striking differences according to the type and temporal position of the conferences. The clinical analyses of individual supervisory groups indicate that M.O.S.A.I.C.S. has potential for examining intragroup dynamics that might be useful both for research and for supervisor training. The comparative analysis of supervisory interactions with teaching interactions demonstrates that such studies might help to illuminate the functioning of these related enterprises.

As with any research instrument, M.O.S.A.I.C.S. has both advantages and shortcomings. It produces an enormous amount of data for even short periods of interaction, but the very volume of this data makes interpretation and summarization difficult. The dimensions and ratios facilitate data reduction, but they add still other factors to be considered in analysis. Research on instructional supervision, however, is in such a nebulous state that this volume of data is a virtual necessity, chiefly for the generation of questions and hypotheses for future research of a more specific nature.

M.O.S.A.I.C.S. provides a comprehensive and multidimensional analysis of pedagogical, substantive, and logical factors in supervision. Computer analysis permits the study of interrelationships between and among these dimensions of meaning, thus increasing the potentialities of the instrument for investigating the "fine structure" of these complex interactions. This focus, however, essentially neglects the affective or social-emotional aspects of supervision which might in the last analysis be the most crucial factors. While it would be possible to add other dimensions to M.O.S.A.I.C.S. to include these areas, a more reasonable approach would probably be to use different instruments specifically designed for this purpose. The instrument developed in this study must be considered one that is limited to research on certain specific aspects of supervision. Research that is truly comprehensive must consider the use of different instruments, each designed for the purpose to which it is best suited.

M.O.S.A.I.C.S. focuses entirely on verbal interaction, excluding nonverbal factors in supervision. These factors would include the examination of audio, video, and written feedback; the demonstration and modeling of teaching techniques; the production of teaching materials; and the subtle, often unconscious gestures, expressions, and nuances that are important in the communication of substantive and interpersonal meanings. This instrument also focuses on formal supervision as carried out in structured conference settings. Much actual supervision is carried out informally, and the supervisor's major impact on the supervisee may frequently occur in such unstructured settings. Although M.O.S.A.I.C.S. could be used in nonconference settings, it is probable that quite different research techniques, such as participant observer techniques, would be better suited to such a research focus.

M.O.S.A.I.C.S. does not require the use of typescripts, and in this respect it is easier to use and less expensive than similar research systems. It is nevertheless a difficult system to use. It contains a large number of categories that must be memorized, and the distinctions between these categories are often difficult to remember during coding. The multiple-analysis system reduces this problem somewhat by permitting coding in small discrete steps as the tape recording is replayed for different dimensions of meaning. The fact remains that this is not an easy system to learn or to use reliably. Even with a very experienced coder the coding time is approximately ten times the duration of the actual conference being analyzed.

In conclusion, M.O.S.A.I.C.S. appears to be a potentially useful and comprehensive research instrument, moderately practical and efficient in terms of the amount and type of data produced. It must be considered only one step in the attempt to understand the complexities of instructional supervision. It is, however, a step. Instructional supervision has been too long neglected as a focus for research, and instruments such as this appear to hold considerable promise in this important educational field.

Outline of Blumberg's System (Supervision)

Unit: 3-second time interval
Type: Verbal behavior, by direct observation, single scoring
Categories:
I. Supervisor Behavior
   1. Support-inducing communications behavior: makes statements that help build a "healthy" climate, release tension, accept feelings.
   2. Praises: makes statements that connote "good" value judgments.
   3. Accepts or uses teacher's ideas: makes statements that clarify, build on, or develop ideas or suggestions made by the teacher.
   4. Asks for information: asks factually oriented questions.
   5. Gives information: makes factually oriented statements or responses.
   6. Asks for opinions: asks the teacher to analyze or evaluate something.
   7. Asks for suggestions: asks for new or alternate ways of doing things.
   8. Gives opinions: gives his own analysis or evaluation.
   9. Gives suggestions: gives new or alternate ways of doing things.
   10. Criticizes: expresses negative value judgments about the teacher.

II. Teacher Behavior
   11. Asks for information, opinions, or suggestions.
   12. Gives information, opinions, or suggestions.
   13. Positive social emotional behavior: makes statements that convey agreement by choice, release tension, accept feelings.
   14. Negative social emotional behavior: makes statements that tend to disrupt the relationship, produce tension, or convey defensiveness.
   15. Silence or confusion.

Outline of Flander's System (Teaching)

Unit: 3-second time interval
Type: Verbal behavior, by direct observation, single scoring
Categories:
I. Teacher Talk
  A. Indirect Influence
    1. Accepts feeling: accepts or clarifies student's feeling tone.
    2. Praises or encourages student action or behavior.
    3. Accepts or uses ideas of students: clarifies, builds, or develops student ideas.
    4. Asks questions re content or procedure with intent of student answer.
  B. Direct Influence
    5. Lectures: gives facts or opinions about content or procedures.
    6. Gives directions: gives directions, commands, or orders expecting compliance.
    7. Criticizes or justifies authority: bawls out, refers to self.

II. Student Talk
    8. Student talk-response: student response to teacher initiation or solicitation.
    9. Student talk-initiation: student self-initiated talk.
    10. Silence or confusion.

Outline of Brown-Hoffman System (Supervision)

Unit: Utterance, or uninterrupted verbal behavior of a participant
   Thought Unit, or expression of one complete idea
Type: Verbal behavior, from typescripts, multiple scoring
Categories:
A. Problem-Solving Domain
   1. Comprehending Processes
      a. Identifying procedures: verbalization of problems for discussion.
      b. Defining procedures: clarification of problems through data-gathering techniques.
   2. Analyzing Processes
      a. Interpreting-evaluating procedures: gaining of insight into problems by diagnosing and assessing performance in terms of stated objectives.
      b. Hypothesizing procedures: postulation of action based on relationships among causal factors.
B. Affective Domain
   a. Catharsis procedures: "talking-out" of emotions, motivations, feelings, and thoughts.
   b. Rapport-building procedures: supportive statements.
   c. Social amenities procedures: polite formalities.
C. Structuring Domain
   1. Routine processes
      a. Administrative procedures: development of policy concerning role expectations.
      b. Summary procedures: recapitulations and terminations.
   2. Directing processes
      a. Leading procedures: attempts to persuade or encourage.
      b. Controlling procedures: attempts to direct and regulate.
D. Noncodable

Outline of Heidelbach's System (Supervision)

Unit: Larger Unit, or uninterrupted talk by a participant
Smaller Unit, or one operational category and one or more substantive areas
Type: Verbal behavior, from typescripts, multiple scoring
Categories:
A. Operational Verbal Behavior
  1. Focusing operations: referring or asking
  2. Descriptive operations: clarifying, describing, summarizing, agreeing, disagreeing, restating, or reacting
  3. Prescriptive operations: thinking or guessing the nature of a teaching behavior, considering a proposal, making a proposal, anticipating or hypothesizing, or generalizing
B. Substantive Verbal Behavior
  1. Student teacher teaching behavior
  2. Cooperating teacher teaching behavior
  3. Generalized teaching behavior
  4. Characteristics of children
  5. Content
  6. Instructional materials
  7. The conference
  8. The lesson
  9. The student teaching experience
  10. Special teachers
  11. The curriculum
  12. Parents and family
  13. Administrative/supervisory behavior
  14. Other teachers' behavior
  15. School nurse
  16. Plan of teaching
  17. Community agencies
  18. School monitor
  19. Professional sequence
  20. Routines

Outline of Bellack's System (Teaching)

Unit: Pedagogical Move, or uninterrupted talk by a participant
Lines, or number of lines of 4½-inch elite type contained in a
pedagogical move
Type: Verbal behavior, from typescripts, multiple scoring
Categories:
    I. Speaker
        T: Teacher
        P: Pupil
        A: Audio-visual device
    II. Pedagogical Move
        STR: Structuring, setting context for subsequent behavior
            by launching or halting-excluding interaction, focus-
            ing attention
        SOL: Soliciting, eliciting a verbal response, physical re-
            sponse, or attention; includes questions, commands,
            imperatives, requests
        RES: Responding, fulfilling the expectation of a solicita-
            tion, answers
        REA: Reacting, a move occasioned by another move but
            not directly elicited; may clarify, synthesize, or ex-
            pand a previous move; rating moves
        REA: Summary reaction, reaction occasioned by more than
            one previous move; a genuine summary or review
        NON: Noncodable reaction, missed statements, etc.
    III. Substantive Meaning
        Specific concepts derived from the subject matter of inter-
        national trade, such as trade barriers, etc.

IV. Substantive-Logical Meaning

    Analytic Process

        DEF: Defining, connotative or denotative

        INT: Interpreting, rephrasing

    Empirical Process

        FAC: Fact stating, reporting, an account, description, statement

        XPL: Explaining, giving effects, reasons, or relationships

    Evaluative Process

        OPN: Opinions of what should or ought to be done, or estimations of worth, value, importance, etc.

        JUS: Justification, reasons, justification, support or criticism of opinions

V. Number of lines of 4½-inch typescript contained in substantive portion of move

VI. Instructional Meaning

        ASG: Assignment, suggested or required activities

        MAT: Materials, teaching aids and instructional devices

        PER: Person, reference to person or personal experiences

        PRC: Procedure, plan of activities or course of action

        STA: Statement, reference to meaning, truth, etc., of verbal utterance

        LOG: Logical process, reference to function of language or logic

        ACT: Action, generalized action

        ACV: Action, verbal

        ACC: Action, cognitive

        ACP: Action, physical

        ACE: Action, emotional

        LAM: Language mechanics, rules of grammar and usage

VII. Instructional-Logical Meanings

    Logical process (same as in IV above)

        DEF: Defining

        INT: Interpretation

        FAC: Fact stating

        XPL: Explanation

        OPN: Opining

        JUS: Justifying

    Rating Process

        POS: Distinctly positive rating of statement

        ADM: Admitting statement to be true

        RPT: Repeat of statement

QAL: Qualified admission of a statement

NAD: Not admitting a statement to be true

NEG: Rejection of statement

AON: Solicitation of admitting/not-admitting reaction

PON: Solicitation of positive or negative answer

Extra-logical Process

PRF: Performing, physical action

DIR: Directing

NCL: Not clear

VIII. Number of lines of 4½-inch typescript contained in instructional portion of move

Teaching cycles

1. STR
2. STR SOL
3. STR REA
4. STR REA REA ...
5. STR SOL RES
6. STR SOL RES RES ...
7. STR SOL REA
8. STR SOL REA REA ...
9. STR SOL RES REA
10. STR SOL RES REA REA ...
11. STR SOL RES REA RES ...
12. STR SOL RES REA RES REA ...
13. SOL
14. SOL RES
15. SOL RES RES ...
16. SOL REA
17. SOL REA REA ...
18. SOL RES REA
19. SOL RES REA REA ...
20. SOL RES REA RES ...
21. SOL RES REA RES ... REA ...

Outline of the Multidimensional Observational System for the Analysis of Interactions in Clinical Supervision (M.O.S.A.I.C.S.)

Unit: Pedagogical Move, or uninterrupted talk by a participant
Unit, or complete thought unit as defined by Bales
Type: Verbal behavior, from tape recordings, multiple scoring
Categories:

  I. Speaker

        S: Supervisor

        T: Teacher who taught specific class being supervised

        O: Observer also interacting in the supervision

  II. Pedagogical Move

        STR: Structuring, launching or halting move that directs the flow of discourse

        SOL: Soliciting, asking for a physical or verbal response

        RES: Responding, answering or fulfilling the expectation of a solicitation

        REA: Reacting, amplifying, qualifying, or otherwise making an unsolicited reaction to a previous move

        RSM: Summary reaction, reaction to more than one move or a genuine summary or review

  III. Substantive Areas (Content Analysis)

    A. Instructional

      1. Generality

          S: Specific, pertinent to the specific class being discussed, the "clinical" aspect of supervision

          G: General, pertinent to theory, generalizations, past experience, the "methods course" aspect of supervision

2. Focus

    O: Objectives and content to be taught

    M: Methods and materials of instruction, relatively strategic and planned aspects of implementation of objectives

    X: Execution, critical incidents, tactical and unexpected interactions

3. Domain

    C: Cognitive, pertaining to knowledge, learning, information, understanding

    A: Affective, pertaining to affective interactions between pupil and subject, such as interest, motivation, attention

    D: Disciplinary and social interactions between teacher-pupil and pupil-pupil

B. Related

    SBJ: Subject being taught, if discussed in terms of the understanding of conference participants

    SPR: Supervision and teacher-training

    GRL: General topics related to education

    GNR: General topics not related to education

IV. Substantive-Logical Meanings (Logical Analysis)

A. Processes Relating to the Proposed Use of Language

    DEF: Defining, definitions and verbal equivalents

    INT: Interpretations and rephrasings

B. Diagnostic Processes

    FAC: Fact stating, accounts, descriptions, or reports

    XPL: Explanations, reasons, or relationships

    EVL: Evaluations

    JUS: Justifications, reasons for evaluations

C. Prescriptive Processes

    SUG: Suggestions, alternatives, and possible actions

    SGX: Explanations, reasons, and relationships for suggestions

    OPN: Opinions, directives or what should or ought to be done

    OPJ: Justifications for opinions, reasons, support, and criticisms

V. Number of Thought Units Contained in Substantive-Logical Area

VI. Procedural Areas

    STA: Statement, reference to a particular statement, usually with respect to its truth, validity, or propriety

      PRC: Procedures, management, assignments, and materials relating to the supervisory conference

      ACT: Action, references to verbal, cognitive, physical, or emotional actions

      PER: Personal interaction and small talk

VII. Procedural-Logical Meanings

  A. Processes Related to the Proposed Use of Language

      DEF: Defining

      INT: Interpreting

  B. Diagnostic Processes

      FAC: Fact stating

      XPL: Explanations

      EVL: Evaluations

      JUS: Justifications

  C. Prescriptive Processes

      SUG: Suggestions

      SGX: Explanations of suggestions

      OPN: Opinions

      OPJ: Justifications for opinions

  D. Rating Processes

      POS: Positive, distinctly positive or affirmative rating

      ADM: Admitting, mildly accepting or equivocally positive rating

      RPT: Repeating, implicit positive rating by a repeat or rephrasing of a previous move

      QAL: Qualifying, a reservation, however mild

      NAD: Not admitting, rejection by a statement of the contrary

      NEG: Negative, distinctly negative rating

  E. Extra-Logical Processes

      PON: Positive or negative, solicitations or responses of either a yes-or-no answer or a positive or negative response

      PRF: Performance, solicitations for action

      NCL: Not clear

VIII. Number of Thought Units Contained in Procedural Area

IX. Teaching Cycles

    1. STR

    2. STR SOL

    3. STR REA

    4. STR REA REA ...

    5. STR SOL RES

    6. STR SOL RES RES ...
    7. STR SOL REA
    8. STR SOL REA REA ...
    9. STR SOL RES REA
    10. STR SOL RES REA REA ...
    11. STR SOL RES REA RES ...
    12. STR SOL RES REA RES REA ...
    13. SOL
    14. SOL RES
    15. SOL RES RES ...
    16. SOL REA
    17. SOL REA REA ...
    18. SOL RES REA
    19. SOL RES REA REA ...
    20. SOL RES REA RES ...
    21. SOL RES REA RES ... REA ...

X. Critical Ratios
  A. Initiatory/Reflexive Ratio:
    $I/R = (STR + SOL) / (RES + REA + RSM)$
  B. Participation Index:
    $P.I. = (\%$ moves by participant$)$
                  $/ (\%$ membership of participant$)$
  C. Analytic/Evaluative Ratio:
    $A/E = (FAC + XPL + SUG + SGX)$
               $/ (EVL + JUS + OPN + OPJ)$
  D. Diagnostic/Prescriptive Ratio:
    $D/P = (FAC + XPL + EVL + JUS)$
               $/ (SUG + SGX + OPN + OPJ)$
  E. Complex/ Simple Ratio:
    $C/S = (XPL + JUS + SGX + OPJ)$
               $/ (FAC + EVL + SUG + OPN)$
  F. Positive/Negative Ratio:
    $P/N = (POS + ADM + RPT) / (QAL + NAD + NEG)$

Detailed Coding Instructions* for
Use with M.O.S.A.I.C.S.

1. General Coding Instructions

1.1. Coding is from the viewpoint of the observer, with pedagogical meaning inferred from the speaker's verbal behavior.

1.2. Grammatical form may give a clue, but it is not decisive in coding. For example, SOL may be found in declarative, interrogative, or imperative form. Likewise, RES may be in the form of a question, indicating a tentative answer on the part of the speaker.

1.3. Coding is done in the general context of the discussion. When two people are speaking at once, or when a person makes an interruption that is not acted upon (the interrupted party continues speaking on the original topic), the interruption is not counted and coding continues in the basic context.

1.4. When one individual is making an extended pedagogical move that is periodically encouraged by grunts and statements such as "uh-huh" and "go on," without actually changing his discourse or pausing for longer than two seconds, these interruptions are not counted as separate pedagogical moves.

1.5. Individual thought units are scored according to the basic rules devised by Bales: simple sentences are scored as one unit; compound sentences joined by "and," "but," etc., are broken down into their component simple parts, each of which is separately scored; one thought unit is scored for each additional predicate when a series of predicates follow a single subject.

° Adapted from the coding instructions for use with the Bellack instrument.

1.6. Complex sentences ordinarily involve more than one score, particularly if the subordinate clause is an adverbial clause. This is especially true when such clauses appear in sentences containing "when . . . then," "if . . . then," and "because." Noun clauses are generally not scored, especially when the clause is used as the subject or the direct object of a sentence. Adjective clauses are not scored unless the speaker's voice places unusual stress on the clause.

1.7. In general, grammatical form may give a clue, but it is not decisive in coding. The above rules serve only as guidelines. Vocal inflections and the general context of discussion will often indicate a thought unit for sentence fragments, phrases, subordinate clauses, and even single words.

2. Pedagogical Moves

2.1. STR moves form an implicit directive by launching discussion in specific directions and focusing on topics or procedures. The function of STR is either launching or halting-excluding, generally by the method of announcing or stating propositions. When a choice must be made between STR and REA, code STR for statements that move the discourse forward or bring it back on the track after a digression. For example, a new SUG or OPN is almost invariably found in a structuring move.

2.2. In general, internal or parenthetical shifts of topic or emphasis are not separately coded unless they constitute a relatively permanent change in the discourse. The discourse is coded in the overall context.

2.3. Solicitations that give someone permission to speak are coded as procedural moves: ACT/PRF. These are not separately coded in the context of a larger solicitation.

2.4. Checking statements (e.g., "Follow me?") are not coded as SOL within the context of another move unless some cue indicating a desired RES is present.

2.5. Implicit in any SOL is the concept of knowing or not knowing. Therefore, code RES for any of the range of possible responses, including invalid ones and those indicating knowing or not knowing alone (e.g., "I don't know").

2.6. A SOL that calls for a fact is coded FAC, but if the RES gives both a fact and an explanation, the response is coded RES/XPL. In the same way, complex responses to solicitations of EVL, SUG, and OPN are coded as JUS, SGX, and OPJ.

2.7. A speaker cannot respond to his own solicitation. An immediate answer of his own question indicates that it was a rhetorical question, which is not coded SOL in the first place. If a speaker answers his own question after an intervening incorrect answer, his correction is coded as a reaction to the incorrect answer. If the speaker answers his own question after a pause, the answer is coded as a reaction to the absence of an expected response.

2.8. When a reaction to a previous move is followed by a genuine summary reaction (RSM), both moves are scored for the same speaker.

2.9. RSM frequently occurs when a unit of discussion is concluded by a speaker, who then turns to a new topic. The coder must determine when RSM ends and STR begins.

2.10. A reaction to a solicitation occurs only when the reaction is about the solicitation and not a response to the SOL.

2.11. A reaction may follow the absence of other reactions to a move such as STR. For example, a speaker may make a proposal and then react to the absence of any positive reactions from the other participants.

3. Teaching Cycles

3.1. All solicitations that only give another speaker permission to speak are ignored for the purposes of coding teaching cycles.

3.2. When a teaching cycle is resumed after an intervening cycle (such as an interpretation cycle: SOL/INT followed by RES/INT), the resumption is coded as part of the original cycle.

4. Substantive Areas

4.1. Coding of Substantive Areas is in terms of the main context of discussion. However, in nondirective discussions shifts of substantive area are common. In order to code these shifts, which are an important aspect of supervision, the following rules are observed:

4.2. Code Instructional Areas in preference to Related Areas if a conflict arises. For example, if it is difficult to determine whether discussion of subject content (e.g., biology) is in the context of content objectives for the pupils (SOC) or in the context of the understanding of the content by the conference participants (SBJ), code SOC in preference to SBJ.

4.3. Code Instructional Domain (Cognitive, Affective, or Disciplinary-social) first. This is the most general of the content dimensions, it tends to persist longest in the discourse, and it is the most difficult to code out of context. If a conflict arises in coding, code Cognitive in preference to Affective and Affective in preference to Disciplinary-social.

4.4. Code Instructional Focus (Objectives and content, Methods and materials, or eXecution) second. Significant shifts in these areas occur more frequently than changes in Instructional Domain. If a conflict arises in coding, code Objectives in preference to Methods and Methods in preference to eXecution.

4.5. Code Instructional Generality (Specific or General) last. Moves commonly shift from Specific to General and back again. For a single move, code the area that occupies the most time or emphasis in the move, and code each move separately. If a conflict arises, code Specific in preference to General.

4.6. Indicate the Substantive Area of each move even if it is not explicitly referred to. For example, procedural moves are coded in the Substantive Area of the general or immediately preceding context.

4.7. Examples of content in each Substantive Area:

SOC: Content and skill aims for pupils; short- and long-term goals; Specific and pervasive content objectives; lab skills and content objectives for pupils; predictions with respect to cognitive objectives; specific questions to be asked to pupils.

SMC: Methods and materials for implementation of cognitive goals; strategic plans and intentions, as well as predictions as to their effectiveness; content sequencing and logical flow; teaching patterns, organization, structure, transitions; grouping; homework as method; test construction.

SXC: Classroom interactions re cognition and learning; interactions with individual pupils; tactical, spontaneous, and critical interactions and incidents; abilities and understandings and learning problems of individual pupils, including events outside of class with a bearing on classroom activities or problems.

SOA: Similar to SOC but with respect to motivations, attitudes, and interests of pupils, especially concerning subject matter; motivational content; values; predictions with respect to affective objectives and content.

SMA: Similar to SMC but with respect to affective goals; predictions re motivational methods.

SXA: Similar to SXC but with respect to motivation and interest.

SOD: Disciplinary and social aims; content aimed at securing attention and discipline; Objectives re leadership, authority, courtesy, and group interactions; predictions with respect to control and social objectives.

SMD: Similar to SMC but with respect to methods for control, discipline, authority, and social interactions.

SXD: Similar to SXC but with respect to classroom interactions and incidents based on questions of control, discipline, and social interactions.

GOC, GMC, GXC, GOA, GMA, GXA, GOD, GMD, GXD: Similar to their specific analogues, but extensions to general situations. These include generalizations, discussions of theory and practice from the broad fields of education and related behavioral sciences, incidents from past experience and other situations, etc.

SBJ: Discussions concerning the subject being taught that have as their purpose the understanding of these subjects by the conference participants themselves. This includes specific information, sources of information, etc.

SPR: Topics relating to supervision, teacher training, the student teaching experience, coursework in education, etc.

GRL: Topics relating to schools and schooling but not instruction *per se.* Included might be Parent's Night, P.T.A. meetings, faculty get-togethers, and the like.

GNR: Topics not relating to schools, education, or learning. Included might be the breakdown of one's car, the current political situation, or the latest league standings.

5. Substantive-Logical Meanings

5.1. Only when DEF or INT are the main focus of the discourse are they coded as such. They are not coded when they are in the immediate context of other Substantive-Logical Meanings.

5.2. In a sequence of complex moves (XPL, SGX, OPJ, or JUS), individual simple moves (FAC, SUG, OPN, or EVL) are coded in the context of the complex moves. For example, in a series of explanations, a move stating a fact will generally be coded as XPL since one can consider that the fact is intimately related to the interrelationships among the other explanations. However, when FAC represents a definite shift to a new topic or when it is in response to SOL/FAC, it is coded as FAC.

5.3. Complex moves (XPL, SGX, OPJ, and JUS) always involve relationships between their simple analogues (FAC, SUG, OPN, and EVL) and other factors, such as generalizations, other simple moves, etc. In the analysis of instruction, particularly for objectives and methods, it is often difficult to determine when relationships are actually involved and when the move represents merely an extended description. As a general rule, these substantive-logical meanings are coded as complex whenever relationships are made to pupils or specific teaching situations. In most other situations these moves are extended descriptions and are coded as simple moves.

5.4. When more than one Substantive-Logical process occurs within a single pedagogical move and the overall context or emphasis is unclear, code according to the following order of priority: OPJ:JUS: SGX:XPL:OPN:EVL:SUG:FAC:INT:DEF. In effect, this means that complex is coded in preference to simple, prescriptive in preference to diagnostic, and evaluative in preference to analytical.

6. Procedural Areas

6.1. Occasionally, within longer moves (e.g., a STR or a REA), reference is made to more than one of the procedural categories.

Identify the primary procedural function of the move and code appropriately.

6.2. Brief introductory or parenthetical comments, such as "I think that . . ." or "It seems like . . . ," are not coded separately as procedural areas (e.g., ACT/FAC) unless there is a clear emphasis on them.

6.3. When more than one of the procedural areas is involved or when the main intent of the discourse cannot readily be determined, the following order of preference is used: STA:FAC:ACT:PER.

7. Procedural-Logical Meanings

7.1. Use the following order of precedence in evaluative reactions when more than one Procedural-Logical meaning is involved: QAL:POS: NEG:ADM:NAD:RPT.

7.2. Any indication of reservation with POS, NEG, ADM, or NAD is coded as QAL.

7.3. When a qualifying statement expresses a brief "but" and goes on to give an explanation, fact, or the like, code a minimum of one unit as STA/QAL (e.g., "But they really *were* involved!" T/REA/SXA/ FAC/1/STA/QAL/1).

7.4. A joke is coded by the convention PER/PRF (e.g., "There's a fungus amongus" T/REA/SXC/-/-/PER/PRF/1).

Completely Coded Ten-Minute Protocol of a Supervisory Conference Recorded at the Harvard-Newton Summer School

T: But there's something that . . . when you're having disciplinary trouble with the class/ . . . I didn't sense any dislike./ I'm calling it dislike/ because I'm not exactly sure what else to call it,/ but today and yesterday and maybe even a little bit the day before, if I was able to realize anything,/ I sensed a certain amount of dislike on the part of some of the students.//   T/STR/SXD/FAC/6
T/4/27

O: I sensed it toward myself when I was teaching.//   O/REA/SXD/FAC/1

S: Dislike of you as a person?//   S/SOL/SXD/INT/1
S/14/2

T: Right.//   T/RES/SXD/INT/1

O: I sensed it toward myself./ D . . . pointed it out to me the first week./ I was really in trouble./ They probably thought I was about that big.//   O/REA/SXD/FAC/4

S: But I don't think it's so much dislike./ I think they want to like you.//   S/REA/SXD/XPL/1/STA/QAL/1

160

O: Yes.//

O/REA/SXD/ – /–/STA/ADM/1

S: But they don't respect you./ That is . . . You know, put yourself in their place./ What if you in the classroom behaved the way they did,/ and got away with it?/ What would you think of the person in the classroom?/ Not only in the classroom,/ because that's kind of a false picture too,/ but as a person?//

S/REA/SXD/XPL/8

T: Yeah.//

T/REA/SXD/ – /–/STA/ADM/1

O: It's quite clear that if a teacher lets things go on,/ that your level of respect for him as a person with any sort of respect for himself decreases./ How can he expect the kids to respect him/ if he doesn't respect himself enough to make certain demands?//

O/REA/GXD/XPL/4

S: You asked me a specific question/ and I want to reply to the question./ I don't want to avoid it./ You asked what can you do./ I think, well, it's kind of a slogan/ but I think that the best thing to do is to earn their respect./ Make this classroom the kind of thing that's enjoyable/ and they're happy with/ and that they're satisfied with,/ and they'll respect you for that./ So far I don't believe that's happened./ I think that what's been going on has been pretty much uninteresting;/ and when it has been interesting,/ like with the project,/ we haven't had these difficulties, I don't think./ But when things get uninteresting,/ they begin to kind of wander away./ Okay, if you can't do that,/ then the alternative, which we discussed earlier this year,/ was that

S/STR/SMD/OPJ/23/ACT/FAC/4
S/4/40

in this case you've got to demand their respect,/ by saying "Wayne, I wish you wouldn't do that."/ Not that,/ but "Wayne, I'M NOT GOING TO HAVE THAT GOING ON IN THIS CLASS-ROOM."/ Or to Ricky./ And I feel that if you would say once to Ricky: "Ricky, I want you to sit down/ and I want you to be-have yourself,/ or I don't want you here at all!"//

O: Yeah!//   O/REA/SMD/ – /–/STA/POS/1

S: Then I think Ricky would stop   S/REA/SMD/OPJ/12
being a problem./ But every time
Ricky does something,/ like
when he threw the airplane/ and
hit Wayne/ and Wayne threw
the airplane back/ and hit Ricky/
and Ricky threw the airplane/
and hit Wayne/ and this went
back and forth six times . . ./
and you let it go on . . . / then
why should he stop,/ and why
should he respect you for letting
him do that?//

O: You know the thing that I think   O/STR/SMD/OPJ/20
gets them away from your get-   O/4/33
ting control is that you're very
apologetic about saying "Be
quiet."/ You say "Let's be quiet
for a minute."/ It's as if you were
talking to people who were going
to behave themselves,/ and were
acting up to test you,/ just because they have forgotten themselves temporarily./ It's like these
little reminders,/ like "Do me a
favor/ and be quiet for a second."/ It has that overtone./ It's
kind of . . . using phrases like
"Well, I think we might do this."/
You know: "We're DOING
this!"/ You're very tentative about
"Well, if we do this,/ is that

going to be okay with you?"/
and "If I ask you to be quiet,/
now would you be quiet?"/ See
what I mean?/ I started out
doing that too,/ because I felt
terribly defensive about the
whole thing./ I was afraid that
authority would make the dis-
tance larger rather than smaller./
Surprisingly enough it doesn't!//

S: Yeah./ It sounds funny that this   S/REA/SMD/OPJ/6/STA/ADM/1
would be a disadvantage,/ but I
think you're so sensitive to kids/
and so afraid of hurting their
feelings/ or something like this,/
that you do the very thing that
you don't want to do./ You're not
helping them at all.//

O: Remember when you were a   O/REA/SMD/OPJ/1
ruffian!//
(laughter)

S: Oh, I can't believe that!//   S/REA/SMD/ − /−/PER/PRF/1

O: You see, I was a goody-goody,/   O/REA/SMD/OPJ/3
so this is totally alien,/ but you
know you've survived.//

T: Yeah.//   T/REA/SMD/ − /−/STA/ADM/1

S: Plus, I really think, in terms of   S/SOL/FAC/1
tomorrow's lesson . . . Tomorrow   S/18/3
you're working on chemicals?//

T: I haven't said yet to them.//   T/RES/SOC/ − /−/ACT/FAC/1

S: Well, that's what you said to us   S/REA/SOC/ − /−/ACT/FAC/1
this morning.// Didn't you?//   S/SOL/SOC/ − /−/ACT/FAC/1
                                        S/19/6

T: Yes.//   T/RES/SOC/ − /−/ACT/FAC/1

S: Okay.//   S/REA/SOC/ − /−/STA/ADM/1

T: Yes./ Tentatively I have them   T/REA/SOC/FAC/1/STA/ADM/1
working on chemicals.//

S: All right.//   S/REA/SOC/ − /−/STA/ADM/1

Then what I would do, I think,   S/STR/SOA/OPN/3/PRC/OPJ/2
is try to be more ingenious than   S/3/6
you've ever been in your whole
life/ as to how you could make

that an interesting/ and exciting lesson for them./ Now, I would be more than happy to help in the preparation of all this,/ but I'm convinced that as a mature person with good intelligence, you can think of something.//

T: Yeah.//   T/REA/SOA/ – /–/STA/ADM/1

I have a couple of ideas about   T/STR/SOA/SUG/9
what to do,/ like making it a   T/4/22
kind of game,/ in a sense a
game-problem type of thing./
Like Mr. Q has a very rare
problem . . . / in that he needs
such and such . . . / and work it
through like that./ He needs
something . . . / Present a problem to them/ where you set the
properties up as part of the
problem.//

S: Uh-huh.//   S/REA/SOA/ – /–/STA/ADM/1

T: And let them use their powers/   T/REA/SOA/SUG/5/ACT/FAC/1
to set up a way that they can
discriminate./ I haven't done any
thinking about the way it might
be worked,/ but set up a problem situation whereby they'll
start,/ given enough information
to get them through to the end,/
and pick something up and . . .//

O: Okay,/ but beware of fairytale-   O/REA/SOA/OPJ/3/STA/QAL/1
like gimmicks/ because that
works when you're on firm
ground with the kids/ but they
may take it for ridiculing them.//

T: Well, I was thinking of some-   T/REA/SOA/SUG/2
thing along the lines of the
Atomic Energy Commission./
Start it off that way.//

S: This is still the development of   S/SOL/SOC/FAC/3
a key?/ Is that correct?/ A key   S/18/6
for chemicals?//

T: Yeah./ I think it can be worked   T/RES/SOC/FAC/2
in on that.//

S: Okay.//   S/REA/SOC/ – /–/STA/ADM/1

T: I got the feeling today, as I was talking to the kids,/ that many of them have the basic idea that you ask questions about big things first,/ and questions about smaller things second,/ and still smaller things third.//   T/STR/SXC/FAC/3/ACT/FAC/1
T/4/12

O: Yeah./ They've been together through the Twenty-Questions thing.//   O/REA/SXC/XPL/1/STA/ADM/1

T: Yeah./ I know they have.//   T/REA/SXC/ – /–/STA/ADM/2

S: Well,/ I'm not sure I have that impression,/ but I haven't seen as many kids as you did/ and we'll have something on Monday anyhow that will give us a little more . . . better evidence.//   S/REA/SXC/ – /–/STA/QAL/4

You know, I want to say another thing too that strikes me might be good./ I don't know whether you can do this or not,/ but I think that one thing that might add effectiveness to your teaching would be to become enthusiastic./ Now I know, or I'm suspicious, that you're probably not very enthusiastic about the subject matter anyhow./ It's kind of hard to be enthusiastic about keys./ Nonetheless, I think your kind of low-keyed, nondirective counseling approach is stilting to the classroom,/ and if you'd listen to your tape/ you'll find that your voice level is about the same.//   S/STR/SMA/OPJ/6/ACT/FAC/2
S/4/24

T: About the only thing I've managed to do is bring it down an octave since I've started.//   T/REA/SMA/FAC/1

S: Yeah,/ and I guess maybe I'm thinking of the way I'd teach the class./ I think I'd come bounding in with red chemicals   S/REA/SMA/OPJ/13/STA/ADM/1 in this hand/ and purple in this hand/ and green in my coat pocket,/ so that they wouldn't have any choice but to pay attention to me for a while./ And it's a dramatic-actory-gimmick,/ . . . well, I don't know if the act is a gimmick,/ but certainly if you can generate some enthusiasm,/ you've got some of these problems licked./ The kids just don't give a toot about what's going on./ And maybe the teacher doesn't either,/ but that's neither here nor there./ Your job is to create a toot in them somehow or other.//

T: Yeah.//

O: Also, you could establish classes starting five minutes sooner/ by having something to do with the class that sort of happens/ and they'd say, "Oh! Let's pay attention!"//

T/REA/SMA/ – /–/STA/ADM/1

O/STR/SMA/SUG/3

O/1/3

M.O.S.A.I.C.S Data for Comparisons of Planning vs. Analysis and Early vs. Late Conferences (Tables 25-48)

TABLE 25

Percentage of Moves by Supervisory Groups in Each Pedagogical
Move Category: Planning and Analysis Conferences

Category by Speaker	% Moves by Group: Planning Conferences						% Moves by Group: Analysis Conferences					
	1	2	3	4	5	$\overline{X}$	1	2	3	4	5	$\overline{X}$
SOL: Supvr.	7.1	8.8	15.0	12.0	8.4	10.0	8.2	8.1	12.6	7.2	6.1	8.2
Tchr.	3.9	4.7	3.9	5.7	5.6	4.7	1.2	4.1	3.0	1.8	3.7	2.6
Obs.	5.6	6.1	6.0	2.0	4.8	4.7	5.0	5.3	3.6	3.9	4.9	4.6
Total	16.6	19.6	24.9	19.7	18.8	19.4	14.4	17.5	19.2	12.9	14.7	15.4
RES: Supvr.	3.5	1.8	3.0	4.9	3.6	3.5	2.8	2.9	3.0	2.5	2.0	2.6
Tchr.	4.9	9.2	13.8	9.9	9.9	8.9	3.0	8.4	8.5	6.8	6.1	6.2
Obs.	5.8	6.7	5.8	3.1	2.8	4.8	7.0	4.5	4.4	2.5	5.9	5.0
Total	14.2	17.7	22.6	17.9	16.3	17.2	12.8	15.8	15.9	11.8	14.0	13.8
STR: Supvr.	4.2	3.7	5.5	5.6	5.6	4.9	2.7	2.6	7.4	6.7	3.5	4.3
Tchr.	3.3	5.3	3.9	5.2	5.1	4.5	2.8	4.1	3.6	2.8	4.1	3.4
Obs.	5.3	3.5	2.5	0.5	4.3	3.4	7.6	5.1	4.9	3.5	5.5	5.5
Total	12.8	12.5	11.9	11.3	15.0	12.8	13.1	11.8	15.9	13.0	13.1	13.2
REA: Supvr.	19.3	12.5	13.4	24.7	21.2	18.9	19.9	16.3	13.4	24.4	17.3	18.8
Tchr.	13.3	16.5	13.8	17.7	15.6	15.4	12.3	21.2	18.4	19.8	18.5	17.6
Obs.	21.9	20.4	11.8	7.9	11.2	15.1	26.4	16.7	16.2	17.7	21.8	20.5
Total	54.5	49.4	39.0	50.3	48.0	49.4	58.6	54.2	48.0	61.9	57.6	56.9
RSM: Supvr.	0.8	0.2	0.9	0.8	1.8	0.9	0.1	0.4	0.5	0.5	0.6	0.4
Tchr.	0.2	0.4	0.5	0.0	0.0	0.2	0.5	0.0	0.3	0.0	0.0	0.2
Obs.	0.5	0.2	0.2	0.0	0.0	0.2	0.4	0.2	0.3	0.0	0.0	0.2
Total	1.5	0.8	1.6	0.8	1.8	1.3	1.0	0.6	1.1	0.5	0.6	0.8
Total: Supvr.	34.9	27.0	37.8	48.0	40.6	38.2	33.7	30.3	36.9	41.3	29.5	34.3
Tchr.	25.6	36.1	35.9	38.5	36.2	33.7	19.8	37.8	33.8	31.0	32.4	30.0
Obs.	39.6	36.9	26.3	13.5	23.1	28.2	46.4	31.8	29.4	27.6	38.1	35.8
I/R: Supvr.	0.48	0.86	1.17	0.58	0.53	0.64	0.48	0.55	1.18	0.51	0.48	0.57
Tchr.	0.39	0.38	0.28	0.39	0.42	0.38	0.25	0.28	0.24	0.17	0.32	0.25
Obs.	0.40	0.35	0.48	0.23	0.65	0.40	0.37	0.49	0.41	0.37	0.38	0.39

SOL = Solicitation
RES = Response
STR = Structuring
REA = Reacting
RSM = Summary reaction
I/R = (STR + SOL) / (RES + REA + RSM)

TABLE 26

Percentage of Units by Supervisory Groups in Each Pedagogical
Move Category: Planning and Analysis Conferences

Category by Speaker	% of Units by Group: Planning Conferences						% Units by Group: Analysis Conferences					
	1	*2*	*3*	*4*	*5*	$\overline{X}$	*1*	*2*	*3*	*4*	*5*	$\overline{X}$
SOL: Supvr.	5.1	5.9	6.9	7.4	5.9	6.2	4.7	4.0	6.3	3.7	4.7	4.6
Tchr.	2.4	2.1	1.9	3.5	2.7	2.5	0.8	2.3	0.7	0.9	1.6	1.3
Obs.	3.1	3.8	3.4	1.1	1.6	2.6	2.0	1.9	1.4	2.0	2.1	1.9
Total	10.6	11.8	12.2	12.0	10.2	11.3	7.5	8.2	8.4	6.6	8.4	7.8
RES: Supvr.	2.9	6.2	2.7	6.1	4.1	4.4	2.6	1.9	3.8	2.3	2.2	2.5
Tchr.	7.1	11.3	13.5	10.3	11.1	10.5	3.5	10.5	12.0	6.0	5.3	7.2
Obs.	3.3	7.3	2.7	1.9	2.1	3.4	8.2	3.8	4.3	1.1	3.7	4.4
Total	13.3	24.8	18.9	18.3	17.3	18.3	14.3	16.2	20.1	9.4	11.2	14.1
STR: Supvr.	5.1	5.8	21.7	12.9	19.4	12.4	4.5	4.1	16.2	20.0	14.3	11.4
Tchr.	8.2	7.5	6.5	6.1	11.0	7.9	4.9	10.4	6.6	4.2	9.3	7.1
Obs.	9.2	4.8	5.4	0.6	4.7	5.1	13.9	8.7	10.4	4.8	6.6	9.0
Total	22.5	18.1	33.6	19.6	35.1	25.4	23.3	23.2	33.2	29.0	30.2	27.5
REA: Supvr.	18.1	9.2	12.2	30.3	17.0	17.7	19.7	13.8	9.8	29.3	16.0	17.9
Tchr.	13.5	18.0	13.5	14.0	10.9	14.0	10.6	21.5	13.4	12.8	16.3	14.8
Obs.	17.7	17.6	7.0	5.0	6.9	11.1	23.3	16.4	13.9	12.0	16.6	16.8
Total	49.3	44.8	32.7	49.3	34.8	42.8	53.6	51.7	37.1	54.1	48.9	49.5
RSM: Supvr.	3.2	0.1	1.5	0.8	2.6	1.7	0.1	0.5	0.5	0.9	1.3	0.6
Tchr.	0.1	0.4	0.4	0.0	0.0	0.2	0.8	0.0	0.5	0.0	0.0	0.3
Obs.	0.8	0.1	0.7	0.0	0.0	0.3	0.3	0.3	0.1	0.0	0.0	0.2
Total	4.1	0.6	2.6	0.8	2.6	2.2	1.2	0.8	1.1	0.9	1.3	1.1
Total: Supvr.	34.4	27.2	45.0	57.5	49.0	42.4	31.6	24.3	36.6	56.2	38.5	37.0
Tchr.	31.3	39.3	35.8	33.9	35.7	35.1	20.6	44.7	33.2	23.9	32.5	30.7
Obs.	34.1	33.6	19.2	8.6	15.3	22.5	47.7	31.1	30.1	19.1	29.0	32.3
I/R: Supvr.	0.42	0.72	1.74	0.55	1.07	0.78	0.41	0.50	1.60	0.73	0.97	0.76
Tchr.	0.51	0.32	0.31	0.40	0.62	0.42	0.38	0.40	0.28	0.27	0.50	0.38
Obs.	0.56	0.34	0.85	0.25	0.70	0.52	0.50	0.52	0.65	0.52	0.53	0.51

SOL = Solicitation
RES = Response
STR = Structuring
REA = Reacting
RSM = Summary reaction
I/R = (STR + SOL) / (RES + REA + RSM)

TABLE 27

Percentage of Moves by Supervisory Groups in Each Pedagogical
Move Category: Early and Late Conferences

Category by Speaker	% Moves by Group: Early Conferences						% Moves by Group: Late Conferences					
	1	2	3	4	5	$\bar{X}$	1	2	3	4	5	$\bar{X}$
SOL: Supvr.	5.4	8.7	15.4	10.3	8.8	9.1	9.7	8.2	12.4	9.7	5.9	9.1
Tchr.	3.2	3.6	2.5	3.9	3.4	3.3	2.1	5.1	4.5	4.1	5.3	4.0
Obs.	5.4	8.5	5.5	1.5	3.2	4.9	5.3	3.0	4.3	3.6	6.1	4.5
Total	14.0	20.8	23.4	15.7	15.4	17.3	17.1	16.3	21.2	17.4	17.3	17.6
RES: Supvr.	3.3	2.2	3.0	3.9	2.9	3.1	3.1	2.5	3.0	3.9	2.5	3.1
Tchr.	3.7	8.7	9.9	9.1	5.6	7.0	4.3	9.0	12.9	8.2	9.4	8.1
Obs.	4.9	7.3	5.7	1.7	5.0	4.9	7.7	4.0	4.5	3.5	4.2	5.0
Total	11.9	18.2	18.6	14.7	13.5	15.0	15.1	15.5	20.4	15.6	16.1	16.2
STR: Supvr.	3.3	2.4	5.2	7.9	5.6	4.7	3.7	3.8	7.6	4.9	3.6	4.5
Tchr.	3.6	3.8	5.2	3.5	3.4	3.9	2.6	5.5	2.3	4.6	5.3	4.0
Obs.	6.0	4.5	4.7	1.5	6.6	4.7	7.1	4.2	2.5	2.0	3.8	4.1
Total	12.9	10.7	15.1	12.9	15.6	13.3	13.4	13.5	12.4	11.5	12.7	12.6
REA: Supvr.	20.8	13.0	11.9	27.1	17.5	18.7	18.3	15.8	14.9	22.9	20.0	18.9
Tchr.	14.3	13.8	14.6	19.3	17.2	15.7	11.4	23.6	17.2	18.2	17.2	17.0
Obs.	24.7	22.9	15.1	9.7	11.8	19.0	23.2	14.5	12.4	13.7	16.0	16.6
Total	59.8	49.7	41.6	56.1	46.5	53.4	52.9	53.9	44.5	54.8	53.2	52.5
RSM: Supvr.	0.6	0.4	0.2	0.6	1.9	0.7	0.4	0.2	1.3	0.7	0.6	0.6
Tchr.	0.3	0.2	0.7	0.0	0.0	0.2	0.5	0.2	0.0	0.0	0.0	0.2
Obs.	0.3	0.0	0.2	0.0	0.0	0.1	0.6	0.4	0.3	0.0	0.0	0.3
Total	1.2	0.6	1.1	0.6	1.9	1.0	1.5	0.8	1.6	0.7	0.6	1.1
Total: Supvr.	33.4	26.7	35.7	49.8	36.7	36.3	35.2	30.5	39.2	42.1	32.6	36.2
Tchr.	25.1	30.1	32.9	35.8	29.6	30.1	20.9	43.4	36.9	35.1	37.1	33.3
Obs.	41.3	43.2	31.2	14.4	26.6	33.6	43.9	26.1	24.0	22.8	30.1	30.5
I/R: Supvr.	0.35	0.71	1.36	0.50	0.65	0.61	0.61	0.65	1.04	0.53	0.41	0.60
Tchr.	0.37	0.33	0.31	0.26	0.30	0.31	0.29	0.32	0.23	0.33	0.40	0.32
Obs.	0.38	0.43	0.49	0.26	0.58	0.40	0.39	0.38	0.40	0.33	0.49	0.39

SOL = Solicitation
RES = Response
STR = Structuring
REA = Reacting
RSM = Summary reaction
I/R = (STR + SOL) / (RES + REA + RSM)

TABLE 28

Percentage of Units by Supervisory Groups in Each Pedagogical
Move Category: Early and Late Conferences

Category by Speaker	% Units by Group: Early Conferences						% Units by Group: Late Conferences					
	1	2	3	4	5	$\overline{X}$	1	2	3	4	5	$\overline{X}$
SOL: Supvr.	3.7	5.1	7.9	5.0	6.5	5.5	6.1	4.7	5.2	6.1	4.3	5.3
Tchr.	2.3	1.4	0.7	1.9	1.4	1.6	1.0	3.0	1.9	2.6	2.7	2.2
Obs.	2.5	3.9	2.8	0.7	1.2	2.3	2.5	1.7	2.0	2.4	2.3	2.2
Total	8.5	10.4	11.4	7.6	9.1	9.4	9.6	9.4	9.1	11.1	9.3	9.7
RES: Supvr.	3.0	5.3	3.2	2.7	2.6	3.4	2.5	2.6	3.3	5.6	3.5	3.5
Tchr.	4.4	11.0	11.1	8.6	3.7	7.6	6.2	10.7	14.5	7.9	11.7	9.9
Obs.	3.8	7.4	4.3	0.7	3.5	4.0	7.7	3.6	2.6	2.1	2.6	3.9
Total	11.2	23.7	18.6	12.0	9.8	15.0	16.4	16.9	20.4	15.6	17.8	17.3
STR: Supvr.	4.1	4.3	11.1	24.8	21.9	12.7	5.4	5.6	27.1	8.9	12.6	11.2
Tchr.	7.1	8.3	9.5	4.5	8.5	7.5	6.1	9.7	3.4	5.7	11.4	7.4
Obs.	13.0	7.3	11.6	2.1	7.5	8.5	10.2	6.4	4.2	3.1	4.2	5.8
Total	24.2	19.9	32.2	31.4	37.9	28.7	21.7	21.7	34.7	17.7	28.2	24.4
REA: Supvr.	19.8	10.7	8.5	29.6	17.1	17.3	18.0	12.4	13.5	30.0	16.0	18.3
Tchr.	12.7	12.6	15.3	11.4	10.7	12.5	11.5	27.4	11.6	15.2	16.1	16.2
Obs.	22.2	22.2	12.2	7.2	12.5	15.7	19.0	11.4	8.7	9.5	11.5	12.4
Total	54.7	45.5	36.0	48.2	40.3	45.5	48.5	51.2	33.8	54.7	43.6	46.9
RSM: Supvr.	1.0	0.4	0.7	0.8	2.9	1.1	2.3	0.2	1.3	0.9	1.0	1.2
Tchr.	0.1	0.2	0.9	0.0	0.0	0.2	0.8	0.2	0.0	0.0	0.0	0.2
Obs.	0.4	0.0	0.1	0.0	0.0	0.1	0.8	0.4	0.7	0.0	0.0	0.4
Total	1.5	0.6	1.7	0.8	2.9	1.4	3.9	0.8	2.0	0.9	1.0	1.8
Total: Supvr.	31.6	25.8	31.4	62.9	51.0	40.0	34.3	25.5	50.4	51.5	37.4	39.5
Tchr.	26.6	33.5	37.5	26.4	24.3	29.4	25.6	51.0	31.4	31.4	41.9	35.9
Obs.	41.9	40.8	31.0	10.7	24.7	30.6	40.2	23.5	18.2	17.1	20.6	24.7
I/R: Supvr.	0.33	0.57	1.53	0.90	1.26	0.84	0.50	0.68	1.78	0.41	0.82	0.72
Tchr.	0.55	0.41	0.37	0.32	0.69	0.45	0.38	0.33	0.20	0.36	0.51	0.37
Obs.	0.59	0.38	0.87	0.35	0.54	0.55	0.46	0.53	0.52	0.47	0.46	0.48

SOL = Solicitation
RES = Response
STR = Structuring
REA = Reacting
RSM = Summary reaction
I/R = (STR + SOL) / (RES + REA + RSM)

TABLE 29

Percentage* of Each Initiator's Cycles for Major Teaching Cycle
Types: Planning and Analysis Conferences

Cycle Types by Initiator	% Cycles by Group: Planning Conferences						% Cycles by Group: Analysis Conferences					
	1	2	3	4	5	$\bar{X}$	1	2	3	4	5	$\bar{X}$
Type 3: Supvr.	8.5	5.7	6.8	1.7	2.0	4.8	4.2	2.2	6.5	4.2	4.9	4.4
Tchr.	8.6	8.5	9.7	15.1	22.9	12.7	8.0	12.5	25.0	14.3	9.1	12.9
Obs.	10.3	4.3	6.1	0.0	12.1	8.0	11.2	13.5	23.1	11.4	12.0	13.1
$\bar{X}$	9.3	6.2	7.3	6.3	11.0	7.9	8.1	9.4	13.9	7.7	8.8	9.3
Type 4: Supvr.	20.7	18.9	8.2	18.5	26.5	18.1	18.1	19.6	19.4	31.9	19.5	22.2
Tchr.	27.6	31.9	16.1	21.9	17.1	23.8	44.0	25.0	20.0	28.6	27.3	28.8
Obs.	35.6	21.7	15.2	21.4	33.3	28.2	43.8	28.8	26.9	28.6	40.0	36.1
$\bar{X}$	28.2	23.9	11.6	20.0	26.0	22.4	33.9	24.6	21.3	30.5	29.9	28.6
Type 5: Supvr.	4.9	5.7	5.5	8.4	4.1	6.1	0.0	0.0	8.1	4.2	4.9	3.4
Tchr.	0.0	2.1	9.7	2.7	8.6	3.7	8.0	5.0	5.0	0.0	12.1	6.5
Obs.	2.3	2.2	6.1	7.1	3.0	3.3	1.1	0.0	7.7	5.7	0.0	2.0
$\bar{X}$	2.7	3.5	6.6	6.4	5.2	4.7	1.6	1.4	7.4	3.9	4.8	3.5
Type 9: Supvr.	2.4	1.9	2.7	3.4	4.1	2.9	0.0	0.0	1.6	0.0	2.4	0.7
Tchr.	5.2	4.3	6.5	1.4	5.7	4.1	4.0	2.5	5.0	4.8	0.0	2.9
Obs.	1.1	4.3	3.0	0.0	0.0	1.9	0.0	0.0	0.0	0.0	0.0	0.0
$\bar{X}$	2.6	3.5	3.7	2.4	3.4	3.0	0.5	0.7	1.8	0.8	0.8	0.9
Type 10: Supvr.	3.7	0.0	4.1	2.5	4.1	2.9	4.2	4.3	4.8	4.2	7.3	4.8
Tchr.	3.4	4.3	6.5	5.5	0.0	4.1	16.0	2.5	10.0	23.8	15.2	12.2
Obs.	3.4	4.3	0.0	0.0	3.0	2.8	4.5	1.9	11.5	8.6	0.0	4.4
$\bar{X}$	3.5	2.8	3.7	3.4	2.6	3.2	6.0	2.8	7.5	8.5	6.4	6.1
Type 14: Supvr.	14.6	17.0	26.0	21.0	16.3	19.4	25.0	21.7	16.1	9.7	19.5	18.1
Tchr.	17.2	12.8	19.4	23.3	20.0	18.9	8.0	20.0	10.0	14.3	6.1	12.2
Obs.	14.9	13.0	15.2	14.3	33.3	17.4	10.1	19.2	19.2	11.4	18.0	14.7
$\bar{X}$	15.4	14.4	21.9	21.4	27.2	18.7	15.6	20.2	15.8	10.9	15.4	15.6
Type 18: Supvr.	15.9	22.6	13.7	19.3	10.2	16.8	13.9	17.4	9.7	8.3	12.2	11.9
Tchr.	13.8	8.5	9.7	6.8	11.4	9.8	0.0	2.5	10.0	0.0	9.1	4.3
Obs.	6.9	10.9	12.1	14.3	6.1	8.9	4.5	7.7	3.8	2.9	10.0	6.0
$\bar{X}$	11.8	14.3	12.4	14.6	9.4	12.8	7.6	9.4	8.4	5.5	10.4	8.2
Type 19: Supvr.	17.1	20.8	9.6	15.1	12.2	14.9	20.8	23.9	11.3	16.7	14.6	17.4
Tchr.	13.8	19.1	9.7	12.3	8.6	13.1	0.0	22.5	5.0	4.8	18.2	12.2
Obs.	14.9	17.4	30.3	35.7	6.1	17.8	18.0	13.5	7.7	20.0	16.0	15.9
$\bar{X}$	15.4	19.2	14.6	15.5	9.4	15.1	16.7	19.6	9.3	15.7	16.1	15.8

Type 3 = STR-REA
Type 4 = STR-REA-REA...
Type 5 = STR-SOL-RES
Type 9 = STR-SOL-RES-REA

Type 10 = STR-SOL-RES-REA-REA...
Type 14 = SOL-RES
Type 18 = SOL-RES-REA
Type 19 = SOL-RES-REA-REA...

*Percentages are based on 100% for each initiator.

TABLE 30

Percentage* of Each Initiator's Units for Major Teaching Cycle
Types: Planning and Analysis Conferences

Cycle Types by Initiator	% Units by Group: Planning Conferences						% Units by Group: Analysis Conferences					
	1	2	3	4	5	$\bar{X}$	1	2	3	4	5	$\bar{X}$
Type 3: Supvr.	3.8	5.8	11.8	1.5	2.0	4.7	1.8	0.7	5.9	4.1	6.3	4.0
Tchr.	5.7	7.1	8.7	11.5	25.0	11.6	4.0	14.0	25.7	7.8	11.5	12.0
Obs.	4.8	3.5	6.5	0.0	10.1	5.2	8.0	10.2	22.7	6.7	9.0	10.7
$\bar{X}$	4.7	5.5	9.7	4.2	10.2	6.6	5.2	8.4	14.6	5.5	8.6	8.2
Type 4: Supvr.	25.5	23.9	16.2	24.0	41.4	26.4	34.9	35.7	37.0	47.4	22.9	36.2
Tchr.	55.1	36.6	21.8	32.5	16.6	33.6	50.0	37.2	36.1	38.2	37.2	39.4
Obs.	58.2	29.7	24.4	44.5	54.2	45.0	58.6	50.7	27.5	35.9	49.7	47.1
$\bar{X}$	46.9	29.6	19.5	29.0	37.5	33.4	49.1	41.0	33.7	42.5	35.7	40.9
Type 5: Supvr.	2.8	13.0	10.1	6.5	4.6	7.2	0.0	0.0	9.5	2.7	5.3	3.7
Tchr.	0.0	1.0	8.7	2.2	13.3	4.6	4.9	6.0	6.5	0.0	12.6	6.7
Obs.	2.2	1.2	6.5	20.0	3.2	4.5	0.8	0.0	2.9	2.3	0.0	1.1
$\bar{X}$	1.8	5.7	8.9	6.9	6.7	5.7	1.2	2.1	6.8	2.1	5.7	3.4
Type 9: Supvr.	2.2	3.5	6.5	4.3	8.6	5.1	0.0	0.0	1.6	0.0	0.9	0.5
Tchr.	4.3	11.3	11.5	1.4	4.9	6.2	3.7	2.7	2.6	2.0	0.0	2.1
Obs.	0.5	5.9	4.8	0.0	0.0	2.2	0.0	0.0	0.0	0.0	0.0	0.0
$\bar{X}$	1.9	6.5	7.2	3.0	5.6	4.6	0.6	0.9	1.2	0.4	0.3	0.7
Type 10: Supvr.	9.8	0.0	10.6	5.3	5.1	6.2	5.2	5.9	6.4	7.6	11.2	7.3
Tchr.	5.9	4.4	14.0	14.5	0.0	7.5	31.6	2.3	12.2	36.8	15.4	17.1
Obs.	5.6	5.3	0.0	0.0	2.9	3.7	6.6	4.5	21.3	10.6	0.0	7.9
$\bar{X}$	7.0	3.0	8.7	7.2	3.2	5.8	10.4	4.1	12.2	13.7	8.7	9.7
Type 14: Supvr.	7.8	9.7	7.8	7.9	10.2	8.6	13.1	8.8	8.9	2.5	8.4	8.0
Tchr.	6.3	6.5	11.8	13.7	8.4	9.2	2.6	4.5	3.9	2.4	1.2	2.9
Obs.	5.0	5.5	9.3	4.5	10.6	6.6	2.7	7.4	6.4	2.7	7.1	5.0
$\bar{X}$	6.1	7.4	9.1	9.2	9.8	8.2	6.1	6.9	7.3	2.5	5.8	5.8
Type 18: Supvr.	15.2	15.5	8.1	17.7	5.4	12.5	10.3	14.1	5.9	4.9	5.5	7.7
Tchr.	8.7	5.0	4.0	4.6	7.5	6.1	0.0	3.7	6.1	0.0	6.2	3.4
Obs.	3.6	14.5	9.3	4.5	8.5	7.7	2.1	3.7	3.5	0.8	6.3	3.2
$\bar{X}$	8.5	12.0	7.4	12.3	6.7	9.4	4.5	7.1	5.2	2.8	6.0	5.1
Type 19: Supvr.	24.3	25.7	12.9	24.6	11.8	19.8	30.2	32.8	14.9	15.9	18.7	21.6
Tchr.	11.3	19.0	6.9	12.5	18.8	14.1	0.0	22.3	5.7	5.4	15.0	12.1
Obs.	7.7	23.0	33.1	25.5	5.8	20.0	19.4	13.6	15.7	32.6	25.5	21.0
$\bar{X}$	18.4	22.9	16.6	21.3	12.4	18.3	19.7	23.0	13.8	18.9	19.9	19.2

Type 3 = STR-REA
Type 4 = STR-REA-REA...
Type 5 = STR-SOL-RES
Type 9 = STR-SOL-RES-REA

Type 10 = STR-SOL-RES-REA-REA...
Type 14 = SOL-RES
Type 18 = SOL-RES-REA
Type 19 = SOL-RES-REA-REA...

*Percentages are based on 100% for each initiator.

TABLE 31°

Percentage* of Each Initiator's Cycles for Major Teaching Cycle
Types: Early and Late Conferences

Cycle Types by Initiator	% Cycles by Group: Early Conferences						% Cycles by Group: Late Conferences					
	1	2	3	4	5	$\overline{X}$	1	2	3	4	5	$\overline{X}$
Type 3: Supvr.	5.1	0.0	3.0	2.4	2.2	2.7	7.4	7.0	10.1	2.8	4.5	6.2
Tchr.	10.0	5.7	24.1	16.1	25.0	14.5	6.1	13.5	4.5	14.3	12.5	11.5
Obs.	7.2	9.7	20.0	14.3	20.0	12.2	14.0	8.3	4.2	5.7	6.2	9.3
$\overline{X}$	7.3	5.7	12.3	7.1	12.9	8.8	10.0	9.7	7.9	6.9	7.8	8.5
Type 4: Supvr.	28.8	16.7	6.1	28.9	17.4	20.3	13.7	21.1	20.3	19.4	29.5	19.6
Tchr.	32.0	28.6	24.1	16.1	20.0	25.5	33.3	28.8	9.1	27.0	22.9	25.7
Obs.	42.2	17.7	20.0	35.7	48.6	32.8	37.6	38.9	20.8	22.9	29.2	32.2
$\overline{X}$	35.4	20.1	13.9	26.5	28.7	25.7	26.7	28.3	18.2	22.4	27.2	24.8
Type 5: Supvr.	1.7	4.8	10.6	6.0	4.3	5.7	3.2	1.8	2.9	7.4	4.5	4.3
Tchr.	0.0	2.9	6.9	3.2	5.0	3.0	6.1	3.8	9.1	1.6	12.5	6.0
Obs.	1.2	1.6	2.9	0.0	0.0	1.3	2.2	0.0	12.5	8.6	2.1	3.8
$\overline{X}$	1.0	2.8	7.7	4.7	3.0	3.6	3.2	2.1	6.0	5.9	6.4	4.6
Type 9: Supvr.	3.4	2.4	3.0	3.6	2.2	3.0	0.0	0.0	1.4	0.9	4.5	1.1
Tchr.	4.0	8.6	3.4	0.0	5.0	4.2	6.1	0.0	9.1	3.2	2.1	3.2
Obs.	0.0	3.2	2.9	0.0	0.0	1.3	1.1	0.0	0.0	0.0	0.0	0.4
$\overline{X}$	2.0	4.3	3.1	2.3	2.0	2.7	1.4	0.0	2.6	1.5	2.1	1.4
Type 10: Supvr.	3.4	2.4	4.5	2.4	10.9	4.4	4.2	1.8	4.3	3.7	0.0	3.2
Tchr.	6.0	2.9	6.9	19.4	10.0	8.5	9.1	3.8	9.1	4.8	6.2	6.0
Obs.	4.8	3.2	5.7	7.1	0.0	3.9	3.2	2.8	4.2	5.7	2.1	3.4
$\overline{X}$	4.7	2.8	5.3	7.1	7.0	5.2	4.6	2.8	5.2	4.4	2.8	4.1
Type 14: Supvr.	8.5	14.3	24.2	12.0	13.0	14.5	26.3	22.8	18.8	20.4	22.7	22.3
Tchr.	10.0	17.1	3.4	25.8	0.0	12.1	21.2	15.4	31.8	19.0	18.7	19.7
Obs.	10.8	17.7	20.0	7.1	17.1	14.8	14.0	13.9	12.5	14.3	29.2	16.9
$\overline{X}$	9.9	16.5	18.5	14.8	11.8	14.0	20.4	17.9	20.0	18.9	23.5	20.0
Type 18: Supvr.	15.3	26.2	10.6	9.6	13.0	13.9	14.7	15.8	13.0	19.4	9.1	15.3
Tchr.	10.0	0.0	6.9	0.0	15.0	6.1	9.1	9.6	13.6	7.9	8.3	9.2
Obs.	7.2	8.1	8.6	0.0	8.6	7.4	4.3	11.1	8.3	8.6	8.3	7.2
$\overline{X}$	10.4	11.5	9.2	6.2	11.9	9.8	9.5	12.4	12.1	14.1	8.7	11.4
Type 19: Supvr.	22.0	23.8	10.6	15.7	13.0	16.6	16.8	21.1	10.1	15.7	13.6	15.5
Tchr.	12.0	28.6	10.3	12.9	20.0	16.4	6.1	15.4	4.5	9.5	10.4	10.1
Obs.	6.9	17.7	11.4	21.4	2.9	14.4	16.1	11.1	33.3	25.7	18.7	19.1
$\overline{X}$	17.2	22.3	10.8	15.6	10.9	15.8	14.9	16.6	14.0	15.6	14.3	15.1

Type 3 = STR-REA   Type 10 = STR-SOL-RES-REA-REA...
Type 4 = STR-REA-REA...   Type 14 = SOL-RES
Type 5 = STR-SOL-RES   Type 18 = SOL-RES-REA
Type 9 = STR-SOL-RES-REA   Type 19 = SOL-RES-REA-REA...

*Percentages are based on 100% for each initiator.

TABLE 32

Percentage* of Each Initiator's Units for Major Teaching Cycle
Types: Early and Late Conferences

Cycle Types by Initiator	% Units by Group: Early Conferences						% Units by Group: Late Conferences					
	1	2	3	4	5	$\bar{X}$	1	2	3	4	5	$\bar{X}$
Type 3: Supvr.	2.3	0.0	7.1	2.6	1.0	2.5	3.1	6.6	9.9	3.0	7.3	5.9
Tchr.	5.0	11.1	22.5	8.2	37.2	15.5	5.0	10.8	3.1	11.6	8.0	8.7
Obs.	4.5	7.3	23.3	7.3	18.6	11.1	8.6	6.3	3.2	3.1	2.4	5.3
$\bar{X}$	4.1	5.8	16.6	4.4	13.5	8.5	5.8	8.3	7.5	5.2	6.1	6.6
Type 4: Supvr.	45.8	22.4	13.9	38.1	22.3	29.0	20.2	36.4	35.2	31.2	44.4	33.0
Tchr.	48.0	23.7	36.4	26.8	16.9	31.7	60.2	45.1	11.5	40.5	32.9	40.3
Obs.	56.6	36.8	25.1	35.1	65.2	45.3	60.3	48.4	28.0	40.5	41.0	47.2
$\bar{X}$	51.5	28.7	23.3	35.3	32.9	35.3	44.6	42.6	30.4	35.8	39.5	39.1
Type 5: Supvr.	1.1	11.0	14.9	4.9	2.6	6.5	1.5	2.7	6.5	4.5	7.6	4.6
Tchr.	0.0	2.2	4.7	2.0	2.2	2.1	5.0	4.8	13.6	0.9	18.4	8.6
Obs.	1.5	0.9	1.7	0.0	0.0	1.0	1.4	0.0	9.0	12.1	2.2	4.2
$\bar{X}$	1.0	4.7	7.6	3.5	1.8	3.7	2.0	3.0	8.0	5.5	9.6	5.5
Type 9: Supvr.	2.7	3.7	8.8	3.9	3.2	4.4	0.0	0.0	0.9	0.5	7.0	1.6
Tchr.	4.0	16.9	2.8	0.0	1.2	5.4	4.1	0.0	17.3	2.9	2.8	3.4
Obs.	0.0	4.3	3.2	0.0	0.0	1.6	0.4	0.0	0.0	0.0	0.0	0.2
$\bar{X}$	1.7	7.2	5.3	2.5	1.9	3.7	0.9	0.0	2.9	1.0	3.5	1.6
Type 10: Supvr.	5.5	3.3	7.1	4.1	15.2	7.2	8.7	2.4	9.4	8.9	0.0	6.4
Tchr.	20.0	3.4	14.4	35.0	8.6	16.2	11.4	3.2	11.0	13.6	8.0	8.4
Obs.	9.0	5.6	14.0	10.2	0.0	7.9	3.2	3.5	9.3	5.7	2.0	4.2
$\bar{X}$	10.9	4.2	11.3	11.7	9.6	9.5	6.7	2.9	9.6	9.3	3.3	6.2
Type 14: Supvr.	2.7	5.3	9.5	3.8	7.7	5.7	15.7	13.2	7.7	7.1	11.1	10.7
Tchr.	3.4	5.3	0.6	10.5	0.0	4.0	6.7	5.4	23.6	8.7	6.9	8.2
Obs.	3.2	6.3	9.1	1.2	7.1	5.5	4.4	6.9	5.1	4.4	9.5	5.9
$\bar{X}$	3.1	5.7	7.1	4.8	5.9	5.2	9.1	8.6	9.3	6.8	9.2	8.6
Type 18: Supvr.	10.6	20.1	9.0	6.7	6.4	9.8	14.1	9.7	5.7	17.5	4.4	10.5
Tchr.	6.2	0.0	2.5	0.0	8.0	3.4	3.5	6.9	9.4	5.1	6.2	6.1
Obs.	4.0	9.8	4.7	0.0	6.2	5.5	1.5	6.9	8.0	3.1	7.8	4.7
$\bar{X}$	6.3	10.9	5.9	4.2	6.7	6.8	6.8	8.0	6.8	10.9	6.0	7.7
Type 19: Supvr.	25.9	32.6	17.6	17.1	13.6	20.2	28.3	25.8	11.5	24.5	16.6	21.0
Tchr.	8.8	29.3	7.5	11.7	25.8	16.3	3.5	15.6	4.2	8.5	12.2	10.5
Obs.	19.2	19.4	15.3	37.6	2.1	17.6	17.9	15.6	36.3	26.4	29.9	23.9
$\bar{X}$	18.3	26.4	14.3	19.0	13.0	18.4	19.6	19.4	16.0	21.0	18.9	19.1

Type 3 = STR-REA
Type 4 = STR-REA-REA...
Type 5 = STR-SOL-RES
Type 9 = STR-SOL-RES-REA

Type 10 = STR-SOL-RES-REA-REA...
Type 14 = SOL-RES
Type 18 = SOL-RES-REA
Type 19 = SOL-RES-REA-REA...

*Percentages are based on 100% for each initiator.

TABLE 33

Percentages of Cycles and Units for Teaching Cycles
According to Initiatory Pattern of Cycle:
Planning and Analysis Conferences

Pattern by Initiator	% Cycles by Group: Planning Conferences						% Cycles by Group: Analysis Conferences					
	1	2	3	4	5	$\overline{X}$	1	2	3	4	5	$\overline{X}$
STR... : Supvr.	11.0	9.6	9.5	11.7	12.0	10.9	8.6	7.2	14.8	25.0	8.9	12.4
Tchr.	9.2	13.7	6.5	15.5	11.9	11.5	7.5	10.8	8.3	7.8	9.7	8.7
Obs.	17.7	8.2	5.1	1.5	12.8	9.2	26.4	17.4	12.1	10.9	20.9	18.4
Total	37.9	31.5	21.1	28.7	36.7	31.6	42.5	35.4	35.2	43.7	39.5	39.5
STR-SOL... : Supvr.	5.3	3.4	8.1	8.7	6.8	6.3	2.2	1.5	10.2	5.3	5.7	4.6
Tchr.	3.2	4.8	5.9	3.3	5.1	4.4	3.8	4.5	3.7	4.7	7.3	4.7
Obs.	3.5	4.1	3.0	0.4	1.7	2.6	3.7	2.3	4.6	4.6	1.6	3.4
Total	12.0	12.3	17.0	12.4	13.6	13.3	9.7	8.3	18.5	14.6	14.6	12.7
SOL... : Supvr.	19.8	23.3	35.7	37.4	23.1	27.9	27.9	24.6	32.4	25.9	18.5	25.8
Tchr.	13.2	13.7	10.2	16.6	12.9	13.4	2.1	13.7	6.5	3.9	9.6	6.9
Obs.	17.1	19.2	16.0	4.9	13.7	13.8	17.7	18.0	7.4	11.8	17.8	15.0
Total	50.1	56.2	61.9	58.9	49.7	55.1	47.7	56.3	46.3	41.6	45.9	47.7
Total : Supvr.	36.1	36.3	53.3	57.8	41.9	45.1	38.7	33.3	57.4	56.2	33.1	42.8
Tchr.	25.6	32.2	22.6	35.4	29.9	29.3	13.4	29.0	18.5	16.4	26.6	20.3
Obs.	38.3	31.5	24.1	6.8	28.2	25.6	47.8	37.7	24.1	27.3	40.3	36.8

Pattern by Initiator	% Units by Group: Planning Conferences						% Units by Group: Analysis Conferences					
	1	2	3	4	5	$\overline{X}$	1	2	3	4	5	$\overline{X}$
STR... : Supvr.	10.2	11.9	17.4	15.1	21.3	14.8	12.4	11.9	22.2	33.1	17.6	19.0
Tchr.	14.9	13.7	7.5	13.6	11.5	12.5	9.5	18.2	9.6	8.4	13.9	12.0
Obs.	27.2	10.4	7.7	5.6	14.9	13.8	32.6	20.2	16.5	12.2	19.2	20.8
Total	52.3	36.0	32.6	34.3	47.7	41.1	54.5	50.3	48.3	53.7	50.7	51.8
STR-SOL... : Supvr.	5.9	6.5	16.0	9.8	13.3	10.3	1.8	2.0	10.4	5.8	7.1	5.2
Tchr.	3.0	6.9	8.5	5.2	6.6	5.6	7.1	6.0	3.4	6.8	8.0	6.2
Obs.	3.9	4.7	3.7	2.5	1.3	3.3	4.2	3.0	7.8	4.6	0.9	3.7
Total	12.8	18.1	28.2	17.5	21.2	19.2	13.1	11.0	21.6	17.2	16.0	15.1
SOL... : Supvr.	16.2	20.1	18.8	34.2	14.4	20.6	19.5	18.9	19.0	14.6	13.9	17.2
Tchr.	6.7	9.7	6.7	9.5	9.7	8.6	0.7	11.2	2.6	2.5	6.7	4.8
Obs.	12.0	16.1	13.7	4.5	7.0	10.5	12.2	8.6	8.5	11.9	12.8	11.1
Total	34.9	45.9	39.2	48.2	31.1	39.7	32.4	38.7	30.1	29.0	33.4	33.1
Total : Supvr.	32.3	38.5	52.2	59.1	49.0	45.7	33.7	32.8	51.6	53.5	38.6	41.4
Tchr.	24.6	30.3	22.7	28.3	27.8	26.7	17.3	35.4	15.6	17.7	28.6	23.0
Obs.	43.1	31.2	25.1	12.6	23.2	27.6	49.0	31.8	32.8	28.7	32.9	35.6

STR... = Teaching cycles 1, 3, 4
STR-SOL... = Teaching cycles 2, 5, 6, 7, 8, 9, 10, 11, 12
SOL... = Teaching cycles 13, 14, 15, 16, 17, 18, 19, 20, 21

TABLE 34

Participation Indices (P.I.) of Cycles and Units for Teaching Cycles
According to Initiatory Pattern of Cycle: Planning and Analysis Conferences

Pattern by Initiator	Participation Index (Cycles): Planning Conferences						Participation Index (Cycles): Analysis Conferences					
	1	2	3	4	5	$\overline{X}$	1	2	3	4	5	$\overline{X}$
STR... : Supvr.	1.74	2.03	2.66	1.93	2.07	2.04	1.21	1.35	2.49	2.71	1.43	1.86
Tchr.	1.29	1.19	0.92	1.64	0.99	1.17	0.94	0.84	0.70	0.54	0.76	0.71
Obs.	0.72	0.54	0.49	0.11	0.68	0.56	0.96	1.01	0.70	0.54	1.03	0.89
STR-SOL... : Supvr.	2.64	1.84	2.82	3.33	3.16	2.80	1.36	1.21	2.36	1.22	2.47	2.14
Tchr.	1.42	1.06	1.03	0.81	1.15	1.07	2.08	1.48	0.60	0.98	1.53	1.19
Obs.	0.45	0.69	0.36	0.06	0.24	0.37	0.59	0.57	0.50	0.69	0.21	0.51
SOL... : Supvr.	2.36	2.77	3.42	3.01	2.94	3.00	3.50	2.92	4.14	2.95	2.56	3.20
Tchr.	1.41	0.67	0.49	0.86	0.80	0.78	0.24	0.67	0.42	0.29	0.64	0.47
Obs.	0.53	0.71	0.52	0.18	0.54	0.48	0.57	0.66	0.32	0.62	0.75	0.60
Total : Supvr.	2.16	2.42	3.15	2.74	2.65	2.68	2.32	2.22	3.39	2.62	2.10	2.55
Tchr.	1.36	0.88	0.67	1.08	0.92	0.95	0.71	0.79	0.55	0.50	0.81	0.66
Obs.	0.59	0.65	0.49	0.15	0.55	0.49	0.74	0.78	0.49	0.59	0.78	0.70

Pattern by Initiator	Participation Index (Units): Planning Conferences						Participation Index (Units): Analysis Conferences					
	1	2	3	4	5	$\overline{X}$	1	2	3	4	5	$\overline{X}$
STR... : Supvr.	1.17	2.21	3.15	2.08	2.83	2.13	1.37	1.58	2.72	2.92	2.20	2.17
Tchr.	1.52	1.04	0.69	1.20	0.74	0.98	0.93	0.99	0.59	0.47	0.84	0.75
Obs.	0.81	0.60	0.48	0.36	0.61	0.64	0.93	0.83	0.69	0.49	0.73	0.77
STR-SOL... : Supvr.	2.75	2.39	3.36	2.65	3.97	3.17	0.82	1.21	3.85	1.60	2.81	2.03
Tchr.	1.25	1.04	0.90	0.90	0.95	0.94	2.88	1.49	0.47	1.20	1.53	1.32
Obs.	0.47	0.54	0.26	0.31	0.12	0.33	0.50	0.56	0.73	0.58	0.11	0.47
SOL... : Supvr.	2.78	2.92	2.84	3.36	2.93	3.07	3.60	3.26	3.74	2.39	2.64	3.08
Tchr.	1.02	0.55	0.51	0.60	0.95	0.70	0.17	0.79	0.26	0.26	0.61	0.47
Obs.	0.53	0.72	0.71	0.20	0.44	0.51	0.58	0.46	0.57	0.89	0.74	0.64
Total : Supvr.	1.93	2.56	3.09	2.80	3.10	2.72	2.02	2.18	3.05	2.53	2.44	2.46
Tchr.	1.31	0.83	0.68	0.86	0.85	0.86	0.92	0.97	0.46	0.54	0.88	0.74
Obs.	0.67	0.64	0.51	0.27	0.45	0.53	0.76	0.66	0.66	0.62	0.64	0.68

STR... = Teaching cycles 1, 3, 4
STR-SOL... = Teaching cycles 2, 5, 6, 7, 8, 9, 10, 11, 12
SOL... = Teaching cycles 13, 14, 15, 16, 17, 18, 19, 20, 21
Participation Indices (P.I.) = (% Units by initiator) / (% Participation in conference)

TABLE 35

Percentages of Cycles and Units for Teaching Cycles According to
Initiatory Pattern of Cycle: Early and Late Conferences

Pattern by Initiator	% Cycles by Group: Early Conferences						% Cycles by Group: Late Conferences					
	1	2	3	4	5	$\overline{X}$	1	2	3	4	5	$\overline{X}$
STR... : Supvr.	10.5	5.0	5.4	24.2	9.9	10.9	9.6	11.8	19.2	12.2	10.7	12.1
Tchr.	11.4	8.6	11.6	8.6	9.0	10.0	5.9	15.8	2.6	15.1	12.2	10.5
Obs.	21.3	12.2	10.8	5.5	23.7	15.0	21.7	13.2	5.2	4.9	12.1	12.1
Total	43.2	25.8	27.8	38.3	42.6	35.9	37.2	40.8	27.0	32.2	35.0	34.7
STR-SOL... : Supvr.	3.5	3.0	10.8	8.6	11.0	6.8	4.0	1.9	6.9	6.6	2.8	4.6
Tchr.	3.2	5.1	4.5	5.5	3.8	4.4	3.5	4.3	5.1	2.9	7.8	4.6
Obs.	2.7	4.4	3.7	0.7	1.1	2.6	4.5	1.9	3.5	2.8	2.2	3.2
Total	9.4	12.5	19.0	14.8	15.9	13.8	12.0	8.1	15.5	12.3	12.8	12.4
SOL... : Supvr.	16.7	22.2	34.6	32.0	24.6	25.2	29.4	25.6	33.9	33.6	17.9	28.4
Tchr.	11.4	11.5	6.2	10.1	7.0	9.5	5.5	15.8	11.4	12.6	14.3	11.3
Obs.	19.2	28.0	12.4	4.7	9.9	15.6	15.9	9.7	12.2	9.3	20.0	13.2
Total	47.3	61.7	53.2	46.8	41.5	50.3	50.8	51.1	57.5	55.5	52.2	52.9
Total : Supvr.	30.7	30.2	50.8	64.8	45.5	42.9	43.0	39.3	60.0	52.4	31.4	45.1
Tchr.	26.0	25.2	22.3	24.2	19.8	23.9	14.9	35.9	19.1	30.6	34.3	26.4
Obs.	43.2	44.6	26.9	10.9	34.7	33.2	42.1	24.8	20.9	17.0	34.3	28.5

Pattern by Initiator	% Units by Group: Early Conferences						% Units by Group: Late Conferences					
	1	2	3	4	5	$\overline{X}$	1	2	3	4	5	$\overline{X}$
STR... : Supvr.	12.8	7.7	9.1	31.0	19.4	15.9	9.8	16.3	31.0	17.7	19.3	18.2
Tchr.	13.7	8.7	14.8	7.5	11.5	11.3	10.8	23.6	2.0	14.1	13.8	13.1
Obs.	29.3	18.1	17.3	6.5	23.0	19.3	30.5	12.9	6.9	10.9	12.5	15.6
Total	55.8	34.5	41.2	45.0	53.9	46.5	51.1	52.8	39.9	42.7	45.6	46.9
STR-SOL... : Supvr.	2.9	6.2	13.8	8.5	15.8	9.1	4.8	2.1	12.4	7.1	5.5	6.1
Tchr.	6.3	7.5	6.1	8.1	2.6	6.2	3.6	5.5	5.7	4.4	11.0	6.1
Obs.	5.1	5.2	7.4	1.6	0.2	3.9	3.0	2.3	4.1	5.2	1.9	3.2
Total	14.3	18.9	27.3	18.2	18.6	19.2	11.4	9.9	22.2	16.7	18.4	15.4
SOL... : Supvr.	11.0	20.4	17.1	23.9	16.0	17.3	24.5	18.4	21.0	25.4	12.6	20.4
Tchr.	5.4	8.6	3.4	5.8	7.2	6.0	2.3	12.4	5.9	6.3	8.9	6.9
Obs.	13.6	17.6	11.0	7.2	4.3	11.0	10.8	6.5	11.1	8.9	14.5	10.5
Total	30.0	46.6	31.5	36.9	27.5	34.3	37.6	37.3	38.0	40.6	36.0	37.8
Total : Supvr.	26.7	34.3	40.0	63.4	51.2	42.3	39.1	36.8	64.4	50.2	37.4	44.7
Tchr.	25.4	24.8	24.3	21.4	21.3	23.5	16.7	41.5	13.6	24.8	33.7	26.1
Obs.	48.0	40.9	35.7	15.3	27.5	34.2	44.3	21.7	22.1	25.0	28.9	29.3

STR... = Teaching cycles 1, 3, 4
STR-SOL... = Teaching cycles 2, 5, 6, 7, 8, 9, 10, 11, 12
SOL... = Teaching cycles 13, 14, 15, 16, 17, 18, 19, 20, 21

TABLE 36

Participation Indices (P.I.) of Cycles and Units for Teaching Cycles
According to Initiatory Pattern of Cycle: Early and Late Conferences

Pattern by Initiator	Participation Index (Cycles): Early Conferences						Participation Index (Cycles): Late Conferences					
	1	2	3	4	5	$\overline{X}$	1	2	3	4	5	$\overline{X}$
STR... : Supvr.	1.46	1.29	1.15	3.00	1.47	1.80	1.54	1.93	4.21	1.80	1.94	2.07
Tchr.	1.40	0.91	1.24	0.68	0.65	0.90	0.84	1.06	0.25	1.43	1.07	0.98
Obs.	0.76	0.97	0.78	0.31	1.08	0.80	0.90	0.67	0.39	0.33	0.67	0.67
STR-SOL... : Supvr.	2.22	1.60	3.36	2.76	4.38	2.92	1.99	1.57	2.63	2.54	1.39	2.20
Tchr.	1.81	1.12	0.71	1.13	0.73	1.03	1.55	1.46	0.98	0.72	1.86	1.20
Obs.	0.44	0.73	0.39	0.10	0.13	0.36	0.58	0.48	0.46	0.50	0.33	0.49
SOL... : Supvr.	2.11	2.40	3.25	3.24	3.75	2.97	3.46	3.34	3.49	2.87	2.17	3.18
Tchr.	1.28	0.51	0.35	0.66	0.52	0.61	0.62	0.85	0.59	0.69	0.84	0.69
Obs.	0.63	0.93	0.47	0.22	0.46	0.59	0.58	0.39	0.43	0.36	0.74	0.48
Total : Supvr.	1.84	2.01	3.00	3.07	2.88	2.55	2.58	2.62	3.55	2.48	1.99	2.69
Tchr.	1.38	0.69	0.66	0.74	0.61	0.77	0.79	0.98	0.57	0.93	1.05	0.85
Obs.	0.67	0.92	0.52	0.24	0.67	0.64	0.65	0.51	0.42	0.37	0.67	0.55

Pattern by Initiator	Participation Index (Units): Early Conferences						Participation Index (Units): Late Conferences					
	1	2	3	4	5	$\overline{X}$	1	2	3	4	5	$\overline{X}$
STR... : Supvr.	1.38	1.49	1.31	3.27	2.28	2.02	1.15	2.06	4.60	1.97	2.68	2.30
Tchr.	1.31	0.69	1.07	0.51	0.65	0.78	1.13	1.23	0.15	1.01	0.93	0.90
Obs.	0.81	1.08	0.85	0.31	0.83	0.79	0.92	0.50	0.35	0.55	0.53	0.64
STR-SOL... : Supvr.	1.21	2.19	3.00	2.21	5.38	2.80	2.52	1.41	3.30	2.01	1.89	2.34
Tchr.	2.34	1.08	0.66	1.35	0.43	1.04	1.68	1.52	0.77	0.80	1.83	1.27
Obs.	0.55	0.57	0.55	0.19	0.02	0.39	0.41	0.48	0.37	0.68	0.20	0.40
SOL... : Supvr.	2.20	2.91	3.21	3.07	3.69	2.99	3.90	3.29	3.27	2.97	2.21	3.19
Tchr.	0.96	0.51	0.32	0.48	0.80	0.56	0.31	0.91	0.46	0.47	0.76	0.59
Obs.	0.70	0.78	0.71	0.42	0.30	0.61	0.44	0.36	0.59	0.48	0.78	0.53
Total : Supvr.	1.60	2.29	2.37	3.00	3.24	2.52	2.34	2.45	3.81	2.38	2.37	2.66
Tchr.	1.35	1.35	0.72	0.65	0.65	0.76	0.89	1.14	0.40	0.75	1.03	0.84
Obs.	0.74	0.74	0.72	0.33	0.53	0.65	0.69	0.45	0.45	0.54	0.56	0.56

STR... = Teaching cycles 1, 3, 4
STR-SOL... = Teaching cycles 2, 5, 6, 7, 8, 9, 10, 11, 12
SOL... = Teaching cycles 13, 14, 15, 16, 17, 18, 19, 20, 21
Participation Indices (P.I.) = (% Units by initiator) / (% Participation in conference)

TABLE 37

Percentage of Moves by Supervisory Groups in Each Substantive Area
and Dimension: Planning and Analysis Conferences

Category	% Moves by Group: Planning Conferences						% Moves by Group: Analysis Conferences					
	1	*2*	*3*	*4*	*5*	$\overline{X}$	*1*	*2*	*3*	*4*	*5*	$\overline{X}$
SOC	37.5	18.8	18.4	17.6	33.4	25.8	2.4	0.0	3.6	13.3	5.1	4.9
SOA	0.5	0.0	0.7	0.7	1.8	0.6	1.9	0.4	8.8	1.4	1.0	2.3
SOD	0.1	1.6	0.2	0.0	0.0	0.3	0.1	0.0	10.1	0.0	0.0	1.4
SMC	45.6	35.9	40.8	55.9	42.1	45.4	16.4	11.0	6.8	24.0	17.3	15.9
SMA	1.1	0.0	7.4	0.0	0.3	1.4	4.2	6.1	8.2	1.2	3.5	4.3
SMD	0.8	4.3	12.0	0.0	0.0	2.8	2.2	1.6	1.9	1.1	0.0	1.4
SXC	2.8	17.5	0.7	4.8	7.1	6.1	38.9	16.3	24.7	24.4	36.0	29.1
SXA	0.7	2.5	6.7	0.0	0.3	1.7	13.6	13.4	23.0	1.9	26.1	14.7
SXD	0.0	7.5	2.5	0.4	0.0	1.8	15.0	31.8	8.2	3.5	0.6	12.1
GOC	0.0	0.2	1.6	0.1	1.0	0.4	0.0	0.2	1.4	0.9	0.2	0.4
GOA	0.0	0.0	0.0	0.0	0.0	0.0	0.0	0.0	0.8	0.2	0.0	0.1
GOD	0.0	0.0	0.0	0.3	0.0	0.1	0.0	0.0	0.0	0.0	0.0	0.0
GMC	0.0	1.0	2.8	1.2	0.8	1.1	0.3	0.0	0.0	0.4	3.5	0.8
GMA	0.2	0.0	0.0	0.0	0.0	0.0	0.0	3.9	0.0	0.4	0.0	0.8
GMD	0.1	0.4	0.0	3.2	0.0	0.9	1.2	0.2	0.5	2.3	0.0	0.9
GXC	0.5	2.4	0.2	0.0	0.0	0.6	0.1	3.7	0.5	3.0	3.1	2.0
GXA	0.2	0.0	0.0	0.0	0.0	0.1	0.1	0.0	0.3	0.2	0.0	0.1
GXD	0.0	1.0	0.0	0.9	0.0	0.4	0.0	1.6	0.5	0.9	0.0	0.6
O	38.1	20.6	21.0	18.7	36.2	27.3	4.5	0.6	24.7	15.8	6.3	9.2
M	47.8	41.8	62.9	60.3	43.1	51.5	24.2	22.8	17.5	29.3	24.4	24.1
X	4.2	30.8	10.1	6.1	7.4	10.6	67.8	66.8	57.3	33.9	65.8	58.6
C	86.6	75.7	64.5	79.6	84.4	79.4	58.1	31.2	37.0	66.0	65.2	53.2
A	2.6	2.5	14.7	0.7	2.3	3.8	19.9	23.8	41.1	5.3	30.6	22.4
D	0.9	14.7	14.7	4.8	0.0	6.2	18.5	35.2	21.4	7.7	0.6	16.4
S	89.1	88.2	89.4	79.3	84.9	85.9	94.7	80.6	95.3	70.9	89.6	86.1
G	1.1	4.9	4.6	5.7	1.8	3.5	1.8	9.6	4.1	8.1	6.9	5.9
Instr. total	90.1	93.1	94.0	85.1	86.7	89.5	96.5	90.2	99.5	78.9	96.5	92.0
SBJ	6.5	1.4	6.0	9.6	5.4	6.2	0.0	2.0	0.5	20.0	1.2	4.9
SPR	2.2	5.5	0.0	4.5	6.6	3.6	3.2	6.5	0.0	0.2	2.4	2.6
GRL	0.2	0.0	0.0	0.0	1.3	0.2	0.0	0.0	0.0	0.9	0.0	0.2
GNR	0.9	0.0	0.0	0.8	0.0	0.5	0.3	1.4	0.0	0.0	0.0	0.3
Rel. total	9.8	6.9	6.0	14.9	13.3	10.5	3.5	9.9	0.5	21.1	3.6	8.0

O = Objectives   C = Cognitive   S = Specific   SBJ = Subject
M = Methods   A = Affective   G = General   SPR = Supervision
X = Execution   D = Social   GRL = Related
GNR = Nonrelated

180

TABLE 38

Percentage of Units by Supervisory Groups in Each Substantive Area
and Dimension: Planning and Analysis Conferences

Category	% Units by Group: Planning Conferences						% Units by Group: Analysis Conferences					
	1	2	3	4	5	$\overline{X}$	1	2	3	4	5	$\overline{X}$
SOC	42.8	20.4	18.3	16.5	43.4	29.1	3.1	0.0	2.6	11.1	5.7	4.5
SOA	1.1	0.0	0.8	0.4	1.1	0.7	1.6	0.4	8.1	1.2	1.3	2.3
SOD	0.0	2.3	0.3	0.0	0.0	0.5	0.3	0.0	9.9	0.0	0.0	1.8
SMC	39.8	32.4	34.6	52.1	38.1	39.7	14.9	10.9	6.2	32.5	14.5	15.9
SMA	1.0	0.0	7.4	0.0	0.1	1.5	4.6	4.0	12.3	1.0	3.1	4.8
SMD	0.8	3.5	13.4	0.0	0.0	3.1	1.6	1.5	4.2	1.6	0.0	1.7
SXC	3.0	17.1	0.8	5.4	5.4	6.3	38.8	21.1	18.7	20.5	32.9	27.2
SXA	0.9	4.6	4.7	0.0	0.1	1.9	12.3	11.9	21.1	2.6	25.4	14.6
SXD	0.0	10.3	2.7	0.2	0.0	2.4	16.5	35.5	11.3	3.9	0.2	13.5
GOC	0.0	0.5	3.4	0.2	1.5	1.0	0.0	0.1	0.5	1.2	0.2	0.4
GOA	0.0	0.0	0.0	0.0	0.0	0.0	0.0	0.0	0.5	0.1	0.0	0.1
GOD	0.0	0.0	0.0	0.1	0.0	0.0	0.0	0.0	0.0	0.0	0.0	0.0
GMC	0.3	0.8	8.4	2.6	0.9	2.4	0.7	0.0	0.0	1.5	3.4	1.2
GMA	0.9	0.0	0.0	0.0	0.0	0.2	0.0	2.5	0.0	0.4	0.0	0.6
GMD	0.0	0.2	0.0	9.4	0.0	2.0	1.3	0.1	2.0	6.2	0.0	1.9
GXC	1.2	3.3	0.8	0.0	0.0	1.1	0.5	3.7	0.9	2.4	4.6	2.4
GXA	0.4	0.0	0.0	0.0	0.0	0.1	0.8	0.0	0.4	0.2	0.0	0.3
GXD	0.0	0.8	0.0	3.5	0.0	0.9	0.0	1.6	0.5	0.5	0.0	0.5
O	44.0	23.2	22.7	17.2	46.0	31.3	5.1	0.5	21.7	13.6	7.2	9.1
M	42.9	36.9	63.7	64.1	39.2	49.0	23.1	19.1	24.7	43.2	21.0	26.0
X	5.6	36.0	9.0	9.2	5.5	12.7	68.9	73.9	52.9	30.3	63.1	58.5
C	87.2	74.5	66.3	76.8	89.3	79.5	58.0	35.8	29.0	69.2	61.3	51.6
A	4.4	4.6	12.8	0.4	1.3	4.4	19.3	18.9	42.5	5.6	29.8	22.7
D	0.8	17.0	16.3	13.3	0.0	8.9	19.8	38.7	27.9	12.2	0.2	19.4
S	89.5	90.6	82.9	74.6	88.2	85.3	93.7	85.4	94.6	74.4	83.1	86.3
G	2.9	5.5	12.6	15.8	2.4	7.6	3.4	8.0	4.7	12.6	8.2	7.3
Instr. total	92.4	96.1	95.5	90.5	90.6	92.9	97.1	93.4	99.3	87.0	91.3	93.6
SBJ	5.1	1.2	4.5	5.9	4.1	4.2	0.0	1.8	0.7	12.1	0.6	2.9
SPR	1.8	2.7	0.0	3.3	4.7	2.5	2.8	4.3	0.0	0.5	8.1	3.3
GRL	0.2	0.0	0.0	0.0	0.6	0.2	0.0	0.0	0.0	0.4	0.0	0.1
GNR	0.5	0.0	0.0	0.3	0.0	0.2	0.1	0.5	0.0	0.0	0.0	0.1
Rel. total	7.6	3.9	4.5	9.5	9.4	7.1	2.9	6.6	0.7	13.0	8.7	6.4

O = Objectives   C = Cognitive   S = Specific   SBJ = Subject
M = Methods   A = Affective   G = General   SPR = Supervision
X = Execution   D = Social   GRL = Related
                                                          GNR = Nonrelated

TABLE 39

Percentage of Moves by Supervisory Groups in Each Substantive Area
and Dimension: Early and Late Conferences

Category	% Moves by Group: Early Conferences						% Moves by Group: Late Conferences					
	1	2	3	4	5	$\overline{X}$	1	2	3	4	5	$\overline{X}$
SOC	22.1	12.6	7.9	19.0	14.6	16.3	20.3	6.5	15.4	13.7	19.5	15.4
SOA	0.5	0.0	5.7	0.2	0.0	1.1	1.7	0.4	3.0	1.5	2.3	1.7
SOD	0.3	1.6	8.7	0.0	0.0	1.8	0.0	0.0	0.8	0.0	0.0	0.1
SMC	35.4	12.8	19.4	35.6	30.5	27.8	28.7	33.5	31.3	46.3	26.3	34.1
SMA	1.2	1.4	9.2	1.4	0.3	2.4	3.8	4.6	6.3	0.0	3.4	3.2
SMD	1.5	5.1	12.9	0.8	0.0	3.6	1.4	1.0	1.8	0.2	0.0	0.8
SXC	20.3	16.8	5.0	19.3	24.1	17.6	18.9	17.0	18.4	9.3	22.9	16.7
SXA	2.7	2.6	19.6	1.5	14.1	6.8	10.6	13.0	8.6	0.4	15.5	8.9
SXD	9.0	27.9	6.5	3.7	0.0	9.9	5.0	11.8	3.8	0.5	0.6	4.1
GOC	0.0	0.0	1.2	1.2	1.3	0.6	0.0	0.4	1.8	0.0	0.0	0.3
GOA	0.0	0.0	0.7	0.0	0.0	0.1	0.0	0.0	0.0	0.1	0.0	0.0
GOD	0.0	0.0	0.0	0.0	0.0	0.0	0.0	0.0	0.0	0.2	0.0	0.1
GMC	0.5	0.4	0.2	1.0	5.0	1.2	0.0	0.6	2.8	0.7	0.4	0.7
GMA	0.0	0.0	0.0	0.2	0.0	0.0	0.1	3.8	0.0	0.1	0.0	0.7
GMD	0.0	0.6	0.5	1.7	0.0	0.5	1.1	0.0	0.0	3.5	0.0	1.2
GXC	0.6	2.0	0.7	3.3	0.8	1.5	0.0	4.0	0.0	0.0	2.5	1.1
GXA	0.0	0.0	0.2	0.0	0.0	0.0	0.4	0.0	0.0	0.1	0.0	0.1
GXD	0.0	1.2	0.2	1.0	0.0	0.5	0.0	1.3	0.3	0.9	0.0	0.5
O	22.9	14.2	24.3	20.3	15.9	19.9	22.0	7.2	21.0	15.6	21.8	17.6
M	38.6	20.2	42.2	40.6	35.8	35.6	35.1	43.6	42.2	50.9	30.2	40.8
X	32.7	50.6	32.3	28.8	39.0	36.2	34.9	47.0	31.1	11.2	41.4	31.4
C	79.0	44.5	34.5	79.3	76.4	65.1	67.9	61.9	69.7	70.1	71.6	68.3
A	4.4	4.0	35.5	3.3	14.3	10.4	16.6	21.7	17.9	2.2	21.2	14.7
D	10.8	36.4	28.8	7.2	0.0	16.2	7.5	14.1	6.6	5.4	0.6	6.8
S	93.1	80.8	94.8	81.4	83.6	87.2	90.4	87.8	89.4	72.0	90.5	85.0
G	1.2	4.3	4.0	8.3	7.2	4.5	1.6	10.1	4.8	5.7	2.9	4.8
Instr. total	94.2	85.0	98.8	89.7	90.7	91.7	92.0	97.9	94.2	77.7	93.3	89.8
SBJ	1.2	3.0	1.2	5.4	2.4	2.6	5.7	0.4	5.8	19.7	3.4	8.1
SPR	3.1	10.5	0.0	3.9	6.6	4.7	2.3	1.7	0.0	1.9	2.5	1.8
GRL	0.3	0.0	0.0	1.0	0.3	0.3	0.0	0.0	0.0	0.0	0.8	0.1
GNR	1.3	1.4	0.0	0.0	0.0	0.7	0.0	0.0	0.0	0.7	0.0	0.2
Rel. total	5.9	14.9	1.2	10.3	9.3	8.3	8.0	2.1	5.8	22.3	6.7	10.2

O = Objectives   C = Cognitive   S = Specific   SBJ = Subject
M = Methods   A = Affective   G = General   SPR = Supervision
X = Execution   D = Social   GRL = Related
                                              GNR = Nonrelated

TABLE 40

Percentage of Units by Supervisory Groups in Each Substantive Area
and Dimension: Early and Late Conferences

Category	% Units by Group: Early Conferences						% Units by Group: Late Conferences					
	1	2	3	4	5	$\overline{X}$	1	2	3	4	5	$\overline{X}$
SOC	21.4	14.1	6.6	14.4	20.5	15.7	24.6	5.5	14.2	13.4	26.2	17.5
SOA	1.1	0.0	7.1	0.5	0.0	1.6	1.6	0.4	1.8	1.0	2.2	1.4
SOD	0.4	2.1	9.2	0.0	0.0	2.2	0.0	0.0	1.0	0.0	0.0	0.2
SMC	32.5	11.5	15.1	43.3	27.8	26.3	22.4	31.6	25.5	41.8	24.1	28.9
SMA	0.9	0.8	8.7	1.0	0.1	2.2	4.6	3.4	11.1	0.0	2.9	4.1
SMD	1.2	3.8	12.9	0.9	0.0	3.5	1.2	1.1	4.4	0.7	0.0	1.3
SXC	23.3	19.8	3.4	16.1	19.3	16.9	18.5	18.6	16.7	9.9	20.2	16.8
SXA	2.2	2.3	19.7	1.8	9.8	6.7	10.8	14.7	6.1	0.8	16.2	9.9
SXD	10.4	32.3	9.4	3.6	0.0	11.4	6.2	13.7	4.7	0.7	0.2	4.9
GOC	0.0	0.0	0.5	1.4	1.8	0.7	0.0	0.6	3.4	0.0	0.0	0.6
GOA	0.0	0.0	0.5	0.0	0.0	0.1	0.0	0.0	0.0	0.1	0.0	0.0
GOD	0.0	0.0	0.0	0.0	0.0	0.0	0.0	0.0	0.0	0.1	0.0	0.0
GMC	1.1	0.4	1.6	2.9	4.5	2.0	0.0	0.4	6.8	1.4	0.4	1.5
GMA	0.0	0.0	0.0	0.4	0.0	0.1	0.9	2.7	0.0	0.1	0.0	0.7
GMD	0.0	0.3	2.0	4.4	0.0	1.3	1.3	0.0	0.0	10.8	0.0	2.5
GXC	1.8	2.4	1.7	2.6	1.1	1.9	0.0	4.7	0.0	0.0	3.4	1.6
GXA	0.0	0.0	0.4	0.0	0.0	0.1	1.3	0.0	0.0	0.2	0.0	0.3
GXD	0.0	0.9	0.2	0.5	0.0	0.3	0.0	1.5	0.3	3.4	0.0	1.0
O	22.9	16.2	23.9	16.3	22.3	20.3	26.2	6.5	20.4	14.6	28.3	19.8
M	35.7	16.8	40.2	52.8	32.4	35.4	30.4	39.2	47.7	54.8	27.4	39.2
X	37.6	57.7	34.8	24.6	30.3	37.3	36.7	53.2	27.7	15.0	40.1	34.5
C	80.1	48.1	28.9	80.6	75.0	63.6	65.5	61.3	66.6	66.4	74.3	67.0
A	4.2	3.1	36.5	3.7	10.0	10.7	19.1	21.2	19.0	2.3	21.3	16.5
D	12.0	39.4	33.6	9.4	0.0	18.7	8.7	16.4	10.3	15.7	0.2	10.0
S	93.4	86.8	92.1	81.6	77.5	86.6	89.9	89.2	85.4	68.3	92.0	85.0
G	2.8	3.9	6.9	12.1	7.5	6.4	3.4	9.8	10.4	16.1	3.8	8.4
Instr. total	96.2	90.7	99.0	93.7	85.0	93.0	93.3	99.0	95.8	84.4	95.8	93.5
SBJ	0.7	2.7	1.0	3.2	1.8	1.8	4.3	0.2	4.2	14.0	2.7	5.2
SPR	2.2	6.1	0.0	2.7	13.0	4.7	2.3	0.8	0.0	1.3	1.2	1.2
GRL	0.2	0.0	0.0	0.4	0.2	0.2	0.0	0.0	0.0	0.0	0.4	0.1
GNR	0.7	0.5	0.0	0.0	0.0	0.3	0.0	0.0	0.0	0.3	0.0	0.1
Rel. total	3.8	9.3	1.0	6.3	15.0	7.0	6.6	1.0	4.2	15.6	4.3	6.6

O = Objectives   C = Cognitive   S = Specific   SBJ = Subject
M = Methods   A = Affective   G = General   SPR = Supervision
X = Execution   D = Social   GRL = Related
                                               GNR = Nonrelated

TABLE 41

Percentage of Moves by Supervisory Groups in Each Substantive-Logical
Category and Dimension: Planning and Analysis Conferences

Category	% Moves by Group: Planning Conferences						% Moves by Group: Analysis Conferences					
	1	2	3	4	5	$\overline{X}$	1	2	3	4	5	$\overline{X}$
DEF	0.0	0.8	0.0	0.0	0.5	0.2	0.0	0.0	0.5	0.0	1.2	0.3
INT	4.9	4.1	8.1	4.9	7.7	5.6	2.3	4.5	6.0	3.7	4.1	3.9
FAC	26.7	24.5	19.8	28.5	19.9	24.9	24.9	25.5	15.1	20.5	26.5	23.1
XPL	7.5	17.6	17.1	8.7	14.3	11.9	17.8	25.7	24.4	22.6	20.2	21.7
SUG	8.0	7.3	4.8	5.1	9.7	6.9	2.7	2.0	1.9	3.2	4.9	3.0
SGX	7.2	6.3	4.1	4.7	9.7	6.3	3.1	2.8	2.5	4.4	3.1	3.2
EVL	5.4	2.9	3.9	3.6	4.8	4.2	8.8	5.5	3.8	5.6	4.5	6.0
JUS	4.5	2.7	8.3	2.0	3.3	3.9	10.8	9.0	4.4	4.9	8.4	8.7
OPN	4.3	4.1	0.9	4.4	1.8	3.5	3.4	2.0	9.9	4.0	3.3	3.4
OPJ	4.9	8.6	5.8	6.4	4.3	6.0	5.9	3.3	8.8	7.0	5.9	6.1
FAC + XPL	34.2	42.1	36.9	37.2	34.2	36.8	42.7	51.2	39.5	43.1	46.7	44.8
EVL + JUS	9.9	5.6	12.2	5.6	8.1	8.1	19.6	14.5	8.2	10.5	12.9	14.7
SUG + SGX	15.2	13.6	8.9	9.8	19.4	13.2	5.8	4.8	4.4	7.6	8.0	6.2
OPN + OPJ	9.2	12.7	6.7	10.8	6.1	9.5	9.3	5.3	18.7	11.0	9.2	9.5
Anal.	49.4	55.7	45.8	47.0	53.6	50.0	48.5	56.0	43.9	50.7	54.7	51.0
Eval.	19.1	18.3	18.9	16.4	14.2	17.6	28.9	19.8	26.9	21.5	22.1	24.2
A/E	2.58	3.04	2.42	2.87	3.78	2.84	1.64	2.83	1.63	2.36	2.48	2.11
Diagn.	44.1	47.7	49.1	42.8	42.3	44.9	62.3	65.7	47.7	53.6	59.6	59.5
Presc.	24.4	26.3	15.6	20.6	25.5	22.7	15.1	10.1	23.1	18.6	17.2	15.7
D/P	1.81	1.81	3.15	2.08	1.66	1.98	4.13	6.50	2.06	2.88	3.21	3.78
Complex	24.1	35.2	35.3	21.8	31.6	28.1	37.6	40.8	40.1	38.9	37.6	39.7
Simple	44.4	38.8	29.4	41.6	36.2	39.5	39.8	35.0	30.7	33.3	39.2	35.5
C/S	0.54	0.91	1.20	0.52	0.87	0.71	0.95	1.17	1.31	1.17	0.96	1.12

Anal. / Eval. = A/E = (FAC + XPL + SUG + SGX) / (EVL + JUS + OPN + OPJ)
Diag. / Presc. = D/P = (FAC + XPL + EVL + JUS) / (SUG + SGX + OPN + OPJ)
Complex/Simple = C/S = (XPL + SGX + JUS + OPJ) / (FAC + EVL + SUG + OPN)

TABLE 42

Percentage of Units by Supervisory Groups in Each Substantive-Logical
Category and Dimension: Planning and Analysis Conferences

Category	% Units by Group: Planning Conferences						% Units by Group: Analysis Conferences					
	1	*2*	*3*	*4*	*5*	$\overline{X}$	*1*	*2*	*3*	*4*	*5*	$\overline{X}$
DEF	0.0	0.3	0.0	0.0	0.2	0.1	0.0	0.0	0.1	0.0	0.8	0.2
INT	5.2	1.9	3.9	2.6	2.6	3.3	1.1	2.1	1.9	1.7	1.6	1.7
FAC	22.3	18.2	12.8	21.8	21.2	19.6	19.5	21.1	8.0	13.6	18.0	16.4
XPL	12.2	26.8	21.5	17.9	19.5	19.1	24.7	31.7	29.9	22.8	32.2	28.1
SUG	8.3	5.3	6.0	5.5	14.3	7.9	1.7	1.7	1.6	2.5	3.3	2.2
SGX	8.2	7.3	7.4	5.4	15.5	8.7	4.6	4.1	3.4	7.0	3.6	4.6
EVL	3.4	1.5	2.0	1.8	2.6	2.3	5.7	2.8	1.3	2.6	2.3	3.1
JUS	4.8	6.0	13.5	1.9	4.5	5.8	17.1	17.4	16.8	6.6	16.9	15.0
OPN	3.3	3.0	1.1	4.8	1.0	2.7	2.8	1.2	3.1	3.5	2.8	2.7
OPJ	12.3	16.4	15.1	15.4	6.3	13.1	7.9	6.0	21.6	22.8	7.9	12.7
FAC + XPL	34.5	45.0	34.3	39.7	40.7	38.7	44.2	52.8	37.9	36.4	50.2	44.5
EVL + JUS	8.2	7.5	15.5	3.7	7.1	8.1	22.8	20.2	18.1	9.2	19.2	18.1
SUG + SGX	16.5	12.6	13.4	10.9	29.8	16.6	6.3	5.8	5.0	9.5	6.9	6.8
OPN + OPJ	15.6	19.4	16.2	20.2	7.3	15.8	10.7	7.2	24.7	26.3	10.7	15.4
Anal.	51.0	57.6	47.7	50.6	70.5	55.3	50.5	58.6	42.9	45.9	57.1	51.3
Eval.	23.8	26.9	31.7	23.9	14.4	23.9	33.5	27.4	42.8	35.5	29.9	33.5
A/E	2.14	2.14	1.50	2.12	4.90	2.31	1.51	2.14	1.00	1.29	1.91	1.53
Diagn.	42.7	52.5	49.8	43.4	47.8	46.8	67.0	73.0	56.0	45.6	69.4	62.6
Presc.	32.1	32.0	29.6	31.1	37.1	32.4	17.0	13.0	29.7	35.8	17.6	22.2
D/P	1.33	1.64	1.68	1.40	1.29	1.45	3.94	5.62	1.89	1.27	3.94	2.82
Complex	37.5	56.5	57.5	40.6	45.8	46.7	54.3	59.2	71.7	59.2	60.6	60.4
Simple	37.3	28.0	21.9	33.9	39.1	32.5	29.7	26.8	14.0	22.2	26.4	24.4
C/S	1.00	2.02	2.62	1.20	1.17	1.44	1.83	2.21	5.12	2.67	2.30	2.47

Anal. / Eval. = A/E = (FAC + XPL + SUG + SGX) / (EVL + JUS + OPN + OPJ)
Diag. / Presc. = D/P = (FAC + XPL + EVL + JUS) / (SUG + SGX + OPN + OPJ)
Complex/Simple = C/S = (XPL + SGX + JUS + OPJ) / (FAC + EVL + SUG + OPN)

TABLE 43

Percentage of Moves by Supervisory Groups in Each Substantive-Logical
Category and Dimension: Early and Late Conferences

Category	% Moves by Group: Early Conferences						% Moves by Group: Late Conferences					
	1	2	3	4	5	$\bar{X}$	1	2	3	4	5	$\bar{X}$
DEF	0.0	0.8	0.5	0.0	2.1	0.5	0.0	0.0	0.0	0.0	0.0	0.0
INT	4.4	2.8	8.2	5.8	4.5	5.0	3.1	5.7	6.1	3.5	6.5	4.6
FAC	23.7	28.3	13.9	22.8	18.3	22.1	27.9	21.9	21.5	26.5	27.5	25.6
XPL	13.9	19.4	21.8	15.9	19.9	17.5	10.8	23.8	18.9	13.9	16.0	15.8
SUG	4.8	3.4	4.0	3.1	6.1	4.2	6.3	5.7	3.0	5.0	7.6	5.6
SGX	5.9	4.3	3.0	4.3	5.6	4.8	4.7	4.8	3.8	4.7	6.3	4.9
EVL	5.9	4.0	2.0	5.8	4.0	4.6	8.0	4.4	5.8	3.6	5.2	5.5
JUS	6.6	5.1	11.2	3.5	6.4	6.3	8.2	6.7	6.8	3.1	6.1	6.1
OPN	5.0	4.0	2.7	4.1	5.8	4.4	2.8	2.1	2.3	4.4	0.4	2.6
OPJ	7.2	6.3	6.7	7.4	8.8	7.2	3.7	5.7	7.6	6.2	2.7	5.0
FAC + XPL	37.6	47.7	35.7	38.7	38.2	39.6	38.7	45.7	40.4	40.4	43.5	41.4
EVL + JUS	12.5	9.1	13.2	9.3	10.4	10.9	16.2	11.1	12.6	6.7	11.3	11.6
SUG + SGX	10.7	7.7	7.0	7.4	11.7	9.0	11.0	10.5	6.8	9.7	13.9	10.5
OPN + OPJ	12.2	10.3	9.4	11.5	14.6	11.6	6.5	7.8	9.9	10.6	3.1	7.6
Anal.	48.3	55.4	42.7	46.1	49.9	48.6	49.7	56.2	47.2	50.1	57.4	51.9
Eval.	24.7	19.4	22.6	20.8	25.0	22.5	22.7	18.9	22.5	17.3	14.4	19.2
A/E	1.96	2.85	1.89	2.22	2.00	2.16	2.19	2.97	2.10	2.90	3.99	2.70
Diagn.	50.1	56.8	48.9	48.0	48.6	50.5	54.9	56.8	53.0	47.1	54.8	53.0
Presc.	22.9	18.0	16.4	18.9	26.3	20.6	17.5	18.3	16.7	20.3	17.0	18.1
D/P	2.19	3.16	2.98	2.54	1.85	2.45	3.14	3.10	3.17	2.32	3.22	2.93
Complex	33.6	35.1	42.7	31.1	40.7	35.8	27.4	41.0	37.1	27.9	31.1	31.8
Simple	39.4	39.7	22.6	35.8	34.2	35.3	45.0	34.1	32.6	39.5	40.7	39.3
C/S	0.85	0.89	1.89	0.87	1.18	1.02	0.61	1.20	1.14	0.71	0.76	0.81

Anal. / Eval. = A/E = (FAC + XPL + SUG + SGX) / (EVL + JUS + OPN + OPJ)
Diag. / Presc. = D/P = (FAC + XPL + EVL + JUS) / (SUG + SGX + OPN + OPJ)
Complex/Simple = C/S = (XPL + SGX + JUS + OPJ) / (FAC + EVL + SUG + OPN)

TABLE 44

Percentage of Moves by Supervisory Groups in Each Substantive-Logical
Category and Dimension: Early and Late Conferences

Category	% Units by Group: Early Conferences						% Units by Group: Late Conferences					
	1	2	3	4	5	$\overline{X}$	1	2	3	4	5	$\overline{X}$
DEF	0.0	0.3	0.1	0.0	1.1	0.3	0.0	0.0	0.0	0.0	0.0	0.0
INT	2.4	1.2	3.5	2.3	1.6	2.2	3.8	2.9	2.3	2.1	2.5	2.8
FAC	16.5	23.7	9.0	15.5	11.5	15.5	25.1	15.6	11.8	19.9	26.0	20.3
XPL	19.2	28.2	30.7	21.6	30.8	25.7	17.7	30.6	20.6	19.2	22.4	21.8
SUG	4.5	2.4	4.7	2.8	5.8	4.0	5.6	4.6	2.7	5.2	10.7	6.0
SGX	6.7	3.7	5.5	8.0	10.7	6.9	6.1	7.7	5.2	4.6	8.1	6.4
EVL	4.4	2.4	0.7	2.4	1.6	2.4	4.6	1.9	2.5	2.0	3.1	2.9
JUS	10.4	11.8	18.2	4.2	9.7	10.7	11.5	11.9	12.0	4.2	12.0	10.3
OPN	4.1	2.9	2.6	4.1	3.9	3.6	2.0	1.2	1.6	4.2	0.4	1.9
OPJ	15.6	11.2	10.9	22.2	12.0	14.5	4.9	10.9	26.2	16.2	3.3	11.4
FAC + XPL	35.7	51.9	39.7	37.1	42.3	41.2	42.8	46.2	32.4	39.1	48.4	42.1
EVL + JUS	14.8	14.2	18.9	6.6	11.3	13.1	16.1	13.8	14.5	6.2	15.1	13.2
SUG + SGX	11.2	6.1	10.2	10.8	16.5	10.9	11.7	12.3	7.9	9.8	18.8	12.4
OPN + OPJ	19.7	14.1	13.5	26.3	15.9	18.1	6.9	12.1	27.8	20.4	3.7	13.3
Anal.	46.9	58.0	49.9	47.9	58.8	52.1	54.5	58.5	40.3	48.9	67.2	54.5
Eval.	34.5	28.3	32.4	32.9	27.2	31.2	23.0	25.9	42.3	26.6	18.8	26.5
A/E	1.36	2.05	1.54	1.46	2.16	1.67	2.37	2.26	.95	1.84	3.57	2.06
Diagn.	50.5	66.1	58.6	43.7	53.6	54.3	58.9	60.0	46.9	45.3	63.5	55.3
Presc.	30.9	20.2	23.7	37.1	32.4	29.0	18.6	24.4	35.7	30.2	22.5	25.7
D/P	1.64	3.28	2.47	1.18	1.65	1.87	3.16	2.46	1.31	1.50	2.82	2.17
Complex	51.9	54.9	65.3	56.0	63.2	57.8	40.2	61.1	63.0	44.2	45.8	49.9
Simple	29.5	31.4	17.0	24.8	22.8	25.5	37.3	23.3	18.6	31.3	40.2	31.1
C/S	1.76	1.75	3.84	2.26	2.77	2.27	1.08	2.63	3.39	1.41	1.14	1.60

Anal. / Eval. = A/E = (FAC + XPL + SUG + SGX) / (EVL + JUS + OPN + OPJ)
Diag. / Presc. = D/P = (FAC + XPL + EVL + JUS) / (SUG + SGX + OPN + OPJ)
Complex/Simple = C/S = (XPL + SGX + JUS + OPJ) / (FAC + EVL + SUG + OPN)

TABLE 45

Percentage of Moves by Supervisory Groups in Each Procedural and
Procedural-Logical Category: Planning and Analysis Conferences

Category	% Moves by Group: Planning Conferences						% Moves by Group: Analysis Conferences					
	1	2	3	4	5	$\overline{X}$	1	2	3	4	5	$\overline{X}$
STA	9.6	6.1	6.9	14.3	10.5	9.9	10.3	9.0	13.2	11.9	10.2	10.8
ACT	6.9	5.3	13.8	8.4	7.1	8.1	4.6	6.9	5.2	9.6	4.3	6.1
PRC	7.2	5.7	1.8	4.4	4.3	5.0	4.1	2.0	3.0	1.4	2.2	2.6
PER	2.8	3.9	4.6	4.7	2.0	3.6	1.4	1.8	1.4	1.1	1.0	1.3
Proc. total	26.5	21.0	27.1	31.8	23.9	26.6	20.4	19.7	22.8	24.0	17.7	20.8
POS	2.1	0.4	1.4	1.2	2.3	1.5	2.0	1.8	1.1	1.1	2.0	1.6
ADM	4.1	3.7	4.4	10.1	5.6	5.8	4.3	5.3	8.8	8.4	6.5	6.4
RPT	2.1	0.8	0.7	1.7	0.8	1.4	1.5	0.4	0.8	1.2	0.2	0.9
QAL	0.8	1.0	0.5	1.1	1.5	1.0	1.9	1.0	1.9	0.9	1.4	1.4
NAD	0.5	0.2	0.0	0.1	0.0	0.2	0.4	0.6	0.5	0.4	0.2	0.4
NEG	0.0	0.0	0.0	0.0	0.0	0.0	0.1	0.0	0.0	0.0	0.0	0.0
Pos. sum	8.3	4.9	6.5	13.0	8.7	8.7	7.8	7.5	10.7	10.7	8.7	8.9
Neg. sum	1.3	1.2	0.5	1.2	1.5	1.2	2.4	1.6	2.4	1.3	1.6	1.8
P/N	6.4	4.1	13.0	10.8	5.8	7.3	3.3	4.7	4.5	8.2	5.4	4.9
DEF	0.0	0.0	0.0	0.0	0.0	0.0	0.0	0.0	0.0	0.0	0.0	0.0
INT	0.6	0.4	1.6	0.5	0.0	0.6	0.3	0.6	0.5	0.5	0.0	0.4
FAC	7.0	6.2	5.8	8.1	4.4	6.7	4.2	4.7	1.6	8.1	4.9	4.9
SUG	0.5	0.8	0.2	0.7	1.3	0.6	0.4	0.2	0.3	0.0	0.0	0.2
XPL	1.0	0.6	0.2	0.9	1.5	0.9	1.0	0.4	1.4	0.7	0.4	0.8
SGX	0.2	0.6	0.0	0.8	0.5	0.4	0.3	0.4	0.0	0.2	0.4	0.3
EVL	0.2	0.0	0.0	0.1	0.0	0.1	0.0	0.0	0.0	0.0	0.0	0.0
OPN	0.4	0.2	0.4	0.5	0.3	0.3	0.3	0.2	0.3	0.0	0.0	0.1
JUS	0.0	0.0	0.0	0.0	0.0	0.0	0.0	0.0	0.0	0.0	0.0	0.0
OPJ	0.2	0.6	0.0	0.2	0.0	0.2	0.3	0.0	0.0	0.2	0.2	0.1
PRF	2.0	0.8	2.8	0.5	2.0	1.5	1.1	1.0	3.6	1.4	0.6	1.4
PON	0.4	0.4	0.9	0.0	0.0	0.4	0.3	0.0	0.5	0.0	0.0	0.2

Pos. sum = POS + ADM + RPT
Neg. sum = QAL + NAD + NEG
P/N = (Pos. sum) / (Neg. sum)

TABLE 46

Percentage of Units by Supervisory Groups in Each Procedural and
Procedural-Logical Category: Planning and Analysis Conferences

Category	% Units by Group: Planning Conferences						% Units by Group: Analysis Conferences					
	1	*2*	*3*	*4*	*5*	$\overline{X}$	*1*	*2*	*3*	*4*	*5*	$\overline{X}$
STA	8.2	5.5	4.8	10.1	5.4	7.0	7.4	6.1	6.6	9.0	6.7	7.2
ACT	4.7	2.8	6.5	5.3	2.6	4.4	3.4	3.4	2.4	5.8	2.1	3.4
PRC	6.0	3.4	3.9	4.8	3.7	4.5	3.2	1.8	3.1	1.6	1.5	2.2
PER	1.2	1.4	1.5	2.5	0.7	1.5	0.6	0.6	0.4	0.5	0.3	0.5
Proc. total	20.1	13.1	16.7	22.7	12.4	17.4	14.6	11.9	12.5	16.9	10.6	13.3
POS	1.6	0.5	0.8	1.1	1.0	1.0	1.4	1.1	0.5	0.8	0.9	1.0
ADM	3.9	3.1	3.0	7.1	3.2	4.1	3.7	3.5	3.7	5.7	4.1	4.1
RPT	1.0	0.4	0.2	1.0	0.4	0.6	0.7	0.3	0.2	0.8	0.2	0.5
QAL	0.9	1.1	0.6	0.7	0.6	0.8	1.0	0.7	1.4	1.3	0.9	1.1
NAD	0.8	0.2	0.1	0.2	0.1	0.3	0.5	0.4	0.7	0.4	0.4	0.5
NEG	0.0	0.3	0.1	0.0	0.0	0.1	0.0	0.0	0.0	0.0	0.1	0.0
Pos. sum	6.5	4.0	4.0	9.2	4.6	5.7	5.8	4.9	4.4	7.3	5.2	5.6
Neg. sum	1.7	1.6	0.8	0.9	0.7	1.2	1.5	1.1	2.1	1.7	1.4	1.6
P/N	4.2	2.5	5.0	10.2	6.6	4.8	3.9	4.5	2.1	4.3	3.7	3.5
DEF	0.0	0.0	0.0	0.0	0.0	0.0	0.0	0.0	0.0	0.0	0.0	0.0
INT	0.4	0.1	0.6	0.2	0.0	0.3	0.1	0.2	0.3	0.2	0.0	0.2
FAC	5.9	3.2	4.1	5.9	2.3	4.4	3.3	2.4	1.7	5.4	2.8	3.2
SUG	0.3	0.5	0.1	0.3	1.0	0.5	0.2	0.5	0.1	0.0	0.0	0.2
XPL	1.0	0.5	2.0	1.4	1.3	1.2	0.9	0.4	1.8	0.5	0.2	0.8
SGX	0.2	0.5	0.4	1.4	0.5	0.6	0.3	0.4	0.0	0.2	0.2	0.2
EVL	0.1	0.0	0.0	0.1	0.0	0.0	0.0	0.0	0.0	0.0	0.0	0.0
OPN	0.2	0.1	0.2	0.3	0.1	0.2	0.3	0.3	0.1	0.0	0.0	0.1
JUS	0.0	0.0	0.0	0.0	0.0	0.0	0.0	0.0	0.0	0.0	0.0	0.0
OPJ	0.4	0.6	0.0	0.2	0.0	0.2	0.4	0.0	0.0	0.5	0.2	0.2
PRF	1.3	0.5	1.3	0.2	0.7	0.8	0.5	0.4	1.1	0.7	0.3	0.6
PON	0.2	0.2	0.3	0.0	0.0	0.1	0.1	0.0	0.2	0.0	0.0	0.0

Pos. sum = POS + ADM + RPT
Neg. sum = QAL + NAD + NEG
P/N = (Pos. sum) / (Neg. sum)

TABLE 47

Percentage of Moves by Supervisory Groups in Each Procedural
and Procedural-Logical Category: Early and Late Conferences

Category	% Moves by Group: Early Conferences						% Moves by Group: Late Conferences					
	1	2	3	4	5	$\bar{X}$	1	2	3	4	5	$\bar{X}$
STA	10.7	7.1	9.4	12.8	7.4	9.7	9.2	8.0	10.1	13.6	12.4	10.8
ACT	5.5	7.3	9.4	10.4	5.3	7.4	6.1	5.0	10.4	8.0	5.7	6.9
PRC	4.6	3.2	3.0	2.5	4.0	3.6	6.8	4.4	1.8	3.5	2.5	4.1
PER	1.8	3.8	4.2	1.7	1.9	2.6	2.5	1.9	2.0	4.0	1.1	2.5
Proc. total	22.6	21.4	26.0	27.4	18.6	23.3	24.6	19.3	24.3	29.1	21.7	24.3
POS	2.6	1.6	2.2	1.4	2.4	1.1	1.6	0.6	0.3	1.0	1.9	1.1
ADM	4.0	4.3	5.5	9.3	3.2	6.8	4.4	4.8	7.3	9.5	8.2	6.8
RPT	1.8	0.6	0.5	1.5	0.3	1.2	1.8	0.6	1.0	1.5	0.6	1.2
QAL	1.5	0.4	1.0	0.6	1.6	1.3	1.1	1.5	1.3	1.2	1.3	1.3
NAD	0.6	0.2	0.2	0.0	0.0	0.3	0.2	0.6	0.3	0.4	0.2	0.3
NEG	0.1	0.0	0.0	0.0	0.0	0.0	0.0	0.0	0.0	0.0	0.0	0.0
Pos. sum	8.4	6.5	8.2	12.2	5.9	9.1	7.8	6.0	8.6	12.0	10.7	9.1
Neg. sum	2.2	0.6	1.2	0.6	1.6	1.6	1.3	2.1	1.6	1.6	1.5	1.6
P/N	3.8	10.8	6.8	20.3	3.7	5.7	6.0	2.9	5.4	7.5	7.1	5.7
DEF	0.0	0.0	0.0	0.0	0.0	0.0	0.0	0.0	0.0	0.0	0.0	0.0
INT	0.9	0.0	0.5	1.0	0.0	0.6	0.0	1.0	1.8	0.2	0.0	0.4
FAC	5.0	5.3	3.2	9.1	4.8	5.5	6.4	5.7	4.6	7.4	4.6	6.0
SUG	0.6	0.6	0.5	0.6	1.3	0.7	0.2	0.4	0.0	0.2	0.0	0.2
XPL	0.5	0.4	1.0	1.0	0.5	0.6	1.6	0.6	0.5	0.7	1.2	1.0
SGX	0.3	0.8	0.0	0.2	0.5	0.4	0.2	0.2	0.0	0.7	0.4	0.4
EVL	0.1	0.0	0.0	0.0	0.0	0.0	0.1	0.0	0.0	0.1	0.0	0.1
OPN	0.3	0.4	0.2	0.2	0.0	0.2	0.4	0.0	0.6	0.4	0.2	0.3
JUS	0.0	0.0	0.0	0.0	0.0	0.0	0.0	0.0	0.0	0.0	0.0	0.0
OPJ	0.3	0.0	0.0	0.2	0.0	0.1	0.2	0.6	0.0	0.2	0.2	0.2
PRF	1.4	1.2	4.0	0.8	2.1	1.8	1.7	0.6	2.3	1.0	0.6	1.2
PON	0.0	0.4	1.0	0.0	0.0	0.3	0.7	0.0	0.5	0.0	0.0	0.3

Pos. sum = POS + ADM + RPT
Neg. sum = QAL + NAD + NEG
P/N = (Pos. sum) / (Neg. sum)

TABLE 48

Percentage of Units by Supervisory Groups in Each Procedural and
Procedural-Logical Category: Early and Late Conferences

Category	% Units by Group: Early Conferences						% Units by Group: Late Conferences					
	1	*2*	*3*	*4*	*5*	$\overline{X}$	*1*	*2*	*3*	*4*	*5*	$\overline{X}$
STA	8.3	5.2	5.2	7.6	5.2	6.4	7.3	6.5	6.2	11.3	6.8	7.7
ACT	3.2	3.6	4.6	5.8	2.2	3.9	4.9	2.6	4.2	5.3	2.4	3.9
PRC	3.9	2.2	3.0	3.1	3.3	3.1	5.3	2.9	4.0	3.4	1.9	3.5
PER	0.7	1.2	1.1	0.6	0.6	0.8	1.1	0.7	0.7	2.4	0.4	1.1
Proc. total	16.1	12.2	13.9	17.1	11.3	14.2	18.6	12.7	15.1	22.4	11.5	16.2
POS	1.8	0.8	1.1	1.0	1.3	1.2	1.3	0.8	0.2	0.9	0.6	0.8
ADM	3.7	3.1	3.0	5.2	2.9	3.6	3.8	3.6	3.8	7.4	4.4	4.6
RPT	0.9	0.4	0.1	0.7	0.2	0.5	0.9	0.3	0.3	1.1	0.4	0.6
QAL	1.1	0.6	0.6	0.6	0.7	0.7	0.8	1.2	1.3	1.3	0.8	1.1
NAD	0.9	0.2	0.3	0.1	0.0	0.3	0.5	0.4	0.6	0.6	0.5	0.5
NEG	0.1	0.1	0.1	0.0	0.0	0.0	0.0	0.1	0.0	0.0	0.1	0.0
Pos. sum	6.4	4.3	4.2	6.9	4.4	5.3	6.0	4.7	4.3	9.4	5.4	6.0
Neg. sum	2.1	0.9	1.0	0.7	0.7	1.0	1.3	1.7	1.9	1.9	1.4	1.6
P/N	3.0	4.8	4.2	9.9	6.3	5.3	4.6	2.8	2.3	4.9	3.9	3.8
DEF	0.0	0.0	0.0	0.0	0.0	0.0	0.0	0.0	0.0	0.0	0.0	0.0
INT	0.6	0.0	0.3	0.3	0.0	0.3	0.0	0.3	0.6	0.1	0.0	0.1
FAC	3.2	2.9	2.7	5.9	2.6	3.4	5.9	2.6	3.1	5.5	2.5	4.1
SUG	0.5	0.5	0.2	0.2	1.1	0.5	0.1	0.4	0.1	0.2	0.0	0.1
XPL	0.5	0.3	1.6	1.0	0.7	0.8	1.6	0.5	2.3	0.8	0.7	1.1
SGX	0.4	0.5	0.0	0.6	0.3	0.4	0.2	0.4	0.4	1.1	0.4	0.5
EVL	0.1	0.0	0.0	0.0	0.0	0.0	0.0	0.0	0.0	0.1	0.0	0.0
OPN	0.2	0.2	0.1	0.1	0.0	0.1	0.4	0.2	0.2	0.2	0.1	0.3
JUS	0.0	0.0	0.0	0.0	0.0	0.0	0.0	0.0	0.0	0.0	0.0	0.0
OPJ	0.5	0.0	0.0	0.5	0.0	0.2	0.4	0.6	0.0	0.2	0.2	0.3
PRF	1.2	0.7	1.6	0.4	0.9	0.9	0.7	0.2	0.8	0.5	0.2	0.5
PON	0.0	0.2	0.3	0.0	0.0	0.1	0.3	0.0	0.1	0.0	0.0	0.1

Pos. sum = POS + ADM + RPT
Neg. sum = QAL + NAD + NEG
P/N = (Pos. sum) / (Neg. sum)

Preferences of Conference Participants for Changed Emphasis on Selected Factors in Clinical Supervision (Tables 49-54)

TABLE 49

Preferences of Conference Participants for Increased (+) or Decreased (-)
Emphasis* on Selected Substantive Areas in Clinical Supervision:
Planning vs. Analysis Conferences

Supervisory Groups		Planning Conferences						Analysis Conferences					
		1	2	3	4	5	$\bar{X}$	1	2	3	4	5	$\bar{X}$
Specific (S)	Supvr.	.2	.5	.1	.3	.6	.3	.1	.1	.3	.2	.7	.3
	Tchr.	.2	.1	.4	.1	.3	.2	.3	.0	.3	.0	.2	.2
	Obs.	.3	.2	.4	-.1	.4	.2	.1	.3	.2	.3	.2	.2
	Total	.2	.3	.4	.1	.4	.3	.1	.2	.3	.2	.3	.2
General (G)	Supvr.	.8	.2	.0	.5	.7	.4	.6	.5	.0	.6	.9	.5
	Tchr.	.6	.3	.4	.2	.5	.4	-.1	.5	.3	.0	.3	.2
	Obs.	.5	.1	.4	.2	.2	.3	.4	.5	.4	.3	.1	.3
	Total	.6	.2	.3	.3	.4	.4	.3	.5	.3	.3	.4	.4
Objectives (O)	Supvr.	-.3	.3	.0	-.3	.0	-.1	-.2	.0	.2	.0	.0	.0
	Tchr.	-.2	.1	.1	-.3	.2	.0	-.1	.2	.3	.0	.2	.1
	Obs.	.1	.3	.1	-.5	.1	.0	.2	.3	.3	.6	.2	.3
	Total	-.1	.2	.1	-.4	.1	.0	.0	.2	.3	.3	.1	.2
Methods (M)	Supvr.	.4	.7	.0	.4	.4	.4	.2	.0	.3	.2	.5	.2
	Tchr.	.4	.2	.4	.0	.1	.2	.3	.1	.1	-.3	.3	.1
	Obs.	.3	.3	.2	.0	.2	.2	.1	.5	.1	.3	.4	.3
	Total	.4	.4	.3	.1	.2	.3	.2	.3	.2	.1	.4	.2
Execution (X)	Supvr.	.3	.2	.2	.8	.9	.4	.0	.2	.2	.4	.9	.3
	Tchr.	.2	-.1	.7	.6	.5	.4	.4	-.4	.3	.1	.0	.1
	Obs.	.4	-.1	.5	.5	.7	.4	.0	-.2	.1	-.1	.1	.0
	Total	.3	.0	.5	.6	.6	.4	.1	-.2	.1	.1	.3	.1
Cognitive (C)	Supvr.	.5	.8	.0	.0	1.0	.5	1.0	1.0	.3	.6	1.1	.8
	Tchr.	.8	.8	1.2	.6	.4	.8	.0	.4	.5	.0	.2	.2
	Obs.	.6	.5	.6	.4	.5	.5	.4	.4	.6	.2	.3	.4
	Total	.6	.7	.7	.4	.6	.6	.4	.5	.5	.2	.5	.4
Affective (A)	Supvr.	.3	-.2	.2	.3	.4	.2	.0	-.5	.0	.1	.4	.0
	Tchr.	.0	.3	.9	-.1	.3	.3	.4	.0	.0	.3	.3	.2
	Obs.	.3	.3	.5	.2	.5	.4	.2	.5	.3	.0	.3	.3
	Total	.3	.2	.6	.1	.4	.3	.2	.1	.1	.1	.3	.2
Social-Disciplinary (D)	Supvr.	.2	.2	.5	.4	.7	.4	.0	-.1	.1	.3	.7	.2
	Tchr.	.1	.2	.7	.0	.4	.3	.3	-.1	.0	.3	.1	.1
	Obs.	.3	.1	.5	.4	.4	.3	.2	.4	.3	-.1	.4	.2
	Total	.3	.2	.6	.2	.4	.3	.2	.1	.1	-.1	.4	.2

*Based on the difference between participants' estimation of actual and desired emphasis
on an arbitrary 5-point scale: *none, little, some, much, all.* Positive values indicate a
desire for more emphasis, negative values indicate a desire for less.

TABLE 50

Preferences of Conference Participants for Increased (+) or Decreased (-)
Emphasis* on Selected Substantive Areas in Clinical Supervision:
Early vs. Late Conferences

Supervisory Groups		Early Conferences						Late Conferences					
		1	2	3	4	5	$\overline{X}$	1	2	3	4	5	$\overline{X}$
Specific (S)	Supvr.	.1	.2	.2	.3	.6	.3	.2	.4	.2	.2	.7	.3
	Tchr.	.1	.1	.4	.1	.2	.2	.3	.1	.4	-.1	.3	.2
	Obs.	.2	.3	.4	.2	.4	.3	.3	.2	.2	.1	.2	.2
	Total	.2	.2	.3	.2	.4	.3	.3	.2	.3	.0	.4	.2
General (G)	Supvr.	.7	.3	.0	.3	.8	.4	.8	.3	.0	.8	.8	.5
	Tchr.	.1	.3	.4	.1	.4	.3	.2	.6	.2	.1	.5	.3
	Obs.	.5	.0	.5	.5	.2	.3	.3	.7	.2	.0	.1	.3
	Total	.4	.2	.4	.5	.4	.3	.4	.6	.2	.2	.4	.4
Objectives (O)	Supvr.	-.3	.2	.2	.0	.0	.0	-.2	.2	.0	-.2	.0	.0
	Tchr.	-.3	.2	.2	-.1	.3	.1	.0	.1	.2	-.3	.1	.0
	Obs.	.1	.3	.3	.4	.2	.3	.2	.4	.1	.1	.0	.2
	Total	-.1	.2	.2	.1	.2	.1	.1	.2	.1	-.1	.0	.1
Methods (M)	Supvr.	.3	.2	.3	.4	.4	.3	.4	.5	.0	.2	.4	.3
	Tchr.	.4	.1	.4	-.1	.0	.2	.3	.2	.2	-.3	.3	.1
	Obs.	.0	.3	.1	.3	.5	.2	.3	.3	.2	.0	.1	.2
	Total	.2	.2	.2	.2	.4	.2	.3	.3	.1	.1	.3	.2
Execution (X)	Supvr.	.0	.2	.0	.7	.7	.3	.4	.2	.4	.4	1.0	.5
	Tchr.	.1	-.4	.4	.5	.1	.1	.6	-.1	.6	.1	.5	.3
	Obs.	.3	-.1	.4	.1	.5	.2	.2	-.1	.3	.1	.4	.2
	Total	.2	-.2	.3	.3	.4	.2	.3	.0	.4	.2	.6	.3
Cognitive (C)	Supvr.	.8	1.5	.2	.7	1.2	.9	.6	.3	.2	.8	1.0	.6
	Tchr.	.3	.4	.9	.2	.4	.4	.4	.8	.8	.4	.2	.5
	Obs.	.5	.4	.8	.3	.4	.5	.6	.5	.5	.2	.5	.5
	Total	.5	.7	.7	.4	.6	.6	.5	.5	.6	.4	.5	.5
Affective (A)	Supvr.	.0	-.7	.2	.3	.3	.0	.4	.0	.0	.0	.5	.2
	Tchr.	.0	.0	.6	.3	.4	.3	.5	.3	.3	.0	.2	.3
	Obs.	.3	.5	.3	.1	.5	.3	.2	.3	.4	.0	.4	.3
	Total	.1	.1	.4	.2	.4	.2	.3	.2	.3	.0	.3	.2
Social-Disciplinary (D)	Supvr.	-.1	-.1	.4	.3	.5	.2	.3	.2	.2	.3	.8	.4
	Tchr.	-.1	.0	.4	.3	.3	.2	.6	.1	.3	.1	.3	.3
	Obs.	.3	.3	.3	.1	.5	.3	.1	.2	.4	.1	.3	.2
	Total	.1	.1	.4	.2	.4	.3	.2	.1	.3	.2	.4	.2

*Based on the difference between participants' estimation of actual and desired emphasis on an arbitrary 5-point scale: *none, little, some, much, all.* Positive values indicate a desire for more emphasis, negative values indicate a desire for less.

TABLE 51

Preferences of Conference Participants for Increased (+)
or Decreased (-) Emphasis* on Selected Substantive
Areas in Clinical Supervision: All Conferences

Total Conferences

Supervisory Groups		1	2	3	4	5	$\bar{X}$
Specific (S)	Supvr.	.1	.3	.2	.2	.7	.3
	Tchr.	.2	.1	.4	.0	.3	.2
	Obs.	.2	.3	.3	.2	.3	.3
	Total	.2	.2	.3	.1	.4	.2
General (G)	Supvr.	.7	.3	.0	.5	.8	.5
	Tchr.	.2	.4	.3	.1	.5	.3
	Obs.	.4	.3	.4	.3	.1	.3
	Total	.4	.4	.3	.3	.4	.4
Objectives (O)	Supvr.	-.3	.2	.1	-.1	.0	.0
	Tchr.	-.2	.2	.2	-.2	.2	.0
	Obs.	.1	.3	.2	.3	.1	.2
	Total	.0	.2	.2	.0	.1	.1
Methods (M)	Supvr.	.3	.4	.2	.3	.5	.3
	Tchr.	.4	.2	.3	-.2	.2	.2
	Obs.	.2	.4	.2	.2	.3	.3
	Total	.3	.3	.2	.1	.3	.2
Execution (X)	Supvr.	.2	.2	.2	.5	.9	.4
	Tchr.	.3	-.3	.5	.4	.3	.2
	Obs.	.2	-.1	.4	.1	.5	.2
	Total	.2	-.1	.4	.3	.5	.3
Cognitive (C)	Supvr.	.7	.9	.2	.7	1.1	.7
	Tchr.	.4	.6	.9	.3	.3	.5
	Obs.	.5	.4	.6	.3	.4	.5
	Total	.5	.6	.6	.4	.6	.5
Affective (A)	Supvr.	.2	-.3	.1	.2	.4	.1
	Tchr.	.2	.1	.5	.1	.3	.2
	Obs.	.2	.4	.4	.0	.4	.3
	Total	.2	.1	.3	.1	.4	.2
Social-Disciplinary (D)	Supvr.	.1	.1	.3	.4	.7	.3
	Tchr.	.2	.0	.4	.2	.3	.2
	Obs.	.2	.2	.4	.1	.4	.3
	Total	.2	.1	.3	.2	.4	.2

*Based on the difference between participants' estimation
of actual and desired emphasis on an arbitrary 5-point
scale: *none, little, some, much, all.* Positive values indicate a desire for more emphasis, negative values indicate
a desire for less.

TABLE 52

Preferences of Conference Participants for Increased (+) or Decreased (-)
Emphasis* on Selected Factors in, and Overall Evaluations** of,
Clinical Supervision: Planning vs. Analysis Conferences

Supervisory Groups		Planning Conferences						Analysis Conferences					
		1	2	3	4	5	$\bar{X}$	1	2	3	4	5	$\bar{X}$
Diagnostic	Supvr.	.4	.5	.1	.2	1.0	.4	.0	.1	.1	.2	.9	.3
	Tchr.	.1	.0	.5	.3	.2	.2	.1	-.3	.2	.0	.2	.0
	Obs.	.3	.0	.4	.4	.4	.3	.1	.1	.0	.0	.1	.1
	Total	.2	.2	.4	.3	.4	.3	.1	.0	.0	.1	.3	.1
Prescriptive	Supvr.	.5	1.0	.2	.5	.9	.6	.6	.0	.5	.1	1.3	.5
	Tchr.	.5	.4	.5	-.1	.2	.3	.5	.3	.4	-.1	.3	.3
	Obs.	.4	.4	.5	-.2	.3	.3	.1	.8	.3	.3	.4	.4
	Total	.5	.6	.5	.0	.4	.4	.3	.5	.4	.1	.6	.4
Analytic	Supvr.	.4	.8	.0	-.5	1.0	.3	.0	.0	.0	.0	.9	.2
	Tchr.	.0	.1	.3	.0	-.1	.1	-.2	-.1	.1	-.1	.3	.0
	Obs.	.1	.1	.3	.2	.1	.2	.2	.4	-.1	.1	.1	.1
	Total	.1	.3	.2	-.1	.2	.2	.1	.2	.0	.0	.3	.1
Evaluative	Supvr.	-.2	-.7	.0	.0	-.7	-.3	.0	.0	.0	.3	-.9	-.1
	Tchr.	.0	.1	.1	.2	.2	.1	.2	.0	-.2	.1	-.2	.0
	Obs.	-.1	.1	.1	.0	.2	.1	.1	-.2	-.1	-.1	.1	.0
	Total	-.1	-.1	.1	.1	.0	.0	.1	-.1	-.1	.1	-.2	.0
Amt. supvr. initiation	Supvr.	-.2	-.2	-.2	-.3	-.7	-.3	.0	.3	.0	-.1	-.7	-.1
	Tchr.	.2	-.1	-.5	-.3	-.4	-.2	.2	.2	-.1	-.4	-.2	-.1
	Obs.	.1	-.2	-.1	-.5	-.4	-.2	.2	-.5	.0	-.5	-.2	-.2
	Total	.1	-.2	-.3	-.4	-.5	-.3	.1	-.1	.0	-.4	-.3	-.1
Amt. tchr. initiation	Supvr.	.2	-.2	.6	.0	.7	.3	.0	.2	.0	.3	.7	.2
	Tchr.	.2	-.3	.3	.3	.2	.1	.0	-.1	-.4	.4	.3	.2
	Obs.	-.1	-.1	-.1	.0	.4	.0	.1	-.1	-.2	.4	.3	.2
	Total	.0	-.2	.2	.2	.4	.1	.0	-.1	-.3	.3	.4	.2
Amt. obs. initiation	Supvr.	.2	.0	.2	.3	.6	.3	.0	.2	.0	.3	.3	.2
	Tchr.	.2	.3	.4	.1	.1	.2	.0	.5	.2	.5	.3	.3
	Obs.	.1	-.4	.1	.3	.3	.1	.0	-.2	-.1	.5	.3	.1
	Total	.1	-.1	.2	.2	.3	.2	.0	.1	.0	.5	.3	.2
Overall evaluation (0=3)	Supvr.	2.0	2.0	2.0	2.0	1.6	1.9	2.2	1.8	1.6	2.0	1.9	1.9
	Tchr.	2.4	2.0	2.2	2.6	1.6	2.2	2.3	1.5	2.2	2.0	2.1	2.0
	Obs.	1.9	2.0	2.3	2.2	1.8	2.0	2.2	1.6	2.6	2.3	2.2	2.2
	Total	2.0	2.0	2.2	2.2	1.7	2.0	2.2	1.6	2.3	2.2	2.1	2.1

*Based on the difference between participants' estimation of actual and desired emphasis
on an arbitrary 5-point scale: *none, little, some, much, all.* Positive values indicate a
desire for more emphasis, negative values indicate a desire for less.

**Based on the participants' evaluation of overall conference effectiveness or productivity
on an arbitrary 4-point scale: 0 = ineffective, 1 = moderately ineffective, 2 = moderately
effective, 3 = effective.

TABLE 53

Preferences of Conference Participants for Increased (+) or Decreased (-)
Emphasis* on Selected Factors in, and Overall Evaluations** of,
Clinical Supervision: Early vs. Late Conferences

Supervisory Groups		Early Conferences						Late Conferences					
		1	2	3	4	5	$\bar{X}$	1	2	3	4	5	$\bar{X}$
Diagnostic	Supvr.	.1	.5	.0	.3	.8	.3	.3	.2	.2	.1	1.0	.4
	Tchr.	-.1	-.2	.3	.2	.2	.1	.3	-.1	.4	.1	.2	.2
	Obs.	.1	.1	.3	.2	.3	.2	.3	.1	.1	.1	.3	.2
	Total	.1	.1	.3	.2	.4	.2	.3	.1	.2	.1	.5	.2
Prescriptive	Supvr.	.7	.3	.5	.2	1.0	.5	.4	.7	.2	.4	1.1	.6
	Tchr.	.6	.4	.5	-.1	.1	.3	.4	.3	.4	-.1	.4	.3
	Obs.	.1	.7	.5	.2	.5	.4	.4	.4	.3	.0	.2	.3
	Total	.4	.5	.5	.1	.5	.4	.4	.4	.3	.0	.5	.3
Analytic	Supvr.	.2	.7	.0	-.2	.8	.3	.2	.2	.0	-.2	1.0	.2
	Tchr.	-.2	.0	.2	-.1	.2	.0	.0	.0	.2	.0	-.1	.0
	Obs.	-.1	.3	.2	.2	.1	.1	.3	.3	-.1	.1	.1	.1
	Total	.0	.3	.2	.0	.3	.2	.3	.2	.0	.0	.3	.2
Evaluative	Supvr.	-.2	-.5	.0	.0	-.7	-.3	.0	-.2	.0	.4	-.9	-.1
	Tchr.	.2	.1	-.1	.3	.0	.1	.0	.0	.2	.0	.1	.1
	Obs.	-.1	.0	.0	-.2	.0	-.1	-.1	-.1	-.1	.1	.3	.0
	Total	-.1	-.1	.0	.0	-.1	-.1	.0	-.1	.0	.1	-.1	.0
Amt. supvr. initiation	Supvr.	-.2	.3	-.2	-.3	-.8	-.2	.0	-.2	.0	.0	-.6	-.2
	Tchr.	.3	-.1	-.6	-.3	-.6	-.3	.0	.2	.0	-.4	-.1	-.1
	Obs.	.4	-.2	-.2	-.8	-.4	-.2	.1	-.6	.1	-.1	-.2	-.1
	Total	.1	.0	-.3	-.5	-.5	-.2	.1	-.3	.1	-.2	-.3	-.1
Amt. tchr. initiation	Supvr.	.2	-.2	.7	.4	.7	.3	.0	.2	.4	.0	.8	.3
	Tchr.	.2	-.1	.4	.4	.6	.3	.0	-.3	.3	.3	.0	.1
	Obs.	.0	.0	.1	.5	.4	.2	.0	-.3	.1	.0	.4	.0
	Total	.1	-.1	.3	.4	.5	.2	.0	-.2	.2	.1	.4	.1
Amt. obs. initiation	Supvr.	.2	-.2	.2	.5	.3	.2	.0	.3	.0	.2	.5	.2
	Tchr.	.2	.1	.6	.1	.4	.3	.0	.8	.1	.6	.0	.3
	Obs.	.1	-.2	.0	.5	.1	.1	.1	-.3	-.1	.5	.4	.1
	Total	.1	-.1	.2	.4	.3	.2	.0	.2	.0	.5	.3	.2
Overall evaluation (0=3)	Supvr.	1.7	1.7	2.0	2.0	1.7	1.8	2.4	2.2	1.5	2.0	1.8	2.0
	Tchr.	2.3	1.9	2.5	2.0	1.7	2.1	2.4	1.6	2.0	2.3	1.9	2.0
	Obs.	2.4	1.9	2.4	2.3	1.9	2.2	1.8	1.6	2.5	2.3	2.1	2.1
	Total	2.2	1.9	2.3	2.1	1.8	2.1	2.0	1.8	2.2	2.2	1.9	2.0

*Based on the difference between participants' estimation of actual and desired emphasis on an arbitrary 5-point scale: *none, little, some, much, all.* Positive values indicate a desire for more emphasis, negative values indicate a desire for less.

**Based on the participants' evaluation of overall conference effectiveness or productivity on an arbitrary 4-point scale: 0 = ineffective, 1 = moderately ineffective, 2 = moderately effective, 3 = effective.

TABLE 54

Preferences of Conference Participants for Increased (+) or
Decreased (-) Emphasis* on Selected Factors in, and Overall
Evaluations** of, Clinical Supervision: All Conferences

Supervisory Groups		Total Conferences					
		1	2	3	4	5	$\overline{X}$
Diagnostic	Supvr.	.2	.3	.1	.2	.9	.3
	Tchr.	.1	-.2	.4	.2	.2	.1
	Obs.	.2	.1	.3	.2	.3	.2
	Total	.2	.1	.3	.2	.4	.2
Prescriptive	Supvr.	.5	.5	.4	.3	1.1	.6
	Tchr.	.5	.4	.5	-.1	.3	.3
	Obs.	.3	.6	.4	.1	.3	.3
	Total	.4	.5	.4	.1	.5	.4
Analytic	Supvr.	.2	.4	.0	-.2	.9	.3
	Tchr.	-.1	.0	.2	-.1	.1	.0
	Obs.	.1	.3	.1	.2	.1	.2
	Total	.1	.2	.1	.1	.3	.2
Evaluative	Supvr.	-.1	-.3	.0	.2	-.8	-.2
	Tchr.	.1	.1	.0	.2	.1	.1
	Obs.	-.1	-.1	.0	.0	.1	.0
	Total	-.1	-.1	.0	.1	-.1	.0
Amt. supvr. initiation	Supvr.	-.1	.1	-.1	-.2	-.7	-.2
	Tchr.	.2	.0	-.3	-.4	-.3	-.2
	Obs.	.2	-.4	-.1	-.5	-.3	-.2
	Total	.1	-.2	-.1	-.4	-.4	-.2
Amt. tchr. initiation	Supvr.	.1	.0	.5	.2	.7	.3
	Tchr.	.1	-.2	.3	.3	.3	.2
	Obs.	.0	-.1	.1	.3	.4	.1
	Total	.0	-.1	.2	.3	.4	.2
Amt. obs. initiation	Supvr.	.1	.1	.1	.4	.4	.2
	Tchr.	.1	.4	.3	.2	.2	.3
	Obs.	.1	-.3	.0	.5	.3	.1
	Total	.1	.0	.1	.4	.3	.2
Overall evaluation (0=3)	Supvr.	2.1	1.9	1.8	2.0	1.7	1.9
	Tchr.	2.3	1.8	2.2	2.1	1.8	2.0
	Obs.	2.1	1.8	2.5	2.3	2.0	2.1
	Total	2.1	1.8	2.3	2.2	1.9	2.1

*Based on the difference between participants' estimation
of actual and desired emphasis on an arbitrary 5-point
scale: *none, little, some, much, all.* Positive values indicate a desire for more emphasis, negative values indicate
a desire for less.

**Based on the participants' evaluation of overall confer-
ence effectiveness or productivity on an arbitrary 4-
point scale: 0 = ineffective, 1 = moderately ineffective,
2 = moderately effective, 3 = effective.

Bibliography

Amidon, E. "A Technique for Analyzing Counselor-Counselee Interaction." In *Counseling and Guidance: A Summary View*, edited by J. Adams. New York: Macmillan Co., 1965.

Amidon, E., and Hunter, E. "Verbal Interaction in the Classroom, The Amidon System for Interaction Analysis." Temple University, Group Dynamics Center, n.d. Mimeographed.

Anderson, R. H. "Supervision as Teaching: An Analogue." In *Supervision: Perspectives and Propositions*. Washington, D.C.: Association for Supervision and Curriculum Development, 1967.

Ayer, F. C. *Fundamentals of Instructional Supervision*. New York: Harper & Bros., Inc., 1954.

Bales, R. F. *Interaction Process Analysis*. Cambridge, Mass.: Addison Wesley Press, 1951.

Bartky, J. A. *Supervision as Human Relations*. Boston: D. C. Heath & Co., 1953.

Belanger, M. L. "An Exploration of the Use of Feedback in Supervision." Ed.D. dissertation, Harvard University, 1962.

Bellack, A. A., Kliebard, H. M., Hyman, R. T., and Smith, F. L., Jr. *The Language of the Classroom*. New York: Teachers College Press, 1966.

Berman, L. M., and Usery, M. L. *Personalized Supervision*. Washington, D.C.: Association for Supervision and Curriculum Development, 1966.

Binnington, G. H. "Self Acceptance Change in Student Teachers as a Result of Student-Centered University Supervision." Ed.D. dissertation, University of Oregon, 1965.

Blaisdel, R. W. "The Role of the Master Teacher at the Harvard-Newton Summer School." Paper, Harvard Graduate School of Education, 1960.

Bloom, B. S., Engelhart, M. D., Furst, E. J., Hill, W. H., and Krathwohl, D. R. *Taxonomy of Educational Objectives: Cognitive Domain*. New York: Longmans, Green & Co., 1956.

Blumberg, A. "A System for Analyzing Supervisor-Teacher Interaction." In *Mirrors for Behavior*, edited by A. Simon and E. G. Boyer. Vol. 8. Philadelphia: Research for Better Schools, Inc., 1970.

Blumberg, A., and Amidon, E. "Teacher Perceptions of Supervisor-Teacher Interaction." *Administrator's Notebook* 14, no. 1 (September 1965): 1–8.

Brown, A. B., Cobban, M. R., and Waterman, F. T. "The Analysis of Verbal Teaching Behavior: An Approach to Supervisory Conferences with Student Teachers." Ed.D. dissertation, Teachers College, Columbia University, 1965.

Brown, R. V., and Hoffman, M. J. S. "A Promissory Model for Analyzing and Describing Verbal Interaction Between College Supervisors and Student Teachers During Supervisory Conferences." Ed.D. dissertation, Columbia University, 1966.

Bush, R. N., and Allen, D. W. "Microteaching: Controlled Practice in the Training of Teachers." Paper presented at the Santa Barbara Conference on Teacher Education of the Ford Foundation, 1964.

Cogan, M. L. "Supervision at the Harvard-Newton Summer School." Paper, Harvard Graduate School of Education, 1961.

———. "Clinical Supervision by Groups." In *The College Supervisor: Conflict and Challenge*. 43d Yearbook of the Association for Student Teaching. Cedar Falls, Iowa: The Association, 1964.

Edmund, N. R., and Hemink, L. "Ways in Which Supervisors Help Student Teachers." *Educational Research Bulletin* 37, no. 3 (March 1958): 57–60.

Evaluating Student Teaching. 39th Yearbook of the Association for Student Teaching. Cedar Falls, Iowa: The Association, 1960.

Fitts, P. M. "Factors in Complex Skill Training." In *Training Research and Education*, edited by R. Glaser. New York: John Wiley & Sons, Inc., 1965.

Flanders, N. A. *Teacher Influence, Pupil Attitudes, and Achievement.* Cooperative Research Monograph no. 12 OE-25040. Washington, D.C.: U.S. Department of Health, Education, and Welfare, 1965.

Gage, N. L. "Paradigms for Research on Teaching." In *Handbook of Research on Teaching*, edited by N. L. Gage. Chicago: Rand McNally Co., Inc., 1963.

Gage, N. L., ed. *Handbook of Research on Teaching.* Chicago: Rand McNally Co., Inc., 1963.

Glaser, R. "Psychology and Instructional Technology." In *Training Research and Education*, edited by R. Glaser. New York: John Wiley & Sons, Inc., 1965.

Glaser, R., ed. *Training Research and Education.* New York: John Wiley & Sons, Inc., 1965.

Goldhammer, R. *Clinical Supervision: Special Methods for the Supervision of Teachers.* New York: Holt, Rinehart & Winston, 1969.

Goodlad, J. *The Changing American School.* Chicago: University of Chicago Press, 1966.

Greenberg, S. B. "A Comparative Analysis of Selected Studies of Classroom Teaching." Ed.D. dissertation, Columbia University, 1966.

Grey, L., and Greenblatt, E. L. "Experiment in Team Supervision." *Journal of Teacher Education* 14, no. 2 (June 1963): 154–162.

Gwynn, J. M. *Theory and Practice of Supervision.* New York: Dodd, Mead & Co., 1961.

Harris, B. M. "Need for Research on Instructional Supervision." *Educational Leadership* 31, no. 135 (November 1963): 129.

————. "Strategies for Instructional Change: Promising Ideas and Perplexing Problems." In *The Supervisor: Agent for Change in Teaching.* Washington, D.C.: Association for Supervision and Curriculum Development, 1965.

Heidelbach, R. "The Development of a Tentative Model for Analyzing and Describing the Verbal Behavior of Cooperating Teachers Engaged in Individualized Teaching with Student Teachers." Ed.D. dissertation, Columbia University, 1967.

Hollister, G. E. "The Group Conference of the Supervising Teacher." *Journal of Educational Research* 44, no. 9 (September 1950): 54–56.

Hough, J. B. "An Observational System for the Analysis of Classroom Instruction." Paper, Ohio State University, 1965. Mimeographed.

Ishler, R. E. "An Experimental Study Using Withall's Social-Emotional Climate Index to Determine the Effectiveness of Feedback as a Means of Changing Student Teachers' Verbal Behavior." Ed.D. dissertation, Pennsylvania State University, 1965.

Jackson, P. W. "The Way Teaching Is." In *The Way Teaching Is.* Washington, D.C.: Association for Supervision and Curriculum Development, 1966.

Krathwohl, D. R., Bloom, B. S., and Masia, B. B. *Taxonomy of Educational Objectives: Affective Domain.* New York: David McKay Co., Inc., 1956.

Kyte, G. C. "The Effective Supervisory Conference." *California Journal of Educational Research* 13, no. 4 (September 1962): 160–168.

LaGrone, H. "Teaching: Craft or Intellectual Process." In *Action for Improvement of Teacher Education.* 18th Yearbook of the American Association of Colleges for Teacher Education. Washington, D.C.: The Association, 1965.

Lucio, W. H., and McNeil, J. D. *Supervision: A Synthesis of Thought and Action.* New York: McGraw-Hill Book Co., 1959.

Maccia, E. S. "Instruction as Influence Toward Rule-Governed Behavior." In *Theories of Instruction.* Washington, D.C.: Association for Supervision and Curriculum Development, 1965.

MacGraw, F. M. "The Use of 35mm Time Lapse Photography as a Feedback and Observational Instrument in Teacher Education." Ed.D. dissertation, Stanford University, 1965.

McConnell, G. "They Helped Us, But—!" *Journal of Teacher Education* 11, no. 1 (March 1960): 84–86.

McDonald, F. J., Allen, D. W., and Orme, M. E. J. "The Effects of Self-Feedback and Reinforcement on the Acquisition of a Teaching Skill." Paper, Stanford University, 1965.

Medley, D. M., and Mitzel, H. E. "Measuring Classroom Behavior by Systematic Observation." In *Handbook of Research on Teaching*, edited by N. L. Gage. Chicago: Rand McNally Co., 1963.

Molchen, K. "A Study of Changes in Intentions, Perceptions, and Classroom Verbal Behavior of Science Interns and Apprentices." Ed.D. dissertation, Harvard University, 1967.

Morrison, V. B., and Dixon, W. R. "New Techniques of Observation and Assessment of Student Teaching." In *The College Supervisor: Conflict and Challenge*. 43d Yearbook of the Association for Student Teaching. Cedar Falls, Iowa: The Association, 1964.

Moser, J. M. "A Case Study of the Effect of Information Feedback on the Performance of Student Teachers in Mathematics." Ed.D. dissertation, University of Colorado, 1965.

Mosher, R. L. "An Application of Ego Counseling in the Supervision of the Student Teacher." Ed.D. dissertation, Harvard Graduate School of Education, 1964.

Northrop, F. S. C. *The Logic of the Sciences and the Humanities*. New York: The World Publishing Co., 1947.

Oliver, D., and Shaver, J. "A Critique of 'Practice in Teaching.'" *Harvard Educational Review* 31, no. 3 (Fall 1961): 437–448.

Osgood, C. E., Suci, G. J., and Tannenbaum, P. H. *The Measurement of Meaning*. Urbana: University of Illinois Press, 1957.

Roth, L. H. "Selecting Supervising Teachers." *Journal of Teacher Education* 12, no. 4 (December 1961): 476–481.

Schueler, H., and Gold, M. "Video Recordings of Student Teachers: A Report of the Hunter College Research Project." *Journal of Teacher Education* 15, no. 4 (December 1964): 358–364.

Schueler, H., and Lesser, G. S. *Teacher Education and the New Media*. American Association of Colleges for Teacher Education, Washington, D.C.: 1967.

Seager, G. B. "The Development of a Diagnostic Instrument of Supervision." Ed.D. dissertation, Harvard Graduate School of Education, 1965.

Sellitz, C., Jahoda, M., Deutsch, M., and Cook, S. W. *Research Methods in Social Relations*. New York: Henry Holt & Co., 1959.

Shaplin, J. T. "Practice in Teaching." *Harvard Educational Review* 31, no. 1 (Winter 1961): 46.

Simon, A., and Boyer, E. G. *Mirrors for Behavior.* Vols. 1–18. Philadelphia: Research for Better Schools, Inc., 1967.

Smith, B. O., and Meux, M. *A Study of the Logic of Teaching.* U.S. Office of Education Cooperative Research Project no. 258 (7257). Urbana: University of Illinois, 1959.

Stratemeyer, F. B., and Lindsey, M. *Working with Student Teachers.* New York: Bureau of Publications, Teachers College, Columbia University, 1958.

Swineford, E. J. "Analysis of Teaching-Improvement Suggestions to Student Teachers." *Journal of Experimental Education* 32, no. 3 (Spring 1964): 299–303.

Thelen, H. A. "Insights for Teaching from a Theory of Interaction." In *The Nature of Teaching,* edited by L. M. Berman. Milwaukee: University of Wisconsin Press, 1963.

Travers, R. M. W. *An Introduction to Educational Research.* New York: Macmillan Co., 1958.

Trimmer, R. L. "Student Teachers Talk Back." *Journal of Teacher Education* 11, no. 4 (December 1960): 537–538.

————. "Tell Us More, Student Teacher!" *Journal of Teacher Education* 12, no. 2 (June 1961): 229–231.

Weller, R. H. "The Analysis of Supervisor-Teacher Conferences During Practice Teaching." Qualifying paper, Harvard Graduate School of Education, 1967.

Wright, H. F. "Observational Child Study." In *Handbook of Research Methods in Child Development,* edited by P. H. Mussen. New York: John Wiley & Sons, Inc., 1960.

Wright, R. G. "An Analysis of the Techniques of Guiding Student Teaching Experiences." Ed.D. dissertation, University of Southern California, 1965.

Yulo, R. J. "An Exploration of the Flanders System of Interaction Analysis as a Supervisory Device with Science Interns." Ed.D. dissertation, Harvard Graduate School of Education, 1967.

Zahn, R. D. "The Use of Interaction Analysis in Supervising Student Teachers." Ed.D. dissertation, Temple University, 1965.